# And Justice

# And Justice for Some

## EXPLORING AMERICAN JUSTICE THROUGH DRAMA AND THEATRE

Wendy Lement and
Bethany Dunakin

HEINEMANN
Portsmouth, NH

**Heinemann**
A division of Reed Elsevier Inc.
361 Hanover Street
Portsmouth, NH 03801–3912
www.heinemanndrama.com

*Offices and agents throughout the world*

The authors and publisher wish to thank those who have generously given permission to reprint borrowed material:

*Justice at War: The Story of the Japanese American Internment Camps* by Wendy Lement, Jordan Winer, and Mimi Jo Katano. Copyright © 1994 by Wendy Lement. Reprinted by permission of the authors.

Excerpts from *The Rosenberg Letters*, edited by Michael Meeropol. Copyright © 1994 by Michael Meeropol. Published by Garland Publishing, Inc. Reprinted by permission of Michael Meeropol.

Excerpts from *We are Your Sons* by Robert and Michael Meeropol. Copyright © 1975 by Robert and Michael Meeropol. Published by Houghton Mifflin. Reprinted by permission of the authors.

**Library of Congress Cataloging-in-Publication Data**
Lement, Wendy Jean.
And justice for some : exploring American justice through drama and theatre / Wendy Lement and Bethany Dunakin.
    p.  cm.
 Includes bibliographical references.
 ISBN 0-325-00649-0 (alk. paper)
 1. Justice, Administration of—United States—Drama.   I. Dunakin, Bethany.   II. Title.
PS3612. E455A83 2005
812'.6—dc22                                                                                    2004020515

*Editor:* Lisa A. Barnett
*Production coordinator:* Elizabeth Valway
*Production service:* Denise Botelho
*Typesetter:* Argosy
*Cover design:* Night & Day Design
*Cover photography:* Mick Hicks. From *Justice at War*, (*left to right*) Daniel Tarr, Mimi Jo Katano, and
    Keri Tarr
*Manufacturing:* Steve Bernier

Printed in the United States of America on acid-free paper
09  08  07  06  05  VP  1  2  3  4  5

# Contents

# Acknowledgments

The plays in this book could not have been created without the support, dedication, and inspiration of many actors, arts administrators, educators, and funders. We'd like to thank the many Theatre Espresso actors who have contributed to the development of *Justice and War*, *The Trial of Anthony Burns*, and our other plays. Thank you to Susan Zeiger, the women who shared moving and often difficult parts of their lives, and the Regis College students, all of whom helped to create *Voicings*. The plays and study guide materials in this collection were particularly inspired by the work of recognized theatre educators and practitioners, including: Lynne Clark, Dorothy Heathcote, Ron Jenkins, Cecily O'Neill, and Chris Vine.

In addition, we would like to thank the following individuals and organizations for their generous contributions and support: Robert Colby, Christopher Robin Cook, Discovering Justice: The James D. St. Clair Court Education Project, Robert Dunakin, Mimi Jo Katano, Carol Korty, Michael and Robert Meeropol, Pamela Menke, Derek Nelson, Theater in the Open, Virginia Pyne Kaneb Faculty Scholars Program, Regis College, Orchard House, Jeremy Solomons, Jordan Winer, and Young Audiences of Massachusetts.

# Introduction

## From an Interview with Walter Cronkite[1]

*DICK GORDON:* You've made it a priority in your life as a public citizen to do whatever you can to help with the education of children, to get children connected to history.

*WALTER CRONKITE:* It's almost the only way they can be good citizens. It's not a question of degree. It's a question of whether they're going to be good citizens or not. Unless they understand history, as [George] Santayana said, they "are doomed to repeat it." I do not think that history is well taught in most of our schools. The history teachers, perhaps, are told to cover so much ground that they don't get an opportunity to dramatize history the way it should be dramatized in teaching it to young people, to get them caught up in that story. Almost every major decision in history involves a duel of personalities. And that duel of personalities is fascinating stuff. It's the stuff of which much writing has been done. And if we taught that way, the kids would be caught up in the flow of history, the flow of competition, the flow that even leads to combat. We just don't get it like that, and I'd like to see it improved.

## Why American Justice and Theatre?

As a teenager in the early 1970s, my interest in civics was almost nonexistent. I attended a few antiwar rallies, but to be honest, I was more interested in being part of the action than in understanding the American political system. Even with a cool, long-haired teacher, I digested junior high lessons in American history like bad medicine. All that changed in the summer of 1973, with the airing of the Watergate Hearings. As if hooked on a soap opera, I tuned in each day and was transfixed by the real-life drama that unfolded before me. I was incredulous as H. R. Haldeman claimed time after time that

---

1. Walter Cronkite, interviewed by Dick Gordon, *The Connection*, WBUR Radio, 10 October 2002.

he did not recall *anything*. I was appalled at John Ehrlichman's unapologetic defense of the break-in as normal practice. And I was astonished as John Dean implicated Nixon and his top advisors in the cover up. Sam Ervin and Daniel Inouye temporarily replaced rock stars as my idols. There were moments of high drama; I remember holding my breath as one witness conferred with his lawyer for several moments over yet another stinging question from a senator. When he answered "not to the best of my recollection," my sigh of disgust seemed to echo those in the Congressional chamber. There were also moments of comic relief, like when Senator Inouye mumbled "[*expletive*] liar" under his breath, unaware that his microphone was turned on. The tension continued to build until the resignation of Richard Nixon provoked a national catharsis.

In the early 1990s, the nation once again was mesmerized by an unfolding legal proceeding—the televised trial of O.J. Simpson. More recently, Winona Ryder and Kobe Bryant's legal woes have captured our attention. While I find a disturbing voyeuristic element to our society's fixation with celebrity court cases, I see an important benefit from the media's attention on trials: U.S. citizens become engaged in their justice system. We learn about the roles of the judge, jury, and lawyers for the defense and prosecution. The nature, reliability, and admissibility of evidence are examined, as is court procedure. Issues of race, gender, and the law are thrust, at least temporarily, back into the national dialogue. We are motivated to learn how our justice system works, or when we disagree with the outcome, why it fails.

Playwrights have capitalized on the dramatic nature of trials since the ancient Greeks; Orestes was tried by the gods for the murder of Clytemnestra in Aeschylus' *Eumenides*. Portia's defense of Antonio in *Merchant of Venice* stands as perhaps one of the best-known examples of the convention. Modern plays such as George Bernard Shaw's *Saint Joan* and Moisés Kaufman's *Gross Indecency: The Three Trials of Oscar Wilde* continue the tradition of using trials as the stuff of drama. Hollywood has long known the dramatic potential of the courtroom with films like *Adam's Rib, To Kill a Mockingbird, Twelve Angry Men*, and *The Verdict*. In pop culture, we are inundated with courtroom dramas that are "ripped from the headlines," and reality shows such as *Judge Judy*.

What is it about hearings and trials that make them inherently dramatic? Anyone who has sat on a jury, or read transcripts of a congressional hearing knows that court proceedings are full of tedious details. At their core, trials are high-stakes events. In death penalty cases such as the Rosenbergs' trial, actual life or death decisions are made in the courtroom. A person's liberty, career, reputation, health, and family ties may all be on the line. There are victims, be it an individual, a family, a community, or—in the case of Watergate—a nation. Overall questions of guilt or innocence and what the verdict will be drive the dramatic action. Along the way, conflicting testimony, doubts as to the reliability of evidence, and questions about the motivations and tactics of the defendant(s), the appellant, lawyers, witnesses, even the judge and jury all help to grab and maintain our attention. Public opinion and the historical context provide the given circumstances for the drama, and the press and pundits fulfill the role of a Greek chorus. Tension builds to the crisis point: the decision of the judge, jury, or congressional committee.

As a playwright, I did not start out to write a series of plays about the American justice system. Often, I was intrigued by the human struggle of those involved in a historical event. With *Salem's Daughters*, I wanted to know what drove the girls of Salem Village to make their accusations. There were also personal reasons for choosing topics. With *Justice at War*, I was outraged both by the existence of the Japanese Internment Camps, and by the fact that I didn't learn about them until 1983 when I heard a discussion on National Public Radio about reparations. I decided that this was a story that needed to be told. With *Voicings*, the selection of the Rosenberg case as the focus of Regis College's oral history and performance project grew out of a discussion with historian Susan Zeiger about my mother who had been politically active in the 1930s and 1940s. In 1953, the FBI approached my mother with questions about the political affiliations of a lawyer for whom she used to work. Susan and I decided to have our students interview radical women (and their daughters) about the Rosenberg case, which was a defining moment in their lives.

As artistic director of Theatre Espresso—a theatre-in-education company that tours to schools, museums, and courthouses—my interest in exploring history through theatre evolved. Theatre-in-Education (TIE) is a form of theatre that involves both scripted material and improvisation with the audience. Generally in TIE, the audience plays an active role in the drama, often making important decisions. There are many forms of TIE; some pieces start with a self-contained play followed by the interactive component, while others involve the audience throughout the performance. These dramas are usually performed in schools, museums, libraries, and historical sites. The performers in TIE are referred to as actor-teachers, as both skills are employed. Theatre Espresso soon discovered that TIE provided a particularly effective framework for teaching the complexities of history.

Two of Theatre Espresso's early dramas were based on court documents. Once the public became familiar with our work, certain opportunities began to unfold. In 2000, Discovering Justice: The James D. St.Clair Court Education Project commissioned the company to write a play to be in residence at the John Joseph Moakley Courthouse in Boston. Beth Dunakin, then a graduate student at Emerson College, came on board as a research and playwriting assistant. After reviewing several cases, we selected the trial of Anthony Burns as the topic for our drama. Throughout the development process, we worked with historical and legal scholars, lawyers and judges, all of whom have provided important insights into the material.

It's tricky business dealing with history in plays, especially if your target audience is young people. There may be substantial pressure from educators and funders to be absolutely "historically accurate." Even if you attempt this feat, you may have difficulty determining what is true; there are often conflicting interpretations of historical events. Whose truth do you portray? My goal, first and foremost, is to write a dramatically compelling piece of theatre. If I fail in that, I might as well deliver a lecture, or recommend a reading list on the topic. I'm not suggesting that you totally disregard history. Often I do a year of research before I even start to write. But throughout the process you will be faced with choices, and the path you follow should be guided by your goals. In the following chapters, you may notice discrepancies between historical information in the script and that in the study guides. In those cases, assume that the study guides contain a more accurate account of events.

As a playwright, I want to present the messy complexities of real-life situations. I want audiences to be as caught up in the chosen event as I am and to feel the struggles faced by my characters. If I can get across the fundamental conflicts of a situation, I don't mind sacrificing a few historical facts. I might change the sequence of events, combine several historical figures into one character, or alter a location. If watching a play can motivate students to embark on their own research, I don't mind if they learn that a few of my facts were inaccurate. That said, in devising a TIE piece the issue of historical accuracy becomes particularly loaded given the importance of both the educational and artistic goals.

Effective plays prompt more questions than they provide answers. If I see a situation as black and white, I need to either find a gray area to explore—something I don't know—or find a new subject to write about. This was the case with *Justice at War*. It was difficult for our writing team to view the Japanese internment camps as anything but an injustice perpetrated against innocent persons. To merely answer the question, "Was it right or wrong to place American citizens of Japanese ancestry in camps?" would have been too simplistic. By examining the constitutionality of the camps, we discovered a range of viable viewpoints. *Voicings* could also have fallen into this trap if we set out to prove that it was wrong for the U.S. government to execute the Rosenbergs. By focusing on how the Rosenbergs' trial affected the lives of radical women, the students collected a rich tapestry of responses.

Mining legal documents as source material for theatre also offers an ideal opportunity to explore the evolutionary nature of the law. In my youth, I tended to see the law as fixed. But I've learned that people can affect change and that court cases often serve as a catalyst for transforming the law. For example, as the Salem witch hysteria grew in scope, public opinion turned against the trials. Governor Phips eventually caved to public pressure and outlawed the admission of spectral evidence in court; the seeing of specters and spirits had been used to convict those accused of witchcraft. Once the law was changed, the trials ceased. In another case, the arrest and subsequent trial of Anthony Burns prompted the Massachusetts State Legislature to enact laws to counteract the Fugitive Slave Law, and Burns' return to slavery turned average citizens into militant abolitionists and helped propel the Republican Party into power.

I wish I could claim that every young person who sees these plays will vote in every election once they turn eighteen, will attend town meetings, and will always fight for their beliefs. Of course, I can't. What I can say is that these plays prompt students to ask questions, to look at historical events in new and deeper ways, and to view historical figures as real people faced with difficult decisions. Following performances, I've often heard students say, "that's still going on, you know," as they draw connections between the fate of Japanese Americans during World War II and attitudes toward Arab Americans today, or they compare the Salem witch trials to modern day witch hunts.

*And Justice for Some* is meant to provide teachers and artists with a variety of ways to explore American justice though drama and theatre. *Salem's Daughters* is a traditional play for family audiences. *The Trial of Anthony Burns* and *Justice at War* are both TIE pieces, devised for school groups. *Voicings* is an example of a musical based on oral histories. These plays can be staged as full productions, presented as readings, or divided into selected scenes and performed in the classroom. The accompanying study guides offer ideas to extend the learning process. The exercises in these sections should be adapted to your students' needs, rather than followed verbatim. In the final chapter, Beth and I share the processes used to develop each script and offer advice to help you create your own plays.

Developing plays based on court documents offers writers, teachers, and theatre companies opportunities for interesting collaborations. The partnership between Theatre Espresso and Discovering Justice is just one of many possibilities. In November 2003, a chapter of the Inns of Court[2] brought me to Denver to direct judges and lawyers in a staged reading of *Justice at War*. They performed for eighty-five fellow judges and lawyers who, like our traditional school groups, participated in the drama in role as Supreme Court judges. It is our hope that this book will inspire readers to create new plays, discover new venues for performance, and develop new partnerships between artists, educators, and civic institutions.

In closing, I'd like to share the following story. Twenty years ago, when I lived in Denver, Colorado, a friend called me from Durango. Her seven-year-old son, John, had been treated for leukemia and needed to be picked up from a Denver hospital. She asked if he could spend the night at my apartment—she would pick him up the next day. Retrieving him from the hospital wasn't a problem, but I had a technical rehearsal for the musical *1776* that night. I offered to try and get out of the rehearsal, but she insisted that I bring her son with me. "He'll love it," she said. As the clock approached midnight, I watched John sitting in the dark watching the play and felt pangs of guilt. I should have just called the director and told him I couldn't make it. Over the next few years, each time I remembered that night, I kicked myself for dragging an ailing seven year old to the theatre for a late night rehearsal.

John died at age twelve, about four years past his life expectancy. After his death, I visited his parents in Durango. One night his mother said, "John used to talk about that rehearsal you took him all the time." I was stunned. She went on to explain: He identified with the character of Caesar Rodney, who suffered both from asthma and a cancerous growth on his face. Despite his illness, Rodney made the trip from Delaware to vote on the Declaration of Independence, saving it from defeat. Watching the character of Rodney fight his illness to make a vital contribution to his country and alter the course of history had a profound effect on John. It gave him strength. For me, it was an unexpected lesson in the power of theatre and its ability to help us connect with history.

—Wendy Lement

---

2. The Inns of Court is a national organization, based on the tradition from England. The primary purpose of the Inns is mentorship; established judges and lawyers serve as mentors to young attorneys. To learn more, visit their website: *www.innsofcourt.org*.

# 1

## Salem's Daughters (1692)

## Overview

While touring historical sites in Salem in 1988, docents informed me that a group of bored girls accused dozens of innocent persons of witchcraft, and that a slave from Barbados had told them stories that fueled the accusations. I wondered why Salem girls were more evil than those of the surrounding towns. What other factors were involved? At that time, I was the educational director of The Children's Theatre in Residence at Maudslay State Park (now Theater in the Open) in Newburyport, Massachusetts. There were several talented girls in the company who complained that they were tired of playing fairies, animals, and other nonhumans. They wanted to tackle more meaty roles. I wrote *Salem's Daughters* for them.

*Salem's Daughters* explores the motivations of girls who accused scores of people, mostly women, of witchcraft in 1692. The play premiered in 1989 at Maudslay State Park and then toured to the Blackburn Theatre in Gloucester, Massachusetts. Since then, *Salem's Daughters* has been produced at high schools and colleges, and revived in 2003 by Theater in the Open. In 1992, Salem State College produced the play as part of Salem's Tercentenary Commemoration of the witch trials.

## A Note to the Director

My preference is for age-appropriate casting, but I have seen successful college and high school shows. Whatever their ages, the actors should develop characters with distinct personalities. Some of the characters, such as Ann

1

and Betty, are sincere, while others are motivated by self-interest. It is important for the cast to explore the complexity of their roles. It is also crucial that they understand the depth of the Puritan belief in witchcraft. While some of the girls manipulate situations to avoid punishment, they all hold the fundamental belief that witches exist and can cause great harm. During the rehearsal process for the play's premiere, we held a dinner at the Gate House at Maudslay State Park. The cast, in costume, stayed in character for the entire evening. It was a great way for them to flesh out their characters and their relationships with each other.

*A word on the fits:* It's helpful for each girl to work with a specific image for each fit (e.g., a bird pecking at her eyes or snakes crawling up her legs). The energy should be outward. The actors should try to push away whatever is attacking them. Actors may tend to move upstage and down to the ground during the imaginary attacks. The director should encourage more variety. If snakes are crawling up your legs, your impulse would be to move upward to get away. A demon can attack an actor from behind forcing her downstage. Another option is for the actor to be possessed by a familiar (an evil spirit that attends to the needs of a spell caster), like a bird, a dog or a cat; as if a spirit is forcing her to move and make sounds against her will. In order for the audience to take the fits seriously, the actors need to be totally invested in their choices.

# Salem's Daughters[*]

## by Wendy Lement

## *Characters*

*Salem's Daughters* premiered in 1989 at Theater in the Open with the following cast:

| | |
|---|---|
| SAMUEL PARRIS/JOHN HATHORNE | Michael Thurston |
| ANN PUTNAM SENIOR | Theresa Linnihan |
| THOMAS PUTNAM | David Adams |
| ANN PUTNAM | Mara Flynn |

MERCY LEWIS . . . . . . . . . . . . . . . . . . . . . . . . . . . . . . . . . . .Emily Wonson
BETTY PARRIS . . . . . . . . . . . . . . . . . . . . . . .Jessica Solomon-Greenbaum
ABIGAIL WILLIAMS . . . . . . . . . . . . . . . . . . . .Anna Solomon-Greenbaum
DORCY GOOD . . . . . . . . . . . . . . . . . . . . . . . . . . . . . . . . . . .Jessamine Dana
SARAH GOOD . . . . . . . . . . . . . . . . . . . . . . . . . . . . . . . . . . .Michelle Ninacs
TITUBA . . . . . . . . . . . . . . . . . . . . . . . . . . . . . . . . . . . . .Catherine Woods
MARY WARREN . . . . . . . . . . . . . . . . . . . . . . . . . . . . . . . . . . .Juliet Nelson
ELIZABETH HUBBARD . . . . . . . . . . . . . . . . . . . . . . . . . . . .Heather Currier
MALE ASSISTANT . . . . . . . . . . . . . . . . . . . . . . . . . . . . . . . . . .Scott Smith
FEMALE ASSISTANT . . . . . . . . . . . . . . . . . . . . . . . . . . . . .Susan Atwood

The musical score was composed by Peter Stewart. The choreographer was Caroline Bredice. Costumes were designed by Liz Raycroft.

*Setting:* Salem Village

*Time:* November 1689–August 1706

Act 1, Scene 1

*Upstage right of center sits a tall black throne. A ladder is built into the back of the throne so that PARRIS may climb up it. There should be enough room at the top for PARRIS to stand and deliver his sermons. A pulpit of sorts is built into the front. A web of ropes extends from the top of the throne to other areas of the stage. There should be a space for props and costume pieces built into the back of the structure. The throne should sit approximately twelve feet high, including a one-foot base. On both sides of the throne, wooden frames with black scrim extend like wings. These can be back lit, or used as masking. Downstage right of the throne sit three wooden benches.*

*As the music begins, the lights come up on ANN JUNIOR, who lays prone downcenter. ANN SENIOR enters with a rope and hands one end to her daughter. The rest of the cast enter and join in a dance of conspiracy each touching the rope at some point. Then ANN SENIOR, THOMAS PUTNAM, ANN, MERCY, BETTY, ABIGAIL, MARY, ELIZABETH, and the townsfolk take their place at the benches. PARRIS climbs the pulpit and the music ends.*

PARRIS: Good people of Salem Village, on this day, the nineteenth of November, 1689, the honorable Reverend, Mr. Nicholas Noyes, has ordained my most unworthy self: pastor. After this humble village hath been without spiritual guidance for two years, God hath sent me to your door. Therefore, I name my text. Joshua, Chapter 5: Verse 9, the first part. "And the Lord said unto Joshua, this day have I rolled away the reproach of Egypt from off you."

Hence learn, you of this place, this village, that God hath graciously brought you to a good day this day. To all who belong to this small congregation: Oh! Let us be exhorted in our places most heedfully to beware of reproaching and disgracing the work of this day. And for the prevention thereof, there is no better way in all the world than to take direction from the word of God, how we are each of us from this day forward to behave ourselves. In a word: I will begin with myself. Much work is laid upon my weak shoulders. I am to labor that my doctrine may burn, and my conversation may shine. I am to make differences between the clean and unclean, so as to change and purge the one, and confirm and strengthen the other. As I am to give cordials to some, so I must administer corrosives to others. In what I am to do, you must not, you cannot, you ought not to be angry: for so am I commanded.

I will now come to you. There are things you are to do, and not a little, neither. You are to pay me that reverence which is due to an ambassador of Christ Jesus. You are to pray for me, and to pray much and fervently always for me. You are to bear me a great deal of love. You are indeed highly to love every minister of Christ Jesus, but you are to love me best. You are to obey me, at least so far as I watch your souls. And as every lover of God's honor will, so let them, say: Amen.

ANN SENIOR: (*Ann Senior rises and pulls her daughter aside.*) I do believe the tide has changed. God smiles upon us at last. Even the air has a particular fervor about it. Can you not feel it, Ann?

ANN: Aye, Mother. Master Parris' sermon surely sends quivers through my spine.

ANN SENIOR: But I was speaking of the air. Does it not seem to you that it doth possess a penetrating quality?

ANN: (*not sure what her mother means*) I believe it does.

ANN SENIOR: It fills my very bones, Ann. Surely you must feel it.

ANN: (*Ann Junior looks at her apologetically.*) Perhaps my garments are too dense.

ANN SENIOR: Come here, child. (*Ann Senior moves them to a spot out of sight. She whispers.*) One only need close one's eyes and draw breath. (*Ann Senior does this and then shivers.*) It is quite overwhelming. Ann, you must attempt it as well, since you doubt my word.

ANN: I do believe you.

ANN SENIOR: Close your eyes and breathe.

ANN: Aye, Mother. (*Ann Junior makes sure no one is looking and then tries it. She feels nothing and looks at her mother blankly.*)

ANN SENIOR: You barely drew a breath. This time hold it longer. (*Ann Junior does this.*) That's it. Doth the air pervade ye, body and soul? (*Ann shakes her head no as she continues to hold her breath.*) Nay? Then ye must persevere. (*After a few moments Ann opens an eye to beg her mother to let her stop.*) When all doubt has drifted from ye and the Lord fills thy heart, then ye shall release thy breath. (*pause*) He is coming to ye now, is he not?

ANN: (*Finally Ann nods yes and falls to the ground panting.*) It is as you said. The air is so strong it doth penetrate my very soul.

THOMAS: (*Looking for his wife, he calls in a loud whisper.*) Ann, Ann have you gone home?

ANN SENIOR: (*She hears him and rushes to kneel by her daughter.*) Thomas, come quickly.

THOMAS: (*sees his daughter on the ground*) Ann, have you fallen ill?

ANN: I . . .

ANN SENIOR: What would you expect, Thomas? The child has not had a drop of milk since the cow died.

THOMAS: Aye, and there is enough goat's milk about to let it go sour.

ANN: Goat's milk tastes foul.

THOMAS: You will be drinking it tonight, just the same.

ANN: I am not ill, really. (*stands*)

ANN SENIOR: (*diverting attention*) Is the Reverend, Master Parris still about?

THOMAS: I have been chattering away with him for the past quarter hour waiting for you. I cannot speak of the weather much longer.

ANN SENIOR: Patience, Thomas. I am just looking after Ann.

THOMAS: Well, be quick about it. I have not the same gift for idle chatter as you. (*crosses to Parris*)

ANN: What must you speak to Master Parris about?

ANN SENIOR: (*pulls her aside*) Now that the Pastor has graced our congregation, we must move quickly to secure our standing.

ANN: Our standing?

ANN SENIOR: I shall invite the Reverend Master Parris and his wife to our house for tea, while Mercy and you escort his niece and daughter to their home.

ANN: Aye.

*ANN SENIOR:* Take the north path to avoid the thick woods.

*ANN:* I shall.

*ANN SENIOR:* And take these for protection. (*She hands Ann Junior apple seeds.*)

*ANN:* Apple seeds?

*ANN SENIOR:* The forest is a den for Satan and his followers.

*ANN:* Mama . . .

*ANN SENIOR:* Have faith, Ann. If an evil spirit doth afflict thee toss these seeds at the creature. The Lord shall guide ye.

*ANN:* Perhaps Mercy should escort the Pastor's daughter.

*ANN SENIOR:* Mercy can nay be trusted, Ann.

*ANN:* Pray, let me come home with you.

*THOMAS:* (*entering*) Master Parris is preparing to leave, Ann. If the child is ill, I will summon Dr. Griggs.

*ANN:* (*quietly*) Mercy can walk with them.

*ANN SENIOR:* I am well able to care for my own daughter.

*THOMAS:* Is she still ailing?

*ANN SENIOR:* Nay. Shall we attend to Master Parris?

*THOMAS:* Pray we are not too late. (*Thomas and Ann Senior cross to Parris.*)

*ANN:* Mama . . . (*She holds the seeds in her hand and runs off stage.*)

*ANN SENIOR:* (*Ann Senior and Thomas Putnam join Parris.*) That was indeed an inspiring sermon, Master Parris.

*THOMAS:* Aye, Salem Village is truly blessed by your presence. If the congregation had any doubts as to your . . .

*PARRIS:* Yes, I have heard of these "doubts." What kind of soul would question a man of the cloth?

*ANN SENIOR:* What my good husband meant to say was that Salem Village is indebted to you.

*PARRIS:* Yet they refuse to supply my home with firewood.

*ANN SENIOR:* There are those among us . . .

*PARRIS:* And they squabble over my meager salary.

*ANN SENIOR:* We would be honored if you and your wife would join our table this afternoon to discuss these matters.

*THOMAS:* I pray you do not lay blame on us for the disgraceful behavior of our neighbors.

*PARRIS:* I accept your generous offer, Mrs. Putnam, but first I must escort my daughter Betty and her cousin Abigail home.

ANN SENIOR: Our servant Mercy Lewis and my daughter Ann would be most happy to accompany them to your house.

THOMAS: Then, in the privacy of our home, we may speak quite frankly of our good neighbors.

PARRIS: As you wish. (*They exit and the rest of the congregation leave except for Ann Junior, Mercy, Abigail, and Betty.*)

## SCENE 2

*The four girls stare at each other. There is a pause.*

ANN: (*making conversation*) They say you lived in Barbados.

BETTY: Aye, it is a wondrous land.

ABIGAIL: (*with false politeness*) If you would be so kind as to excuse us, we shall be heading home now.

MERCY: And I will be taking you there.

ABIGAIL: We are quite familiar with the path home, Mary Lewis.

MERCY: Mercy.

ABIGAIL: Aye, may God have mercy on this wretched place.

MERCY: I am named Mercy Lewis.

BETTY: She knows this, I am sure.

MERCY: (*with authority*) I will be taking charge of you.

ABIGAIL: (*takes no notice*) Have you a pleasant day, Mercy Lewis, and you too, the smaller Ann Putnam. Come, Betty.

BETTY: I hope we shall see you next Sunday.

ANN: Your father has ordered that you shall see us now, Betty Parris.

MERCY: Did you not hear him say we are to walk you to your door?

ABIGAIL: Aye, but I am very well able to be finding our door.

ANN: But we are to go with you.

ABIGAIL: Do you always do as you are told, Ann Putnam?

ANN: (*lying*) No.

ABIGAIL: Then find a thing to occupy yourself until sunset.

MERCY: You'll not be leaving us, Miss Abigail Williams. Although I must say, I would prefer it.

BETTY: Why can they not come home with us, Abigail?

ABIGAIL: And who says we shall be going home?

BETTY: Father does.

ABIGAIL: Poor little Betty. (*She takes a bite of an apple. Dorcy Good has been watching them for a time. She is four years old and dressed in beggar's clothes.*)

MERCY: I'll not be whipped on the count of you, Abigail Williams.

ABIGAIL: And I'll not be bored on the count of you.

DORCY: (*Dorcy makes her way over to the girls. She looks so pitiful that Betty and Abigail are immediately taken by her presence. Ann and Mercy look at her in disgust.*) Could you spare a small piece of your apple, Miss?

ABIGAIL: (*handing it to her*) You may finish it, surely.

ANN: (*Ann shoves the apple out of Dorcy's hand and pushes her over on the ground.*) Go back to the devil, you horrid creature.

ABIGAIL: (*Abigail and Betty are truly shocked by Ann's behavior.*) I made a gift of the apple, Ann Putnam.

ANN: Would you make such a gift to Satan himself?

ABIGAIL: Be you an imbecile?

SARAH: (*Sarah Good has spotted the girls and runs to Dorcy.*) Dorcy, my child. My poor child. (*Dorcy runs to her arms. Betty and Abigail stand petrified. Ann and Mercy are not affected.*)

ANN: (*spits at her*) The devil take you, Sarah Good.

SARAH: (*Sarah is about to strike Ann, but thinks better of it.*) I should have known it would be the likes of you, Ann Putnam. You are just as hateful as your mother. Shame on you. Shame on all of you. My poor child has not a bite to eat for two days now. Has God not placed one ounce of pity in the cold hearts of you Putnams?

MERCY: Listen to the old witch speak of God.

SARAH: Were I a witch, I would surely cast a spell on you.

ANN: Have you not had enough evil conjuring?

SARAH: God will punish you, Ann Putnam. I need not be concerned with that. (*She picks up Dorcy and starts to leave.*)

MERCY: (*Mercy picks up a rock and throws it at Sarah.*) I shall see you burn in Hell, witch. (*Ann joins in with the rock throwing and harassment.*)

SARAH: (*as she runs off*) A curse on you. A curse on you, I say.

MERCY: (*Betty and Abigail are in shock.*) Ann, look, she has bewitched Abigail and little Betty.

ABIGAIL: (*quickly coming to her senses*) It is not the devil that put us in a state, Mercy. We would surely be flogged for such foulness.

BETTY: Be she really a witch, Ann?

ANN: Aye, and she hath cast her devilment upon us before.

*ABIGAIL:* I have heard no talk of a witch in Salem Village.

*ANN:* There be more than one, and not only in Salem. My mother found the devil in Andover, not more than a year ago. She could not prove the woman to be a witch, and so they set the wench free.

*BETTY:* We saw a witch hung in Boston, did we not, Abigail?

*ABIGAIL:* Aye, if she were truly a witch.

*BETTY:* She must have been, or why should she be hanged?

*ABIGAIL:* I cannot do all your thinking for you.

*BETTY:* What spells has this witch cast upon your house?

*ANN:* My mother speaks of many vile acts. I cannot tell you these.

*BETTY:* Why not?

*ANN:* They would surely make your hair stand up on your neck.

*MERCY:* Aye.

*ABIGAIL:* In Barbados there are evil spirits in every tree. They dance at night and court young girls.

*BETTY:* (*scared*) That is not true.

*ABIGAIL:* They fly above the island and drop the maidens in the ocean, unless they agree to commit vile sins with Satan himself.

*BETTY:* That is a lie!

*ANN:* There is one incident which I myself witnessed.

*MERCY:* Aye, the one with the cow.

*ANN:* About a month ago Goody Good came to our door begging food and such. When my mother turned her away empty handed, she left muttering some evil curse.

*ABIGAIL:* Does your mother not believe in charity for the poor?

*ANN:* (*The girls gather around her.*) Goody Good used to have as much money as anyone. Then her husband died and she lost everything. There must be some reason God would inflict such hardship on a woman. She is a servant of the devil, no doubt.

*MERCY:* Tell them what happened to the cow.

*ANN:* The very next day after the spell had been cast, our milking cow died.

*MERCY:* She was a healthy cow, too.

*ANN:* How can you explain that, if not by witchcraft?

*ABIGAIL:* Perhaps, but even so, it seems like a mild case—hardly worth telling.

*MERCY:* She has done worse than that. She has murdered babies.

*ANN:* Mercy!

*MERCY:* She eats their flesh.

*ABIGAIL:* Every witch does that.

*BETTY:* Let us go home, Abigail.

*ABIGAIL:* Aye, and Tituba can tell these Salem girls about the ways of the devil.

*BETTY:* We are to read the bible.

*ABIGAIL:* Aye, the truth may frighten our new friends.

*MERCY:* I shall not be frightened by talk of the devil.

*ANN:* Nor I.

*BETTY:* Father said . . .

*ABIGAIL:* You may do as you like. Perhaps you should walk behind us, lest our conversation scare you.

*BETTY:* I shall walk with you.

*ABIGAIL:* Then get on with it. (*They exit.*)

SCENE 3

*As the girls exit, the* PUTNAMs *enter with teacups. They sit on the base of the throne.* PARRIS *holds his cup out and drinks seated at his throne.*

*PARRIS: (in mid conversation)* No, Putnam, I blame you. I came to this God forsaken village on your assurances.

*THOMAS:* What would you have me do?

*PARRIS:* Negotiate.

*THOMAS:* With what?

*PARRIS:* Did you know that Judas sold our Lord Jesus Christ for thirty pieces of silver?

*THOMAS:* Aye, but what has that . . .

*PARRIS:* Thirty pieces of silver for the Son of God!

*ANN SENIOR: (getting in his good graces)* He was worth far more.

*PARRIS:* I should say so, Mrs. Putnam, at least three times that sum.

*THOMAS:* Forgive me Master Parris, but what is your point?

*PARRIS:* My point, Putnam, is that your efforts have failed. The whole of my salary, including provisions, stands at a mere sixty pounds.

*THOMAS: (exasperated)* I have taken every possible opportunity . . .

PARRIS: (*dryly*) So you said. Now, I have a proposal that I myself will bring before the council. But I will need the support of the Putnams.

THOMAS: Of course.

PARRIS: Good. (*ending the conversation*) With God's help we can rectify this unfortunate situation once and for all.

THOMAS: What is it that I am supporting? If I may inquire.

PARRIS: (*losing patience*) Worshippers from outside of Salem Village come to my parish, do they not?

THOMAS: There were at least seven such persons this morning.

ANN SENIOR: There were twelve.

PARRIS: Twelve. And these persons, I assume, made donations to the church?

THOMAS: To be sure.

PARRIS: And where do these proceeds go?

THOMAS: To the village coffers, I believe.

PARRIS: I say they will go to me, as a bonus. I want to know who makes the donations and how much they give. In fact, I would like to extend that policy to the entire congregation. As it is I have no record of who supports my presence and who opposes me.

THOMAS: I can certainly give you those names, Master Parris.

PARRIS: (*sharply*) I want records kept, Putnam. I shall do it myself.

THOMAS: As you wish.

ANN SENIOR: Would you care for more tea, Master Parris?

PARRIS: No, thank you. I believe our business is through for today.

THOMAS: (*Ann Senior and Thomas exchange glances.*) Master Parris, could I trouble you for just a moment longer?

PARRIS: If you will be brief.

ANN SENIOR: My husband has a proposal of his own to make.

THOMAS: I can speak for myself, surely.

ANN SENIOR: Then get on with it. Our new reverend has much to do. Have you not, Master Parris?

PARRIS: Indeed, Mrs. Putnam.

THOMAS: I am a simple man, Master Parris, a farmer by trade. I will put it to you plainly.

PARRIS: Go on.

THOMAS: As you know, your main support in this congregation comes from those of the Putnam family. There are, in total, twenty-one Putnams who voted for your appointment.

ANN SENIOR: (*jumps on this*) Twenty-five (*softens*), if you count your sisters' husbands.

THOMAS: At any rate, we Putnams represent over a quarter of your support in this congregation.

PARRIS: What is your point?

THOMAS: Master Parris, with all due respect we have sat patiently listening to all your demands. This sort of thing does not come as easily to me, I not having your experience in commerce.

PARRIS: I see.

ANN SENIOR: There is no need to be in bad temper, Thomas. Master Parris knows how important the Putnams are to him. He'd be more than happy to appoint our kinfolk to positions within the church. After all, he will need deacons, church elders, and such. And why not appoint those who laid the foundation for his employment. (*pause*) Your tea is quite cold.

PARRIS: I will have a drop more, thank you. I believe that such appointments would be beneficial to us all. But, if I consent, Putnam, you must move to end those squabbles with your neighbors. A divided congregation does hurt my standing.

THOMAS: Israel Porter builds a dam, flooding my richest soil and you would have me embrace him.

PARRIS: If it would bring them under the wing of my congregation, I say you must.

THOMAS: His dealings have cheated my family out of our rightful inheritance.

ANN SENIOR: It is strange indeed that a man would pass over his eldest son and leave the bulk of his holdings to his second wife. What kind of power does such a woman possess?

PARRIS: (*bored with this*) My friends, it is clear you have been wronged by these jealous neighbors of yours.

ANN SENIOR: There have been evil deeds worse than this.

THOMAS: I cannot tell you the hardships my wife and I have had to endure.

PARRIS: These are indeed hard times, for all.

ANN SENIOR: Hard enough without the help of Satan.

PARRIS: Are you implying that the devil has played a role in your misfortune?

ANN SENIOR: There be no doubt.

PARRIS: Witchcraft is a serious charge, Mrs. Putnam.

ANN SENIOR: I have suffered many a serious loss. (*She starts to cry. Thomas stares at her admonishingly.*)

THOMAS: You must not talk about it, dear.

ANN SENIOR: Not long ago a curse was placed upon us, killing our milking cow. And me with so many mouths to feed.

PARRIS: One must have evidence to lay such a charge.

ANN SENIOR: Then advise us, Master Parris. (*Ann Senior stands and crosses down right. As she speaks, the nightmare music begins to play. The two assistants enter the playing space with a long rope. During the following speech they dance with the rope and eventually tie it to two trees to be used as a clothesline. They finally bring out a steaming cauldron. They set it on a circle of rocks as if it were on a fire.*) I have heard that there are ways of uncovering such evils. That when one's livestock is cursed and dies, the identity of the witch who cast this wicked spell may be discovered. One only need cut off the ears of the animal and toss them into the fire. Within the heat of the flames the witch's imp shall be released from the ears and its master shall be the first to arrive there. (*Thomas places a firm hand on her shoulder to stop her from continuing.*)

PARRIS: I caution you both. The use of witchcraft, even in defending your-self against the devil, is strictly forbidden, and punishable by death. Do you understand?

THOMAS: My wife had no intention of . . .

ANN SENIOR: Yes, we understand each other. (*The Putnams exit and the music ends.*)

SCENE 4

TITUBA *enters singing the song of the yellow bird. She carries a basket and paddle. She crosses to the cauldron and stirs the contents.*

TITUBA: (*sings*) Yellow Bird, sitting all alone in a tree.
Yellow Bird, sitting all alone like me.
Where's your lady friend?
Say she'll be back again.
Yes she fly away.
You're more luckier than me.
I wish I were a yellow bird.
I would fly away, too.
Since I'm not a yellow bird,
I'm going to stay here with you.

*Toward the end of the song, the four girls enter laughing and out of breath. When* ANN *and* MERCY *catch sight of* TITUBA *over the cauldron, they freeze.* BETTY *runs to hug her.*

*TITUBA:* So, how did your father's first sermon go?

*BETTY:* Very well.

*ABIGAIL:* One more blessed verse, and I would have hurled that bible right in his face. I swear it.

*TITUBA:* One of these days you're going to be talking up a storm, child, and he'll be right around the corner, hearing every word you say. (*Abigail shrugs.*) And who is this you brought home with you?

*ABIGAIL:* Two beggar children we found on the road.

*BETTY:* She is a liar, Tituba.

*TITUBA:* Is that so?

*BETTY:* They are from the Putnam house. Father says they shall join us in our bible reading.

*TITUBA:* (*looks at the two frozen girls and smiles*) Do they have names?

*ANN:* Ann . . . Ann Putnam.

*TITUBA:* It's a pleasure to meet you, Ann.

*MERCY:* (*Prompted by Ann, she speaks.*) And I am Mercy Lewis.

*TITUBA:* Well, sit you down Mercy and Ann. Betty, go fetch your friends some biscuits and tea from the house.

*BETTY:* Aye, Tituba.

*ANN:* (*walks slowly to the cauldron*) What is it that you are cooking?

*MERCY:* It smells foul.

*ANN:* Mercy.

*TITUBA:* Would you not like a taste?

*ANN:* (*shakes her head*) No, thank you.

*TITUBA:* I don't blame you. It's not for eating.

*MERCY:* What is it for, then?

*TITUBA:* Sleeping on. (*laughs*) I'm giving the beddings a good washing.

*ANN & MERCY:* Ah. (*They laugh nervously. Betty enters and hands Tituba the tin. She opens it and hands it back to Betty.*)

*TITUBA:* You can each have one now, and another one later. (*Betty passes them out. Abigail grabs two and stares defiantly at Tituba.*) I suppose Abigail would like both of hers now. (*She takes the tin from Abigail and closes it.*) You better get to your reading.

ABIGAIL: Tituba, what was that song?

TITUBA: Now what song would that be?

ABIGAIL: The one you were singing.

TITUBA: I sing a lot of songs.

BETTY: She means the one you were singing when we came home.

TITUBA: Oh, that one.

ABIGAIL: What is it called?

TITUBA: That's the song of the yellow bird. (*Ann and Mercy stare at each other.*)

ABIGAIL: Can you teach it to us?

TITUBA: (*notices Ann and Mercy's reaction*) I don't know. Your two friends look like they just swallowed a yellow bird.

ANN: A yellow bird is an instrument of Satan, is it not?

TITUBA: No. He is one of God's creatures, don't you know. (*She sees that the two girls are not convinced and decides not to press it.*) There are many birds though.

BETTY: Tituba and I found a robin's nest.

TITUBA: Then maybe you want to sing about the robin.

MERCY: We see blue jays near our house.

TITUBA: Oh, we can sing about them, too.

TITUBA: Betty, Abigail, come let's teach Mercy the song of Chee Chee Bird-O. (*Tituba teaches them the song. Ann watches at first. The other girls are charmed into the song and begin to pick up on Tituba's movements. They finally pull Ann Junior into the dance.*)

> Chee Chee Bird-O (*hold note*)
> Some of them a halla some a ball,
> Some a _____. (*fill in name of bird. Example: robins.*)
> Some of them a halla some a ball,
> Some a _____. (*fill in name of bird. Example: blue jays.*)
> Peel head Jon Crow
> Sit down in a tree top
> Pick off the blossoms.
> Come let me hold your hand gal,
> Come let me hold your hand.
> It's a long time gal me never see you.
> Come let me reel and turn gal,
> Come let me reel and turn.

*When the song is over, the girls fall on the ground.* ANN, BETTY, *and* MERCY *are embarrassed that they let go.*

*TITUBA:* You sing as beautiful as the birds themselves. Now you must go do your reading.

*ABIGAIL:* Tituba, how could you tell if there be witches in Salem Village?

*TITUBA:* What kind of nonsense are you talking now?

*ANN:* It's a fact.

*ABIGAIL:* Tell them about real witchcraft, in Barbados.

*TITUBA:* I don't know anything about witchcraft, in Barbados or anywhere else. Now pick up your bibles and read, before I tell your uncle.

*ABIGAIL:* But you knew of a witch doctor there.

*TITUBA:* And a witch doctor protects a village from evil spirits.

*ABIGAIL:* How could he tell if there be evil spirits about?

*TITUBA:* What's all this talk of witchcraft, or are you trying to get out of your reading?

*ANN:* There are witches in this town that would do harm to me and my kin.

*TITUBA:* Then you best pray to God, child.

*MERCY:* She has been cursed this very day. We all saw it.

*BETTY:* We did.

*ABIGAIL:* What would the witch doctor do if we were in his village?

*TITUBA:* He'd surely take you over his knee for not doing what you're told. Now if you're going to be standing here, you might as well help me with this washing. (*She pulls the wet steaming sheets from the cauldron and slaps them on a rock.*) Lord knows what kind of vermin crawled into that trunk on the boat here. You can't be too careful, you know. (*The girls stare at the sheets.*) You don't think they're going to wring themselves out, do you?

*BETTY:* No.

*TITUBA:* Then get to work. (*Abigail and Betty reluctantly take a sheet and begin wringing it out. Ann and Mercy follow suit.*)

*ANN:* Tituba . . . Abigail told us that on the island of Barbados, there be evil spirits in every tree.

*TITUBA:* (*laughs*) Did she?

*MERCY:* It is not true, is it?

*TITUBA:* Well now, I'm not sure. I haven't inspected every tree.

*ABIGAIL:* There are. I have seen them.

*TITUBA:* And I've seen glorious spirits dancing through the Island trees. But I'll tell you one thing (*looks at Ann*), if you're set and determined to find evil in the world, sooner or later it will find you. (*The girls stare at Tituba.*) Now, are you going to hang those bedclothes up, or stand there with your mouths hanging open? (*The girls catch themselves and hang the sheets on the line.*)

*ANN:* What do spirits look like when they are dancing?

*TITUBA:* It depends who's doing the looking.

*ABIGAIL:* What do you see?

*TITUBA:* Oh, I see the future, and the past and the present, as if they were all rolled up into one time, or no time.

*ABIGAIL:* Tituba can see the future in tealeaves.

*MERCY:* (*Mercy gulps down her tea.*) What do mine say?

*TITUBA:* I didn't say that I would.

*MERCY:* Please.

*TITUBA:* (*pause*) All right, just this once. But you mustn't tell nobody.

*MERCY:* I swear it.

*ANN:* (*Tituba looks at Ann.*) I swear it.

*TITUBA:* Very well then, let's have a look. (*stares into the cup*) Ah . . .

*MERCY:* What?! What do you see?

*TITUBA:* Hush!

*MERCY:* Sorry.

*TITUBA:* (*examines the cup*) Mmmn, that's what I thought.

*BETTY:* What is it, Tituba?

*TITUBA:* The dagger. (*The girls gasp.*) Danger lies ahead.

*MERCY:* What kind of danger?

*TITUBA:* Don't be so curious. It will bring trouble. (*A pause, as the girls stare at each other.*)

*ANN:* Can you . . . speak to the dead?

*TITUBA:* No. And I don't want to!

*ANN:* I do.

*TITUBA:* No you don't, child.

*ABIGAIL:* She can see other things.

*TITUBA:* It's a dangerous business.

*MERCY:* Can you tell me whom I am to marry?

*TITUBA:* No. (*pause*) But I will tell a true story about a young girl who did.

Salem's Daughters, *(left to right) Jessica Rybicki, Samantha Wilkens, Kali Walker, Abigail Davies, and Michaella Scott, photo by Wendy Lement.*

*BETTY:* Did what?

*TITUBA:* Summoned the spirit of her groom to be.

*MERCY:* Then you do know how.

*TITUBA:* Now this girl, you see, couldn't wait for things to take their right and natural course. So she gathered some of her friends into the woods to help her perform a Silent Tea. (*The girls gather around her and sit mesmerized. As the music begins to play, the Female Assistant acts out the ritual, as if it were in the imagination of the girls.*) Before she could begin the ceremony, she had to fast for three full days. And on the third day, she baked a loaf of cornbread. But the girl had to make sure that every step she took, was a step backward. When she mixed the cornbread, she had to add the last thing first and the first thing last. And when she came to the woods, everyone had to be silent, or the spell would break. Then in the silence, always taking her steps back, she set a table for two. One plate for her and one for the spirit of her groom, the cornbread in the center with a knife. And finally she made the tea, pouring the boiling water in first and then the special tealeaves. The girl poured a cup for each of her friends first, then herself, then her guest to be. She took a deep breath and sat down at the table and at the same moment all the girls turned their cups to the left three times and took a sip of the tea. And then it happened.

BETTY: What?

TITUBA: (*The Male Assistant enters in a white, flowing, hooded robe. He passes through the sheets on the clothesline becoming the spirit groom.*) The spirit of her future groom came to her and sat at the table. The figure was like a ghost and only she could see the face of her husband. (*The groom kneels facing the bride. His back is to the audience. He takes off his hood only long enough for his bride to see his face.*) Her friends saw nothing but a white shapeless figure. And then he was gone. And the knife had disappeared. (*The bride and groom exit quickly pulling the clothesline and the sheets off with them. The music ends.*)

MERCY: Did it work?

TITUBA: Have you not been listening?

MERCY: But, was she wed to the man she saw that night?

TITUBA: She was. Ill-fated though she be. For three years they were married, and happy, too. Until one night, she told him about the Silent Tea and how it was his face she saw. He stared at her and then he took out a wood box she had never seen before. You know what was inside the box, don't you? It was the knife, from the table. And he said, "You were the witch who put me through that night of hell!" And he stabbed her with the knife, and left her there to die.

BETTY: Did she . . . die?

TITUBA: Almost, child, almost. But lucky for her, I happen to notice him storming out in a rage and when he was gone, I went in and found her. Or else she'd be dead for sure. That's how I know these things.

MERCY: Do you know of any other ways to see your future husband?

TITUBA: No. (*pause*) Now, isn't it time you go and do what your father asked?

BETTY: He and Mama will be home soon for dinner.

TITUBA: They will? And look at us just sitting around. Go do what you're told.

ANN: Thank you for the tea, Tituba. Mercy and I should be starting home.

MERCY: Could you read Ann's tealeaves?

TITUBA: Enough tea reading today. Remember, not a word. (*They nod and start to leave.*)

SCENE 5

*The music starts and the* FEMALE *and* MALE ASSISTANTS *enter. The* FEMALE ASSISTANT *carries a stake, the other shadows her movements.* TITUBA *and the two remaining girls exit. The* ASSISTANTS *begin to move as if they were being tormented. Finally the* FEMALE ASSISTANT *stabs the stake into the ground marking a grave site. As they exit,* ANN SENIOR *enters and kneels by the grave. With her arms she conjures a baby and holds it close to her.* ANN JUNIOR *has entered with a small bunch of wild flowers. She stands behind her mother watching her.* ANN SENIOR *does not notice her daughter. The music ends. After a pause,* ANN JUNIOR *finally speaks.*

*ANN:* I told Mercy it would be best for her to go straight home.

*ANN SENIOR:* (*Ann Senior starts with fright. After gaining her composure she speaks.*) I am glad you came. (*Pause as Ann Junior places her flowers on the grave and kneels across from her mother.*) I had the dream again.

*ANN:* I heard you last night.

*ANN SENIOR:* It comes almost every night, now.

*ANN:* When I fell back to sleep, it came to me, too.

*ANN SENIOR:* This is truly a sign.

*ANN:* They cried out to me.

*ANN SENIOR:* Poor tormented souls.

*ANN:* They bid me to find who it was that murdered them.

*ANN SENIOR:* What vile creature would inflict such harm, and to one so innocent as a newborn child?

*ANN:* I saw my tiny brother his eyes burning with pain. Then your sister appeared in winding sheets with all her lifeless children about her, their eyes upon me crying for me to help them. How can I help them?

*ANN SENIOR:* I am told I need proof that the evil hand is upon us. Tell me, how does one prove what is invisible?

*ANN:* There are those who are given sight into this invisible world.

*ANN SENIOR:* If only I knew such a person.

*ANN:* I . . . may know of one.

*ANN SENIOR:* Speak up, child.

*ANN:* She claims she cannot speak to the dead. But I believe her to be lying.

*ANN SENIOR:* Tell me what person this is, who speaks with spirits.

*ANN:* She sees the future. Is it not possible she can see the past?

Salem's Daughters, *(left to right) Samantha Wilkens and Libbie Womack-Jorn, photo by Wendy Lement.*

*ANN SENIOR:* Answer me, child. Who is this person?

*ANN:* I cannot say. I made a promise.

*ANN SENIOR:* Ann, if there be someone who may ease our torment, you must tell.

*ANN:* I could ask her for you.

*ANN SENIOR:* Has she some hold on you?

*ANN:* None. I swear.

*ANN SENIOR:* Are you not my own daughter? My namesake?

*ANN:* Aye, but I . . .

*ANN SENIOR:* Then how could you keep this from me? Have I not told you ought of my life? My dreams? You dare not confide in your own mother? Could it be the devil has made you swear?

*ANN:* Nay, by my word.

*ANN SENIOR:* Then how is it you are my daughter?

*ANN:* (*almost in tears*) It is Tituba.

*ANN SENIOR:* Who?

*ANN:* The Parris' serving woman.

*ANN SENIOR:* Tituba.

*ANN:* She read Mercy's tealeaves. And Abigail says she can do more things, too.

*ANN SENIOR:* (*as if trying the word on*) Tituba.

*ANN:* She knows how girls may summon the spirit of the man they are to wed. She told us this.

*ANN SENIOR:* You must have a talk with this Tituba.

*ANN:* Not if the Reverend Master Parris is about.

*ANN SENIOR:* Nay, he must know nothing of this. But next Sunday, I shall invite the Master Parris to our home. And you shall go to theirs. Do you know what to do?

*ANN:* Aye, mother.

*ANN SENIOR:* You are my precious daughter, after all.

ANN SENIOR *gets up as if in a dream and exits.* ANN JUNIOR *sinks by the grave and falls asleep. The music picks up as she dreams. The* MALE ASSISTANT *moves to her and offers his hand, she looks up and slowly takes it. She stands and they begin to waltz in a large circle. The* FEMALE ASSISTANT *enters in the white costume from before. She folds her arms as if holding a baby. She holds the baby out to* ANN. ANN *starts to reach for it, but the* MALE ASSISTANT *makes her continue dancing. In the background the other cast members enter ceremoniously from behind the scrim. They quietly take their place in church. The tempo picks up as* ANN *tries furiously to escape the dancer and reach for the baby. As they reach a climax,* ANN *breaks free of the* MALE ASSISTANT. ANN *turns to the* FEMALE ASSISTANT *who makes a motion as if making the baby disappear. The* FEMALE ASSISTANT *runs to the side of her counterpart.* ANN *turns back to the* MALE ASSISTANT *and raises her arms as if holding on. The* MALE ASSISTANT *also holds his arms up, but makes a motion with his hands of releasing* ANN. *The* ASSISTANTS *exit quickly.* ANN *spirals toward the benches in slow motion as if falling from a great height. The music ends abruptly. She sits up with a start to hear* PARRIS' *booming voice. She is in church.*

SCENE 6

PARRIS *removes his hood and stands. He speaks to the congregation.*

*PARRIS:* From the Book of Revelations, Chapter 17: Verse 14, "These shall make war with the Lamb, and the Lamb shall overcome them: For he is the Lord of Lords, and the King of Kings. And they that are with him are called, and chosen and faithful." Our Lord knows that this war shall last as long as Satan can fight. It shall not be forever and always. Caution and admonition to all and every one of us to beware of making war with the Lamb. For one may do so with pious intent. The temptation is great when a soul is tormented by a servant of the devil; that is when we have been cursed and that curse brings misfortune to our family or property.

What is meant by temptation? Temptation is an instrument of the devil. The devil may offer all kinds of spells. The devil may sayith, "Beware, beware of the Snake. He who summons Satan to expose his servants, becomes a vile slave of the devil." Our Lord sayith, "Have faith. After this life the saints shall no more be tormented with war from devils and their instruments. The city of heaven, provided for saints, is well walled and well gated, so that no devils, nor their instruments shall enter there-in." Amen.

ALL: Amen.

ANN and THOMAS PUTNAM start to leave in a hurry, but are stopped by PARRIS' voice.

PARRIS: Ah, Mr. and Mrs. Putnam, I trust you took my sermon to heart.

THOMAS: Please believe we did indeed heed your warning.

PARRIS: (dryly) I am pleased.

ANN SENIOR: You offered us such good counsel. I was hoping to repay your kindness by inviting you and Mrs. Parris once more to our humble home.

PARRIS: You are too kind, Mrs. Putnam. Shall we say next Thursday?

ANN SENIOR: I was hoping you could join us this afternoon. I have taken the liberty of instructing Mercy and Ann to accompany your daughter and niece home.

PARRIS: Have you?

THOMAS: Thursday would be perfectly acceptable . . .

ANN SENIOR: I am afraid there are urgent matters that concern you, Reverend.

PARRIS: What sort of matters, Mrs. Putnam?

ANN SENIOR: It may not be wise to speak with so many people about. But I can tell you that it concerns your salary.

PARRIS: I thought that business was over and done with.

THOMAS: I can assure you . . .

*ANN SENIOR:* . . . that there are still those who would see you undone. It would be a disservice to you, if I did not speak out.

*PARRIS: (pause)* Very well, dear lady, I am at your disposal.

*ANN SENIOR:* Splendid.

ANN SENIOR *and* THOMAS *exit.* PARRIS *replaces his hood and watches the following scene.*

SCENE 7

BETTY *and* ABIGAIL *enter the space and stop by the tree.*

*BETTY:* They are not here.

*ABIGAIL:* I can see that.

*BETTY:* I am sure they decided not to come.

*ABIGAIL:* And you would go home?

*BETTY:* It may be wise.

*ABIGAIL:* Then go.

*BETTY:* Not by myself.

*ABIGAIL:* Then stay, and do not be such a pest.

*BETTY: (pause)* He knows.

*ABIGAIL:* How would he? Unless you . . .

*BETTY:* I would not! But why should he deliver such a sermon?

*ABIGAIL:* What is it now?

*BETTY:* He spoke of conjuring.

*ABIGAIL: (bored)* Did he?

*BETTY:* Did you not hear him?

*ABIGAIL:* I was not listening.

*BETTY:* We are on the path to Hell no doubt.

*ABIGAIL:* Then we might as well have a bit of sport on the way.

*BETTY:* I do not desire to meet the devil, Abigail.

*ABIGAIL:* And what of a newborn baby?

*BETTY:* What of it?

*ABIGAIL:* Your father is a man of God. Is he not?

*BETTY:* You know he is.

*ABIGAIL:* Then tell me, if a child is born and by some unhappy chance dies before he is blessed, what is his fate?

*BETTY:* He is bound for Hell, although he may dwell in the easiest room of that place.

*ABIGAIL:* And so this child, who could have no knowledge of sin is cast to the devil. Tell me then, what chance do the likes of us have in entering the kingdom of Heaven?

*BETTY:* Aye, but it must be worse for those in league with Satan.

*ABIGAIL:* Would you sign his book?

*BETTY:* Not by my life!

*ABIGAIL:* Neither would I. Please stop worrying. (*Ann and Mercy enter down the hill. Mercy carries a basket.*) You certainly took your time.

*ANN:* My mother kept me after the service. Your uncle will be home before the dinner hour. We must be there by then.

*ABIGAIL:* Then we had best get started.

*MERCY:* Abigail . . .

*ABIGAIL:* What did you forget?

*MERCY:* Not a thing . . . . I . . . it is only that I . . .

*ANN:* I found her filling her face with bread and molasses behind the barn, and on Friday, too.

*ABIGAIL:* I knew we could not trust these Salem girls.

*MERCY:* I was hungry.

*BETTY:* Tituba has baked some fresh muffins at home.

*ABIGAIL:* You have ruined us now. I do not know why you bothered to bring these things.

*ANN:* You need not be concerned. I found someone to take her place.

*BETTY:* Tituba says she must fast for three days.

*ANN:* Aye, and Mary Warren often goes for that and longer without food.

*MERCY:* She says her mistress scarcely feeds her.

*ABIGAIL:* Who else have you told?

*ANN:* No one. I swear.

*ABIGAIL:* We would be in for a beating if this be known.

*ANN:* Mary would not say a word. (*gossiping*) It is the spirit of her Master, John Proctor, she wishes to see.

*ABIGAIL:* He is married, is he not?

*BETTY:* Aye, and his wife is with child.

*ANN:* Even so, Mary has her eye on him, you can be sure. She says his wife is bad tempered.

*MERCY:* It would suit her if Goody Proctor died on the birthing bed.

*ABIGAIL:* No matter. She shall see her groom, whether it be John Proctor or not. But has she baked the bread?

*ANN:* This morning, and in the proper fashion.

*MERCY:* (*Sees Mary Warren and Elizabeth Hubbard and calls out to them.*) Mary! Down here!

*ABIGAIL:* Shhh. Must you tell the entire village.

*MERCY:* (*defiantly*) There be no one else here.

*ABIGAIL:* Who walks with her?

*ANN:* It looks to be Elizabeth Hubbard, niece of Dr. Griggs.

*ABIGAIL:* You swore you told no one else.

*ANN:* It was not me. (*Mercy's face turns red with guilt. The girls stare at her.*)

*ABIGAIL:* Why did you not invite the entire village?

*MERCY:* Elizabeth is my closest friend. She swore she would not tell a soul.

*ABIGAIL:* As I remember, so did you.

*MARY:* (*entering*) What must I do with this bread?

*ABIGAIL:* Eat it for ought I care. Betty, let us go home.

*BETTY:* Aye, I am ready.

*MERCY:* Mary, tell Abigail how long you have fasted.

*MARY:* Today shall be the fourth.

*ABIGAIL:* With so many girls we should be discovered, no doubt. You may do as you please. Betty and I shall find some trustworthy companions.

*ANN:* None of us wishes to be found out. Why should we tell?

*MARY:* My Master would see me horsewhipped. You may believe, I shall not say a word.

*ELIZABETH:* Nor I. I swear by my mother's grave.

*ANN:* We have gathered all that we need (*begins to unload her basket*), the bread, the tea pot, and cups, the boiling water, the knife and the tealeaves.

*ABIGAIL:* (*considers these things, then makes the decision to give it a try*) Those leaves will not do. I found these in Tituba's trunk.

*BETTY:* You stole them?

*ABIGAIL:* One hand full.

*BETTY:* I do not like this.

*ABIGAIL:* Another word from you, and I shall send you home by yourself.

*BETTY:* The end of the world is close at hand. I know it.

*MERCY:* Aye, I have heard that, too. Last week Mary Walcott said . . .

ABIGAIL: This is supposed to be a *silent* tea.

MARY: I am ready.

ANN: Me, too.

ELIZABETH: May I knit during the ceremony?

ABIGAIL: If it will keep you quiet.

BETTY: What is that you are knitting, Elizabeth?

ABIGAIL: Sit and be silent. (*She waits for all to do this.*) Now, first we must make a pledge that no matter what comes of this business, no one shall breathe a word of it to any living soul. (*She scratches a cross in the dirt and kneels. She motions for the other girls to join her. They form a circle and hold hands.*)

ALL: We swear.

ABIGAIL: Then let the Silent Tea begin.

MERCY: (*whispers to Mary*) If it be John Proctor's face you see, you must confess it.

MARY (*Outraged*) Did you tell . . .

ABIGAIL: Shhhh!

ABIGAIL *motions for everyone to take a position around the space.* MARY *stands and walks backward. She sets a table for two on a stump. She places cornbread between the two plates, and carefully places the knife. The girls' attentions are riveted on the knife, except for* ELIZABETH, *who is busy knitting.* MARY *makes the tea and places a cup in front of each girl. She sits at the stump. Off of* MARY's *cue, the girls begin to turn the cups three times to the left.* ABIGAIL *notices that* ELIZABETH *is still knitting. She elbows her to get her to join in. Together they drink it. Then they wait.* ELIZABETH *returns to her knitting. The music begins and the* MALE ASSISTANT *appears in the white costume from before. All the girls, except for* ELIZABETH, *see him and are transfixed on his every move. The figure points at* MARY *and moves to her. He sits across from her and removes his hood exposing an executioner's hood. Only* MARY *sees this. She is terrified and begins to scream. This scares the other girls including* ELIZABETH *who accidentally stabs herself with her knitting needle. They all begin screaming. The figure disappears.* MARY *runs to the other girls, who frantically question her.*

MARY: Death . . . it was death.

MERCY: Who was it you saw?

MARY: His face . . . oh Lord. (*She screams.*)

*MERCY:* But was it John Proctor?

*MARY:* Blackness. . . . Am I to die?

*ELIZABETH:* I did not see him.

ABIGAIL *moves to the knife and steals it with no one looking.*

*MARY:* Did you not see his face, black with death? Is it he that is to die?

*ABIGAIL: (stealing focus)* The knife is gone!

*MERCY:* He claimed the knife!

*This is too much for* BETTY. *She falls on the ground in fits. In the height of the hysteria* PARRIS' *voice stuns all the girls except* BETTY *who continues in her fits.*

*PARRIS:* What in the name of our Lord Jesus Christ is the nature of this spectacle? (*The girls are too scared to speak.*) I asked you girls a question. What mischief is this?

*ABIGAIL: (musters all her strength)* No mischief, Uncle. Our Betty has seen a snake. (*crosses to her*) The beast frightened her so.

*PARRIS:* What sort of snake?

*ABIGAIL:* A common one, Sir. She shall recover soon. (*places a hand on Betty's shoulder*) Will you not, Betty? (*Betty quiets down and goes into a trance-like state.*)

*PARRIS:* She is a frail child, at that. Still it may be wise to have her seen by Dr. Griggs.

*ELIZABETH:* He is my uncle, Sir.

*PARRIS:* Go to him, child. Tell him our Betty is ill.

*ELIZABETH:* I am on my way.

*MARY:* I shall go with her. (*They leave in a hurry.*)

*PARRIS:* Oh, why, has God sent me to this loathsome place? First, I am met with dissension. After, I am told that there is some grievance over my salary. And now my precious Betty is beset with fear. A snake you say?

*ABIGAIL:* I believe it to be one, sir.

*PARRIS:* The devil has done his work today. I must take the child home before confronting these villagers.

*ABIGAIL:* She seems quite calm now, Uncle. With the help of Mercy and Ann, I could bring her home.

*PARRIS:* You are the strong one, are you not?

*ABIGAIL:* Aye.

*PARRIS:* Very well. Inform Dr. Griggs that I shall return momentarily.

*ABIGAIL:* As you wish, Uncle.

PARRIS *replaces his hood and continues to watch.* ANN *and* MERCY *stare at* ABIGAIL. *The three girls burst into laughter.*

*ABIGAIL:* Did you see Mary and Elizabeth run up that hill?

*MERCY:* One would think the devil himself was chasing them.

*ANN:* (*takes deep breaths*) Why am I laughing? I was never so terrified in my life.

*MERCY:* I thought he would beat us for sure.

*ABIGAIL:* Do not make more of it than it was. I am tired of this. We must escort my poor ailing cousin to her bed. (*They look at Betty who is still in a trance.*)

*ANN:* What is it that ails her?

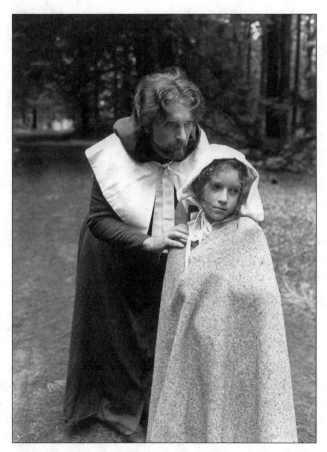

Salem's Daughters, *Michael Thurston and Jessie Solomon-Greenbaum, photo by Douglas R. Gilbert.*

*MERCY:* She looks pale as ashes.

*ABIGAIL:* She jumps at her own shadow. (*tries to snap Betty out of her state*) Betty we are going home now. (*lightly shakes her*) Betty, did you not hear me? You wanted to go home, and now we are. Betty, you are not a baby. Stand up so we can go home. If you think we are going to carry you all the way, we are not.

*ANN:* Maybe she did see a snake.

*MERCY:* Abigail made that up.

*ABIGAIL:* And what do you know of it, Mercy Lewis?

*MERCY:* I know that Betty will not be walking home, poor thing. (*In grand style, Abigail falls to the ground screaming. She imitates Betty's fit. At first Ann and Mercy are frightened, then they see through the act. Abigail sits up with a start and stares ahead as if in a trance. Ann and Mercy look at each other and make a silent agreement to play along.*) Ann, what shall we do?

*ANN:* I suppose we shall have to carry them both home.

*MERCY:* I am much too weak for that. Perhaps the two of us could lift Betty and bring her home.

*ANN:* But what of Abigail? We cannot just leave her here to *die.*

*MERCY:* Nay, we shall send *her uncle* to fetch her when he returns.

*ANN:* That is all we can do. (*They pick up Betty and begin carrying her up the hill.*)

*MERCY:* Poor Abigail.

*ANN:* Poor Abigail.

*When the three girls are out of sight* ABIGAIL *drops the act. She stands up and brushes off her skirt. A brief section of the music is played and the* ASSISTANTS *make a sharp adjustment pointing at her. She does not see this, but senses it and it scares her. She runs up the hill.*

Act 2, Scene 1

ELIZABETH HUBBARD *enters cautiously. She looks around to make sure her companions are not in sight. Content that she is alone, she sits and begins knitting.* MERCY *and* MARY *call her name from backstage. They enter and spot* ELIZABETH. MERCY *calls out to her in a loud whisper.*

*MERCY:* Elizabeth. (*no answer*) Elizabeth, we have been searching for you.

*ELIZABETH:* (*intent on her knitting*) Can I not finish this one row?

MERCY: (*grabs the knitting*) How can you knit at such a time?

ELIZABETH: It soothes me, surely. I would like it back now. (*She tries to grab it.*)

MERCY: Not yet. (*throws it to Mary*)

ELIZABETH: Be careful.

MARY: Tell us what your uncle said.

ELIZABETH: Why should I?

MARY: (*pulling out one of the knitting needles*) Because if you do not . . . I shall start pulling.

ELIZABETH: Stop!

MARY: (*hums as she begins to pull*)

ELIZABETH: I do not know much.

MARY: We know he went to their home.

ELIZABETH: Betty is ill. May I have my yarn, now? (*goes for the yarn*)

MARY: When you tell us something we do not already know. (*She throws it to Mercy.*)

MERCY: What news of Abigail?

ELIZABETH: (*looks at Mercy defiantly*) None.

MERCY: Are we not closest of friends?

ELIZABETH: Mary Walcott is my closest friend.

MERCY: (*begins to pull*) Tis such a pity, all this work.

ELIZABETH: (*stopping her*) Abigail is also afflicted.

MARY: With what ailment?

ELIZABETH: None to speak of.

MERCY: (*hums and pulls the yarn*)

ELIZABETH: I swear. My uncle says it is not an illness at all.

MARY: What is it then?

ELIZABETH: Poor Betty and Abigail are *bewitched*.

MERCY: I knew it.

ELIZABETH: Kindly return my knitting. (*She reaches for the yarn, but Mercy throws it to Mary.*)

MARY: Have our names been mentioned in this?

ELIZABETH: Why should they?

MERCY: If little Betty were frightened she might tell ought.

ELIZABETH: Do you hear what I say? She is not frightened, she is bewitched.

MARY: By whom?

ELIZABETH: She will not say. She does not speak, but stares at the wall, like this. (*She does her imitation.*) Her father hadst ordered her to fast for three days to drive out the evil spirits, but she is only the worse for it.

MARY: Is she to die then?

ELIZABETH: I do not know. Mary Walcott says they will send her away from Salem Village.

MERCY: Where would they send her?

ELIZABETH: (*definite*) That is ought I know.

MERCY: (*considers this*) Give her the stupid yarn.

MARY: (*referring to the knitting*) What is this going to be?

ELIZABETH: My aunt asked me to knit a blanket for Goody Proctor's baby.

MARY: (*furiously ripping out stitches*) Oooooh.

ELIZABETH: (*grabs the yarn from Mary*) I might have told you more, but I shall not say a word, Mary Warren. (*storms off*)

MERCY: (*watching Elizabeth go*) What do you think?

MARY: Our secret will be safe for now.

MERCY: I meant about Abigail and Betty.

MARY: When it happened, I thought she were only scared. But if Dr. Griggs . . .

MERCY: (*getting very nervous*) We summoned the devil. Tituba warned us.

MARY: We are not witches, Mercy.

MERCY: Now Ann is afflicted, as well.

MARY: I have not heard that.

MERCY: I say she is. At night she is tormented in her sleep. And by day she says she is called to the grave of her poor dead brother. And I am living in the same house. Maybe Satan comes for me next.

MARY: I was the one who saw death's face.

MERCY: What if he comes for me?

MARY: Do not sign his book, no matter how horrible his tortures.

MERCY: What do you know of it?

MARY: I know.

MERCY: I suppose he has come to you.

MARY: Nay. (*decides to tease Mercy*) But one of his servants came.

MERCY: You are a liar, Mary Warren.

MARY: A repulsive creature with the face of . . . Goody Proctor. (*She makes a grotesque face and the two girls laugh.*)

MERCY: (*suddenly serious*) It could happen though. My mistress says there are many witches in Salem Village. One only needs proof.

MARY: What sort of proof?

MERCY: I am not sure . . .

MARY: (*pause*) I must get back to my chores before the old witch beats me with her broom.

MERCY: And I should be looking after Ann while the Putnams are out.

MARY: God be with you, Mercy Lewis.

MARY: And you, Mary Warren. (*The two girls exit and the music begins to play.*)


ACT 2, SCENE 2

*As the music begins the FEMALE ASSISTANT enters holding a stake. She beckons to ANN JUNIOR who enters in a trance-like state. She is wearing her nightgown and holds a handful of wild flowers. The FEMALE ASSISTANT leads her to a spot where she marks the grave. ANN places the flowers on the grave. The MALE ASSISTANT enters carrying DORCY GOOD. He places her in front of ANN and then gives DORCY an imaginary apple. DORCY eats it grotesquely and then throws it down on the grave. TITUBA enters and mimes conjuring up a biscuit tin. She opens the tin and offers DORCY a biscuit. DORCY runs to her, hugs her, and reaches for the biscuit. TITUBA mimes slamming the tin lid down on DORCY's hand. DORCY runs to ANN and hugs her for protection. ANN hesitates and then embraces DORCY. DORCY slowly takes ANN'S hand, bites it, and runs back to TITUBA. They hold hands and dance in a circle. They motion for ANN to join them. She refuses. The TWO ASSISTANTS pull ANN there, but she refuses to dance. The ASSISTANTS force her to join the circle. After a couple of turns ANN breaks free of everyone. The dream figures turn in on her. TITUBA shakes her head and motions for DORCY to go to ANN. The ASSISTANTS keep a hold of ANN. DORCY pinches ANN and turns to TITUBA. TITUBA smiles. DORCY pinches her again and ANN tries to break away. The ASSISTANTS bring ANN down to the ground. TITUBA motions for DORCY to continue, then exits laughing. DORCY places her hands around ANN's neck, and mimes a choking action. ANN tries to scream but no sound comes out. She starts to shake. The music ends abruptly, the dream figures disappear, and ANN's screams become audible. ANN SENIOR and THOMAS PUTNAM enter looking for her.*

ANN SENIOR: (*running to her*) Ann, oh my precious daughter. Ann. (*She places her cloak around Ann Junior and holds her until she is fully conscious. At that point Ann Junior begins crying.*) Do not be frightened.

THOMAS: (*trying not to lose patience*) Where is Mercy?

ANN: (*still crying*) I do not know.

ANN SENIOR: (*to her husband*) Shhh.

THOMAS: (*to his wife*) And you would not have her see Dr. Griggs.

ANN SENIOR: There be no need, Thomas.

THOMAS: What is it that ails you, child? (*Ann Junior shrugs.*)

ANN SENIOR: Can you not see this child has been cursed?

THOMAS: Who is it that afflicts thee, Ann?

ANN SENIOR: These faceless demons do harm my family, and we are to do nothing. (*to Thomas*) You must speak to the Reverend Master Parris.

THOMAS: What would I say?

ANN SENIOR: That here lies our proof.

THOMAS: He may not listen to me.

ANN SENIOR: Then you are to make him listen.

THOMAS: His own child and niece are afflicted, yet he does nothing.

ANN SENIOR: Am I to lose another child to Satan?

ANN: Mama, am I dying?

ANN SENIOR: No, my sweet child, your father would not let that happen. (*Mercy enters out of breath.*) Mercy!

MERCY: (*speaks quickly*) When I returned home, Ann was gone. I have been searching all of Salem Village for her. You may ask anyone you wish. Then I remembered this place.

ANN SENIOR: I left her in your charge, did I not?

MERCY: Aye, Mrs. Putnam, but . . .

THOMAS: What evil spirit possessed you to leave this poor child alone?

MERCY: No spirit, Master Putnam.

THOMAS: Have we not taken you into our home, girl? Clothed and fed you?

MERCY: Aye.

THOMAS: And this is our payment?

MERCY: I love Ann as a sister, surely.

THOMAS: Tell me why you should not be flogged . . . (*He grabs her shoulders.*)

MERCY: (*almost in tears*) I did not mean . . .

THOMAS: (*He throws her down.*) And thrown back to the streets.

*MERCY:* It was Mary.

*THOMAS:* You blame your carelessness on Mary Walcott?

*MERCY:* Mary Warren, the Proctor's serving girl.

*THOMAS:* She forced you to leave the side of this afflicted child?

*MERCY:* Mary is afflicted as well.

*ANN SENIOR:* Sweet Lord.

*MERCY:* She begged me to walk her home. She was so frightened.

*ANN SENIOR:* Frightened of what, child?

*MERCY:* Witches, Mrs. Putnam.

*ANN SENIOR:* She hath seen them?

*MERCY:* A repulsive creature, she said, who beat her senseless with a broom.

*ANN SENIOR:* What face did she see?

*MERCY:* Pardon?

*ANN SENIOR:* Who is this witch that hurts our children?

*MERCY: (pause)* It were disguised.

*ANN SENIOR:* Disguised?

*MERCY:* Aye, or a stranger. She could not tell.

*ANN SENIOR:* Oh, Thomas.

*THOMAS:* If this be a falsehood, Mercy . . .

*MERCY:* It is the truth, I swear. A repulsive creature, she said, and with a broom, too.

*ANN SENIOR:* Master Parris must hear of this.

*THOMAS: (pause)* I shall speak to Parris, for ought the good it will do.

*ANN SENIOR:* God save us all.

*They move to their places in church.*

ACT 2, SCENE 3

PARRIS *begins his sermon as the* PUTNAMS *take their place in church.*

*PARRIS:* John, Chapter 6, Verse: 70, "Have I not chosen you twelve, and one of you is a devil." Our Lord Jesus Christ knows how many devils there are in his church, and who they are. There are devils as well as saints in Christ's church. What is meant here by devils? Our bible sayith, "One of you is a devil." Answer: By "devil" is ordinarily meant any wicked angel or spirit. Sometimes it is put for the prince or head of the evil spirits, or fallen angels. Sometimes it is used for vile or wicked persons—the worst of such who for their villainy and impiety do most resemble devils and wicked spirits. There are such devils in church. There are also true saints in church. Here are good men to be found—yea, the very best; and here are bad men to be found, the very worst. Such as shall have the highest seat in glory, and such also as shall be cast to the lowest and fiercest flames of misery. Saints and devils, like Jeremiah's basket of figs. (*The music begins as a tone. A light comes up behind the scrims where the Assistants move as if being tormented.*)

Let none then build their hopes of salvation on this: that they are church members. This you and I may be, and yet devils for all that. (*Ann Junior begins moaning and holding her head. Parris notices this but continues over it.*) Oh! If there be any such among us, forbear to come this day to the Lord's table, lest Satan enter more powerfully into you. (*Ann's moaning becomes louder.*) Lest while the bread be between your teeth, the wrath of the Lord come pouring down upon you. (*Ann stands and screams as she hurls her bible at Parris and then falls into a full-fledged fit. Parris' voice becomes louder.*) If the church of Corinth were called to mourn because of one incestuous person (*Abigail falls into a fit.*), how much more my New England churches mourn (*Mercy falls into a fit. Parris' voice becomes louder.*), that such as work witchcraft, or are vehemently suspected so to do, should be found among them. (*Mary falls into a fit.*) Examine we ourselves well, what we are. We are either saints or devils: the scripture gives us no medium. (*Elizabeth falls into a fit, as does Ann Senior. Parris is now shouting.*) Oh it is a dreadful thing to be a devil and yet to sit down at the Lord's table. Such incur the hottest of God's wrath. (*Abigail begins barking like a dog and prancing around on all fours. Elizabeth and Mary follow suit. Ann Junior and Mercy try to fly like birds.*) Let each church member pray, and pray most fervently for the salvation of Christ's children, and let no man rest until those she-witches are brought forward to face God's wrath. Amen.

THOMAS: Amen.


*The girls collapse into silence. The music ends and the* ASSISTANTS *return to the throne.* THOMAS *rushes to his wife and daughter who are crying.* ELIZABETH *stands, gets her knitting and exits with* MARY WARREN *and* ABIGAIL. MERCY *helps* THOMAS *escort his distraught wife off stage.* ANN JUNIOR *stands. She looks refreshed and starts to leave.*

*PARRIS:* Ann Putnam!

*ANN:* (*stiff with fear*) Aye, Master Parris?

*PARRIS:* (*gently*) You have forgotten your bible.

*ANN:* (*with a sigh of relief*) Thank you, Reverend. (*Ann retrieves her bible and exits.*)

*The music starts and the actor who plays* PARRIS *replaces his hood and climbs down the ladder. He exits followed by the* ASSISTANTS. *INTERMISSION*

ACT 3, SCENE 1

*The music begins. The actor who plays* PARRIS *enters followed by his* ASSISTANTS. *As they move into place,* TITUBA *enters carrying firewood. The music ends and* TITUBA *hums the yellow bird song. She puts down the wood and is about to go for more when she sees* ANN JUNIOR *coming down the hill with a basket. She calls to* ABIGAIL.

*TITUBA:* Abigail! Abigail, would you come here a moment?

*ABIGAIL:* (*entering*) Uncle said I did not have to finish my reading if I felt ill.

*TITUBA:* I'm not bothered about that. Isn't that Ann Putnam coming down the hill?

*ABIGAIL:* Aye.

*TITUBA:* Go fetch some tea then (*with a hint of sarcasm*), if you're not feeling too sick.

*ABIGAIL:* I am a bit better today. (*She goes.*)

*ANN:* Good afternoon, Tituba.

*TITUBA:* What brings you out this way? I heard you were ill.

*ANN:* Nay. (*reconsiders*) I was.

*TITUBA:* Well, sit you down. Abigail will bring you tea.

*ANN:* I only came to give the good Reverend and his wife these preserves.

*TITUBA:* I'm afraid they left for Salem Town early this morning.

*ANN:* Are they expected home soon?

*TITUBA:* I think so.

*ANN:* I see.

ABIGAIL *enters with the tea.*

*TITUBA:* Why don't you drink your tea, and maybe they be home before you're done.

*ANN: (takes the tea from Abigail)* Thank you, Abigail.

*ABIGAIL:* Next time you can get it yourself.

*TITUBA:* Don't be so willful, child.

*ABIGAIL:* I am not.

*ANN:* My mother says one needs strength of spirit in these times.

*TITUBA:* Now don't you fret. Like your bible say, the Lord will protect his children.

*ANN:* Until the devil intervenes.

*TITUBA:* We must pray to God.

*ANN:* That we must. But there is more we can do. Would you be willing to serve the Lord, Tituba? And you, Abigail?

*TITUBA:* What are you talking about, Ann?

*ANN:* Unmasking the devil.

*ABIGAIL:* And you know how?

*ANN:* I know of such a spell.

*TITUBA:* Abigail, go inside now.

*ABIGAIL:* But . . .

*TITUBA:* I said, go!

ABIGAIL *starts to go but hides around the corner.*

*TITUBA:* I think you should go home now. The Reverend wouldn't like this kind of talk in his house.

*ANN:* And what of tea reading and telling fortunes?

*TITUBA:* What do you want from me?

*ANN:* You possess certain gifts.

*TITUBA:* Do you want me to read your tealeaves now?

*ANN:* Dr. Griggs hath said the evil hand is upon us.

*TITUBA:* So I've heard.

*ANN:* This morning Goodwife Sibley called upon my home out of concern for us. She gave my mother a recipe. She is convinced that if these instructions are followed precisely, the wicked demons shall be found and brought to justice. *(She reads from a small piece of paper.)* Rye flour is mixed with the urine of all the afflicted girls. The dough is baked, and then fed to a dog. Now I have brought water passed from both Mercy and myself. (*She pulls out one of the jars in her basket.*) Abigail would only need to collect from Betty, and I from the remaining girls. Then, while the good Reverend and his wife are at church tomorrow, you could complete the spell.

*TITUBA:* Why doesn't your mother bake it?

*ANN:* You are bound to the spirit world.

*TITUBA:* Who told you that?

*ANN:* And baking this cake in the house of a reverend should surely increase its power. (*She hands Tituba the paper.*)

*TITUBA:* I don't read. (*She throws the paper on the ground.*)

*ANN:* Abigail may help you.

*ABIGAIL:* (*running in*) I shall read it to you. (*She picks up the recipe.*)

*TITUBA:* I told you. Go inside.

*ANN:* Abigail, how goes it with your cousin?

*ABIGAIL:* They sent her away.

*TITUBA:* The poor child.

*ABIGAIL:* They say she may die.

*ANN:* (*sounding much like her mother*) I have seen too many children put to their graves. I fear there shall be more. We need only to sit and wait, while Satan does his work.

*ABIGAIL:* Tituba, do you wish us all dead?

*TITUBA:* No, don't talk nonsense.

*ANN:* What harm could it do?

*TITUBA:* I don't know.

*ABIGAIL:* I shall help you collect the water from each girl.

*ANN:* Bless you, Abigail.

*TITUBA:* Do you not hear what I'm saying, girl? I don't want no part of this.

*ANN:* It would be very unfortunate if the Reverend learned of what took place in his home. He might even blame you for his daughter's ailment.

*TITUBA:* They were innocent enough things going on, you know.

*ABIGAIL:* He would not think so.

*ANN:* You must understand how desperate things are.

*ABIGAIL:* It may save us all, Tituba.

*TITUBA:* (*realizes that she is up against a wall*) Then go, but be quick about it. (*Ann hands Abigail the jar.*)

*ABIGAIL:* I promise. (*exits*)

*ANN:* We are indebted to you.

*TITUBA:* Just don't tell nobody, else I be beat for sure.

*ANN:* It shall be our secret. (*exits*)

TITUBA *crosses upstage to watch the girls go. While doing so, she grabs on to the clothesline. The music begins abruptly as the* MALE ASSISTANT *runs around* TITUBA *with one end of the rope, and then stands behind her. The* FEMALE ASSISTANT *runs down stage, diagonal from* TITUBA, *with the other end of the rope.* TITUBA *is forced to swing the rope around. It becomes a jump rope.* MARY *and* ELIZABETH *enter upstage and look at the rope with delight.* MARY *begins jumping rope and* ELIZABETH *joins in.* ABIGAIL *enters with the basket and jar from the previous scene and joins in.* ANN *enters, she does not pause, but moves straight through the game, pulling the rope with her. This causes everyone to get caught in a web of rope. The three girls untangle themselves. The two* ASSISTANTS *move* TITUBA, *still entangled, to the throne. They wrap the rope around the throne with* TITUBA *held facing the pulpit. She remains there during the next two scenes.*

ACT 3, SCENE 2

*The music ends.* ANN *and* ABIGAIL *scout the area, as the other girls become impatient.*

*ELIZABETH:* Abigail.

*ABIGAIL:* Shhh.

*MARY:* (*whispers*) I have to be back before the Proctors return.

*ELIZABETH:* If you will not tell us why you . . .

*ANN:* Shhh.

*ELIZABETH:* I am going home.

*ABIGAIL:* Patience Elizabeth, I must be sure we are alone.

*MARY:* Please hurry.

*ANN:* One moment! (*When she is satisfied they are alone she speaks to Abigail.*) Go to the end of that path and wait for us there.

*ABIGAIL:* Why should I?

*ANN:* If anyone approaches, you may warn us.

*ABIGAIL:* But . . .

*ANN:* You wanted to come. So, either make yourself useful or go home. (*Ann and Abigail stare at each other. Abigail gives in, hands Ann the basket and exits.*)

MARY: (*Mary and Elizabeth are amazed that Abigail was defeated.*) Now can you tell us?

ANN: First, we must take the oath of silence. (*She makes a cross in the dirt. The girls quickly move into place.*) If any one of us does speak of this secret meeting, may the devil cut out her tongue, for she hath betrayed us.

ALL: We swear.

ANN: We are called upon to unmask the vile witch that has tormented us.

ELIZABETH: We are?

ANN: Aye. It is a most serious task.

MARY: How does one expose a witch?

ANN: (*as if everyone should know*) By mixing our urine with rye flour and baking it into a cake.

ELIZABETH: I am not going to eat that.

ANN: Tituba shall feed it to a dog.

ELIZABETH: Oh.

MARY: Then what happens?

ANN: The witch is exposed, and either confesses or is hanged.

MARY: How?

ANN: By a rope.

MARY: How is she exposed?

ANN: (*She doesn't know.*) I have brought a jar. Abigail, Mercy, and I have done our part. Now you must do yours.

ELIZABETH: Is that not enough for your cake?

ANN: Nay, it must be all of us.

MARY: Why?

ANN: Tituba knows these things, better than you.

ELIZABETH: Aye, but . . .

ANN: Betty is close to death, we are sure to be next.

ELIZABETH: But if we are discovered, they may hang *us*.

ANN: Go home if you wish. May this witch choke the life from you for ought I care.

MARY: (*pause*) Give me the jar. (*Ann does this.*) Would you please turn your back? (*Ann and Elizabeth mask Mary from the audience as she squats behind them.*)

ELIZABETH: I have never heard of such an odd recipe.

ANN: I suppose.

*ELIZABETH:* What if the dog refuses to eat it?

*ANN:* She shall starve it until it does.

*ELIZABETH:* Poor dog.

*When* MARY *is done she stands and holds the jar out to* ELIZABETH.

*MARY:* Now you.

*ELIZABETH:* Must I? (*They stare at her until she takes the jar. She moves behind them and squats, there is a pause.*)

*ANN:* Hurry!

*ELIZABETH:* I cannot.

*MARY:* Try.

*ELIZABETH:* I am too nervous. May I go behind a tree instead?

*ANN:* Aye, but be quick about it. (*Elizabeth runs behind a tree.*) She is hopeless.

*MARY:* (*pause, then shouts*) Must you take all day?

*ELIZABETH:* If you holler at me it only takes longer.

*MARY:* (*pause*) When does she bake it?

*ANN:* Tomorrow, while we are in church.

*ABIGAIL:* (*runs on out of breath and terrified*) My uncle . . . my uncle . . .

*ANN:* What?

*ABIGAIL:* My uncle, he is coming this way.

*MARY:* (*in a loud whisper*) Elizabeth . . . come out of there.

*ELIZABETH:* (*behind the tree*) I am almost finished.

*ABIGAIL:* (*loud whisper*) My uncle!

*ELIZABETH:* (*behind the tree*) What?

*MARY:* What shall we do?

*ANN:* (*loud whisper*) Elizabeth!

*ABIGAIL:* Lord, he is coming. Run! (*Mary, Abigail, and Ann start to run. Ann manages to hide—the audience can see her. Abigail and Mary are caught in Parris' gaze.*)

*ELIZABETH:* (*Elizabeth enters from behind the tree, beaming as she holds up the jar.*) I did it!

*PARRIS:* (*removing his hood*) You did what, Elizabeth?

*ELIZABETH:* (*jumps from fear, hurling the jar in the air*) I . . . I . . .

*PARRIS:* Go on. What were you collecting?

*ELIZABETH:* (*not understanding*) Sir?

*PARRIS:* In the jar. Must I bring your uncle here?

*ELIZABETH:* Nay. I wanted no part of it. I swear. *She* made me, for Tituba's cake.

*PARRIS:* Who made you?

ABIGAIL *and* MARY *stare at her.*

*ELIZABETH:* She said she would cut out my tongue. She . . . (*She envisions a spirit coming at her. She gasps.*) Oh!

*PARRIS:* What is wrong child?

*ELIZABETH:* Do you not see her standing there?

*PARRIS:* Tell me what evil spirit is present.

*MARY:* (*picks it up*) She carries a knife!

*PARRIS:* Who is it that afflicts thee?

*ELIZABETH:* Blackness. Go back to the devil!

*PARRIS:* Does . . . Tituba hurt you?

*ELIZABETH:* (*takes the suggestion*) No *Tituba*, stay away. I am not your servant. Oh! She comes for my tongue! Help me. (*She falls to the ground fighting off the imaginary Tituba. The struggle goes on for a few seconds. Mary assists in fighting off the vision. Elizabeth sits up panting.*)

*PARRIS:* Is her spirit still about?

*ELIZABETH:* (*still breathing hard*) Nay, she say she come back for my tongue. (*She places her finger in her mouth and then looks at it.*) Look, here is blood from where she cut.

*PARRIS:* She shall torment you no more. I shall see to that.

*ABIGAIL:* (*musters her strength*) The cake was to help, uncle. To expose the evil one . . .

*PARRIS:* You have been misguided, child. Only a servant of Satan would employ such witchery. (*losing his temper*) Oh, how odious becomes the deed when it is done in the house of the Lord. The sorceress must stand in judgment. And may God have mercy on her soul. (*Parris replaces his hood.*)

*ABIGAIL:* (*Abigail stares at the two girls. They look at her apologetically.*) Boo! (*She stamps her foot, Mary and Elizabeth scream and run off. Ann comes out from hiding. She is devastated by what she has seen. She looks sheepishly at Abigail. Abigail stares at her and starts to leave.*)

*ANN:* Abigail . . .

*ABIGAIL:* You shall burn in hell, Ann Putnam. (*She exits.*)

*The music picks up on her exit. The* MALE ASSISTANT *brings in a rocking chair setting it down so that it continues to rock.* ANN *enters in a daze and sits in the chair. The* FEMALE ASSISTANT *enters with one end of rope that binds* TITUBA. *She places it in* ANN's *lap.* ANN *begins playing with the end of the rope unconsciously. She rocks, staring straight ahead, unaware of where the rope leads. The* ASSISTANTS *exit.*

ACT 4, SCENE 1

MERCY *enters with a basket as the music ends. She puts the basket down, moves to* ANN, *and replaces Ann's hair inside her bonnet. We are outside the Putnam's home. It is the morning of Tituba's trial.* ANN *is off in her own world.*

*MERCY:* Do you think one wedge of cheese is enough? (*pause*) Ann?

*ANN:* (*distracted*) What?

*MERCY:* I have brought one wedge of cheese, three apples, and one half a loaf of bread.

*ANN:* Aye.

*MERCY:* Is it enough, then?

*ANN:* I am not sure.

*MERCY:* It is a long ride. And the trial may last through the day. Perhaps I should fetch another wedge. Do you think so, Ann?

*ANN:* I do not know what to think.

*MERCY:* I shall get two pieces.

*ANN:* I am sorry. Two pieces?

*MERCY:* Of cheese! What ails thee?

*ANN:* Does this not seem odd to you?

*MERCY:* I suppose.

*ANN:* I brought Tituba the recipe.

*MERCY:* Aye. (*pause*) I shall be back with the cheese.

*ANN:* Mercy . . . Must we go?

*MERCY:* We are ordered to do so.

*ANN:* I know this.

*MERCY:* Our testimony is needed.

*ANN:* And if we are found to be witches?

*MERCY:* It is Tituba on trial.

*ANN:* Do you believe her to be a witch?

*MERCY:* Did she not read fortunes? And she came for Elizabeth and Mary with a knife. Even the Reverend Master Parris sayith she is a witch.

*ANN:* She seemed to be a good person.

*MERCY:* The devil is a master of disguise. I thought she were a witch when I first saw her. You heard her sing Satan's song of the yellow bird. Do you forget these things?

*ANN:* Nay. (*pause*) We sang her song, too. We danced with her.

*MERCY:* It were surely the tea.

*ANN:* The tea?

*MERCY:* Her secret leaves lure young girls under her spell, no doubt. And what of your dreams? Did she not come for you, and with the waif, Dorcy Good?

*ANN:* Can a dream be true?

*MERCY:* It may surely be a sign. If she is in league with the likes of Goody Good, they may come for your soul.

*ANN:* Why must they torment my family?

*MERCY:* Perhaps it is as Master Parris says.

*ANN:* Satan's greatest victory lies in the downfall of the Lord's chosen ones.

*MERCY:* Aye.

*ANN SENIOR:* (*enters with a shawl for Ann Junior*) Mercy, have you gathered all we need?

*MERCY:* Ought but a little, Mrs. Putnam.

*ANN SENIOR:* Then finish up, child. Would you make us late?

*MERCY:* Nay, I am on my way. (*exits*)

*ANN SENIOR:* (*places the shawl around her daughter*) Are you still distraught, Ann? (*Ann Junior nods.*) I am not. I feel that dark cloud which hath haunted our family being lifted from us. It is a matter of time. It is all a matter of time.

*ANN:* Mama, if Tituba tells them . . .

*ANN SENIOR:* Of the recipe?

*ANN:* Will they come for me?

*ANN SENIOR:* I have already confessed it.

*ANN:* (*amazed*) Mama.

*ANN SENIOR:* And the good Reverend has forgiven us our sin. He understands now. But he needs our help if he is to protect us.

*ANN:* (*tentatively*) I had a dream.

*ANN SENIOR:* Of my sister?

*ANN:* Of Tituba.

*ANN SENIOR:* When?

*ANN:* A week ago, maybe two.

*ANN SENIOR:* And you kept it from me?

*ANN:* I was frightened.

*ANN SENIOR:* Frightened of your own mother?

*ANN:* Of what might happen.

*ANN SENIOR:* You must always tell me your dreams, Ann.

*ANN:* She came with the man in black, the devil I am sure. And Dorcy danced with her and . . .

*ANN SENIOR:* And what?

*ANN:* She tried to choke me, and Tituba laughed and . . . then I do not remember.

*ANN SENIOR:* Dorcy Good?

*ANN:* Aye.

*ANN SENIOR:* (*definite*) Goody Good were there, too.

*ANN:* I had not seen her.

*ANN SENIOR:* Perhaps she were there as . . . a familiar . . . a bird.

MERCY *enters and decides to stay out of sight, but* ANN SENIOR *notices her.*

*ANN:* (*making the connection*) A yellow bird.

*ANN SENIOR:* Aye, a yellow bird.

*ANN:* But it were only a dream.

*ANN SENIOR:* You are so innocent. Do you think the devil has not the power to make you believe you are dreaming? He is too clever.

*ANN:* Do you say it happened?

*ANN SENIOR:* How could you know these things?

*ANN:* Tituba came to me then?

*ANN SENIOR:* Not in body, perhaps. But her spectre, her spirit were surely there.

*ANN:* (*terrified*) Oh.

*ANN SENIOR:* You must advise the court, my child, before more harm is done.

*ANN:* They may not believe me.

*ANN SENIOR:* (*pulling Mercy into their circle*) If Mercy were to give similar evidence . . .

*MERCY:* It is as though I were there.

*ANN:* (*realizing the implications*) She choked me.

*ANN SENIOR:* Have strength, Ann.

*THOMAS:* (*entering*) Mercy!

*MERCY:* Aye, Master Putnam.

*THOMAS:* Did I not bid you iron my best shirt for this day?

*MERCY:* You did.

*THOMAS:* Then why, pray, does it lie wrinkled upon the floor?

*MERCY:* (*confident*) I was afraid to touch it, Sir.

*THOMAS:* Afraid?

*MERCY:* (*matter of fact*) A black cat lay all upon it, and then it turned into a snake.

*ANN SENIOR:* (*appalled*) And this in our own house.

*THOMAS:* Then come along. The sooner we attend to this business, the better.

*As they exit,* ANN SENIOR *catches* MERCY *with a slight crack of a smile.* MERCY *quickly removes the smile.*

## ACT 4, SCENE 2

*The actor who played* PARRIS *puts on a wig and glasses to become* JOHN HATHORNE. ANN SENIOR *and* THOMAS *stand stage left, and are dimly lit.*

*HATHORNE:* Let the record show that on this day, March ye first, sixteen hundred and ninety-two, in Salem Village, Tituba, an Indian Woman, has been brought before the Magistrates for suspicion of witchcraft by her committed according to ye complaint of Thomas and Ann Putnam of Salem Village. Let the record also show that I, John Hathorne, have required of Constable Joseph Herrik to bring at the same time the following girls of Salem Village as they may give evidence in ye above said case: (*The girls enter and take their positions as their names are called.*) Ann Putnam, Mercy Lewis, Abigail Williams, Mary Warren, Elizabeth Hubbard. As all of the above named persons are present, the examination of Tituba Indian shall commence. (*The Assistants bring in Tituba. She looks very worn and has obviously been beaten. She struggles with them. The Assistants return to their posts.*) Tituba, what evil spirit have you familiarity with?

*TITUBA:* None.

*HATHORNE:* Why do you hurt these children?

*TITUBA:* I do not hurt them.

*HATHORNE:* Who is it then?

*TITUBA:* The devil for ought I know.

*HATHORNE:* Did you never see the devil?

*TITUBA:* Never.

*ANN:* I saw the apparition of Tituba. The devil did bring her and Dorcy Good to torture me most grievously by pricking and pinching me.

*MERCY:* And the spirit of Sarah Good was there. And then she turned into a yellow bird.

*ANN:* And then Tituba choked me until I could no longer breathe.

*MERCY:* She choked me too.

*MARY:* She came at me with a knife.

*ELIZABETH:* She came for my tongue. (*She envisions Tituba coming for her.*) She comes for me now. Help me! (*She screams and falls into a fit.*)

*MARY:* (*picking it up*) She holds the knife. (*screams and points at Tituba*)

*MERCY:* Do you not see the yellow bird? (*She screams and follows suit.*)

*ANN:* It comes for my blood. No Tituba, call it back. I will not sign your book. (*joins in the fits*)

*ABIGAIL:* Lord help us, we are done for. (*She joins in.*)

TITUBA *stands in shock as she watches this. The music begins. The ASSISTANTS come at TITUBA carrying chains. They hold out the chains and then drop them on either side of TITUBA. She reacts as if being tortured and moves toward the girls who are still screaming. On the next drop of a chain TITUBA screams, and touches one of the girls. The girls fall like dominos and stop screaming. The ASSISTANTS place the chains over TITUBA'S shoulders, lift her up, and escort her back to her place. As the dialogue continues, they take the chains off TITUBA and drop them on either side of the throne. The music ends.*

*HATHORNE:* Tituba, why did you hurt these children?

*TITUBA:* I did not.

*HATHORNE:* In such cases in England, afflicted persons have been released from a witch's spell when that demon doth place a hand upon them. Has that not just been proven?

*TITUBA:* No. (*The girls start to moan.*)

*HATHORNE:* But someone hurts the children?

TITUBA: (confused) Yes.

HATHORNE: Who is it then? (pause) Did you never see the devil?

TITUBA: (Pause as she decides to beat them at their own game.) The devil came to me and bid me to serve him.

The girls stop moaning and watch.

HATHORNE: Who have you seen?

TITUBA: Four women sometimes hurt the children. (Tituba stares at Ann Senior.)

HATHORNE: Who were they?

TITUBA: (pause) Sarah Good and Sarah Osborne, and I do not know who the others were. Sarah Good and Osborne would have me hurt the children but I would not. There was a tall man from Boston, too. (Tituba stares at Thomas Putnam.)

HATHORNE: When did you see them?

TITUBA: Last night at Boston.

HATHORNE: What did they say?

TITUBA: They say hurt the children.

HATHORNE: And did you hurt them?

TITUBA: No. There is four women and one man. They hurt the children and they lay all upon me and they tell me if I will not hurt the children, they will hurt me.

HATHORNE: But did you not hurt them?

TITUBA: Yes, but I will hurt them no more.

HATHORNE: Are you sorry you did hurt them?

TITUBA: (emphatic) Yes.

HATHORNE: And why then do you hurt them?

TITUBA: They say, hurt the children or we will do worse to you.

HATHORNE: What have you seen?

TITUBA: A man come to me and say, "serve me."

HATHORNE: What service?

TITUBA: Kill the children (girls gasp), or they will do worse to me.

HATHORNE: What is this appearance you see?

TITUBA: Sometimes it is like a hog and sometimes a great dog.

HATHORNE: What did it say to you?

TITUBA: The great dog say, "serve me." And I say, "I am afraid."

HATHORNE: What else did you say to it?

TITUBA: I say, "I will serve you no longer." And then he looked like a man and he told me he had pretty things he would give me.

HATHORNE: What were these pretty things?

TITUBA *can't think of what to say.*

ANN JUNIOR: A yellow bird.

TITUBA: He said he had more pretty things if I would serve him.

HATHORNE: Why did you go to Thomas Putnam's last night and hurt his child?

TITUBA: They pull and haul me and make me go.

HATHORNE: And what would they have you do?

TITUBA: (*Looking at Ann Junior*) Cut off her head with a knife. (*Ann reacts.*)

HATHORNE: How did you go?

TITUBA: We ride upon sticks and are there presently.

HATHORNE: Do you go through trees or over them?

TITUBA: We see nothing but are there presently.

HATHORNE: What attendants hath Sarah Good?

TITUBA: A yellow bird, and she would have given me one.

HATHORNE: What meat did she give it?

TITUBA: It did suck between her fingers. (*The girls moan.*)

HATHORNE: What hath Dorcy Good?

TITUBA: A yellow dog. She had a thing with the head like a woman, with two legs and wings. Abigail Williams that lives with her Uncle Parris said that she did see the same creature, and it turned into the shape of Dorcy Good.

ABIGAIL: (*all eyes on her*) On two occasions it did come to me and pinch me.

ANN: It tried to choke me.

MERCY: I saw it and then it turned into a wolf and jumped upon me.

ELIZABETH: Oh . . .

HATHORNE: What ails thee now?

ELIZABETH: It is here.

HATHORNE: What, what do you see?

ELIZABETH: The creature, it comes for me. (*She falls into her fit.*)

MARY: Oh look it changes its shape. The great dog. Its face! It has the face of Goody Proctor! (*She falls into a fit.*)

*HATHORNE:* Tituba, do you see who hurts these children now?

*TITUBA:* I am blind now. I cannot see.

*A low hum is heard.* TITUBA *is escorted off by the* ASSISTANTS. *The girls take their positions. The* ASSISTANTS *enter with* DORCY GOOD. SARAH GOOD *is back lit behind a scrim.*

*HATHORNE:* On this day, March ye twenty-fourth, sixteen hundred and ninety-two, Dorcas Good, Daughter of Sarah Good, has been brought before us upon suspicion of witchcraft, by her committed according to complaints made against her by Thomas and Ann Putnam, of Salem Village. Before God, she shall stand to face those she hath afflicted. (*He announces each of the girls and they stand upon hearing their name.*) The deposition of Mercy Lewis:

*MERCY:* The apparition of Dorcy Good, Sarah Good's daughter came to me and did afflict me, urging me to write in her book. And several times since Dorcy Good hath afflicted me biting, pinching and choking me, urging me to write in her book. (*She sits.*)

*HATHORNE:* The deposition of Mary Warren:

*MARY:* I saw the apparition of Dorcy Good. Sarah Good's daughter came to me and bit me, and pinch me and so. She continued afflicting me most grievously until the twenty-fourth of March, being the day of her examination. (*She sits.*)

*HATHORNE:* The deposition of Ann Putnam, daughter of Thomas Putnam.

*ANN:* The apparition of Dorcy Good came to me and tortured me by pinching me several times and choking me until I could not breathe. (*She sits and begins to weep.*)

*HATHORNE:* Dorcas Good ye hath been charged with the most hideous crime of witchcraft. Confess it now, or ye shall be hanged in accordance with law. What say you?

*The girls all shift their faces toward her.*

*DORCY:* (*Terrified, she looks to her mother, who nods her head.*) I am guilty. (*She grabs onto her ears, bends over and starts to shake.*)

*The tone gets louder. The* ASSISTANTS *carry* DORCY *off and bring in* SARAH GOOD, *who fights them.*

*HATHORNE:* Sarah Good, what evil spirit have you familiarity with?

*SARAH:* None.

*HATHORNE:* Have you made no contracts with the devil?

*SARAH:* Nay.

*HATHORNE:* Why do you hurt these children?

*The following is a collage of voices, which should overlap and grow in intensity.*

*ANN:* She killed our cow.

*SARAH:* I do not hurt them.

*MERCY:* She was a healthy cow, too.

*SARAH:* I scorn it.

*HATHORNE:* Who do you employ then to do it?

*ABIGAIL:* She has done worse than that.

*SARAH:* I employ nobody.

*MARY:* She has murdered babies.

*HATHORNE:* What creature do you employ, then?

*ELIZABETH:* She eats their flesh.

*SARAH:* No creature.

*ABIGAIL:* All witches do that.

*SARAH:* I am falsely accused.

*ANN:* She killed our cow.

*HATHORNE:* Why did you go away muttering from the Putnams' home?

*ANN & MERCY:* She eats babies.

*SARAH:* I did not mutter, but pray for food for my child.

*THE GIRLS:* All witches do that.

*HATHORNE:* Who do you serve?

*SARAH:* I serve God.

*THE GIRLS:* (*The following starts as a low chant, with the following words overlapping, and then builds.*) The devil take you, Sarah Good. Confess it witch. Hang the witch.

*HATHORNE:* (*over the chanting*) What do you say when you go muttering from their house?

*SARAH:* It is the Commandments. I may say my Commandments, I hope.

*HATHORNE:* What commandment is it?

*SARAH:* If I must tell you, I will tell: It is a psalm.

*HATHORNE:* What psalm?

*SARAH:* (*mutters some psalm*)

*HATHORNE:* (*As he hits his gavel, the music and the chanting stop.*) Sarah Good, I find you guilty of using witchcraft against several persons of Salem Village. As you refuse to confess to these crimes, I sentence ye to death.

*Three ropes drop from the web above. The music picks up and the ASSISTANTS enter with executioner hoods. The girls move back at the sight of the ropes. The MALE ASSISTANT moves SARAH GOOD, who stares directly at the girls, to the rope. The FEMALE ASSISTANT brings SARAH'S hand up to the rope. In a moment she shifts her weight off her feet and snaps her neck. The girls turn away.*

*HATHORNE:* Bridget Bishop of Salem Village, I sentence ye to death. (*Hathorne hits the gavel.*)

*HATHORNE:* Elizabeth Proctor, I sentence ye to death. However, since ye are with child, I hereby postpone your sentence until after the birth of the child. John Proctor of Salem Village, I sentence ye to . . .

*MARY:* He is innocent. (*a moment of sanity*) They are all innocent.

*THE GIRLS:* (*turn on her chanting*) The devil take you, Mary Warren. Confess it witch. Hang the witch.

*HATHORNE:* Mary Warren of Salem Village, I sentence ye . . .

*MARY:* I saw John Proctor with the devil.

*HATHORNE:* I sentence John Proctor to death. (*He hits the gavel. The girls comfort Mary.*) Mary Esty of Topsfield. (*hits the gavel*) Rebecca Nurse of Salem Village. (*hits the gavel*)

*The following lines overlap. HATHORNE continues hitting his gavel at each name. The girls form an accusing machine pointing a finger in front of them at each accusation and then falling to the ground. The falls and rises are staggered between every other girl.*

*ABIGAIL:* (*coming in*) Sarah Osborne of Salem Village.

*ANN:* (*coming in*) Elizabeth Howe of Topsfield.

*ELIZABETH:* (*coming in*) Sarah Wildes of Topsfield.

*MERCY:* (*coming in*) Susanna Martin of Amesbury.

*MARY:* (*coming in*) The Reverend George Burroughs of Wells, Maine.

THE GIRLS: (*Hathorne's gavel picks up pace, as does the accusing machine. The following names overlap and are repeated until Hathorne's cry for order is heard. During this, the two Assistants jump up and grab the two ropes on either side of Sarah Good. They spin on the ropes until Hathorne's call for order.*) Martha Carrier, George Jacobs, John Willard, Ann Foster, Giles Corey, Martha Corey, Alice Parker, Mary Parker, Ann Pudeator, Wilmont Redd, Margaret Scott, Samuel Wardwell, Sarah Dustin.

HATHORNE: (*He hits the gavel furiously.*) Order! Order! Order! (*The girls freeze in whatever position they land in. Their arms should be extended pointing toward the audience, if possible. The music ends. During the following speech the Assistants release Sarah Good from her rope and one of them carries her off over his shoulder.*) The Governor of Massachusetts, the honorable Sir William Phips, hath declared that "spectral evidence," that is evidence which relies solely upon the seeing of spirits or spectres, inadmissible in a court of law. Therefore . . . (*He takes off the wig and glasses, and speaks to the girls in a neutral voice.*) I shall not be requiring of your services any longer. (*The girls slowly lower their arms. The actor who played Hathorne climbs down from the throne and exits. Ann Putnam watches as everyone turns their back on her and walks away.*)

ACT 5, SCENE 1

*Music begins and the* ASSISTANTS *enter with stakes. They tease and torment* ANN *and throw her to her knees. They mark two gravesites and then exit.* DORCY GOOD *enters. She has been destroyed by the trial and the fate of her mother. She wanders the graveyard searching for the unmarked grave of her mother. She lashes out one minute and sings to herself the next.* ANN *watches this with a mixture of horror, pity, and profound guilt.*

DORCY: (*whispers*) Mama . . . Mama . . . I here. Mama, where . . . ? You said . . . Mama you here? (*calls out wildly*) Mama! (*suddenly calm*) Ah, there . . . Mama. No, no cry. Look, an apple, Mama. (*She pulls out a rotten core.*) You hungry? (*She begins to bite at the core. She sees Ann and whispers to her imaginary mother.*) Mama . . . hide . . . hurt you . . . run . . . they here . . . No, Mama take me . . . they . . . she hurt . . . Mama . . . come . . . (*Dorcy throws herself on the ground and tries to dig through. Ann takes a step toward her and Dorcy runs away. Ann returns to the site of her mother's grave and sobs.*)

ANN SENIOR *enters from behind the scrim. She is a ghost.* ANN JUNIOR *never looks at her, but directs her lines to the sky. The music continues low, underneath.* ANN SENIOR's *first three lines are said by both she and* ANN JUNIOR. *It is as though* ANN JUNIOR *is answering for her mother. On these lines she moves her head downward, then back up for her own line.* ANN SENIOR'S *voice is low on these first three lines.*

*ANN: (slowly)* Mama. . . . Can you hear me? Do you know what has happened?

*ANN SENIOR & JUNIOR:* All things must take their course.

*ANN:* Now I am called the evil one.

*ANN SENIOR & JUNIOR:* Life is a trial. All of life is a trial.

*ANN:* For what?

*ANN SENIOR & JUNIOR:* For the spirit, for the soul . . .

*ANN:* For property. They say we did this to acquire land.

*ANN SENIOR:* I do not remember what I did.

*ANN:* Is it my fault then?

*ANN SENIOR:* We are all guilty. We are all innocent.

*ANN:* I remember you made me give Tituba the recipe, and she was accused.

*ANN SENIOR:* Life is a trial.

*ANN:* And I said nothing.

*ANN SENIOR:* Such an impressionable child.

*ANN:* I had a dream that Dorcy Good and her mother came to me. They told me of their innocence. They said I am Satan's instrument.

*ANN SENIOR:* More dreams.

*ANN:* But you said dreams were true.

*ANN SENIOR:* How was I to know these things?

*ANN:* I do not desire to live any longer.

*ANN SENIOR:* Seek forgiveness then.

*ANN:* How could I be forgiven? I do not deserve to be. *(pause)* Mama!

*ANN SENIOR:* I am here.

*ANN:* I miss you.

*ANN SENIOR:* Our time will come.

*ANN:* I am all alone now. All the other girls have gone. And I am afraid to speak to anyone.

*ANN SENIOR:* I am near you.

*ANN:* Nay. You left me alone. You made me alone.

*ANN SENIOR:* All of us die alone.

*ANN:* Then I am coming soon.

*ANN SENIOR:* Aye. Everyone comes. (*The tone gets louder as Ann Senior exits behind the scrim.*)

*ANN:* (*calls after her*) Mama, do not leave. Do not leave me all alone. (*She bends over and sobs. As Ann Senior exits behind the scrim, the actor who played Parris and Hathorne joins her as she revolves. This is a vision in Ann Junior's mind. The light behind the scrim fades. The music ends.*)

ACT 5, SCENE 2

*ANN:* (*She slowly collects herself and stands facing the audience. It is fourteen years after the trial. Ann is very weak and disheveled. She knows she is close to death. She starts off meekly.*) I have spoken to Reverend Green about my desire to receive full communion and have asked him if I might read the following confession to you. He hath most graciously consented. On this day, August ye twenty-forth, seventeen hundred and six, I desire to be humble before God for that sad and humbling providence that befell my father's family the year about ninety-two. I then being in my childhood should be such a providence of God, be made an instrument for ye accusing of several persons of a grievous crime whereby their lives were taken away from them, whom now I have just grounds and good reason to believe they were innocent persons and that it was a delusion of Satan that deceived me in that sad time. Whereby, I justly fear I have been instrumental with others, though ignorantly and unwittingly to bring upon myself and this land the guilt of innocent blood. Though what was said or done by me against any person I can truly and uprightly say before God and man, I did it not out of any anger, malice, or ill will to any person for I had no such thing against any one of them; but what I did was ignorantly being deluded by Satan. And particularly as I was a chief instrument of accusing of Goodwife Good and her daughter (*She falls to her knees.*), I desire to lie in ye dust and earnestly beg forgiveness of God and from all those unto whom I have given just cause of sorrow and offense, whose relations were taken away or accused. Amen. (*She bows her head.*)

*The cast enters singing the hymn "Morning"** (1832) by Henry K. Oliver for the curtain call.* ANN *stands and joins them.*

---

*Oliver's version contains the phrase "Lo! Salem's daughters weep around." The hymn was first published by Isaac Watts in 1709 under the title of "Christ Dying, Raising and Reigning."*

# Salem's Daughters Study Guide

## Learning Goals

1. to survey Puritan culture in 1692 as it relates to the Salem witch trials
2. to explore the circumstances that led to the witch hysteria
3. to examine the Salem witch trials from the perspective of the accusers
4. to relate Ann Putnam's experience to modern issues of prejudice and peer pressure

## What Happened in History

In the winter of 1691 to 1692, several girls in Salem Village began exhibiting strange behavior including screaming fits, physical contortions, and mysterious trances. The village physician, Dr. Griggs, was unable provide a medical diagnosis for these bizarre occurrences, and instead suggested that the children were afflicted by Satan. The girls were pressured into naming their tormentors, and eventually three women were accused, including Tituba, the Reverend Parris' servant from Barbados, who testified that there was a conspiracy of witches in the village.

Accusations continued over the spring and summer of 1692, and the Special Court of Oyer and Terminer was established to try the cases. In all, twenty-seven people were convicted of witchcraft; of those, nineteen people were hanged and one man was pressed to death. Others died in prison. By the fall of 1692, opposition to the witch trials was strong. Governor Phips of Massachusetts outlawed the use of spectral evidence, on which many of the accused were convicted, and the Special Court was dissolved. Fourteen years later, Ann Putnam wrote a confession to the congregation acknowledging that she was wrong in her accusations. Salem Village's new pastor Reverend Green entered Ann's confession into the church record on 24 August 1706.

## Historical Timeline

*November 1689:* Samuel Parris, a failed merchant from Barbados, is ordained pastor of Salem Village.

*January 1692*: Parris' nine-year-old daughter Elizabeth and eleven-year-old niece Abigail Williams exhibit strange behavior. Other girls in the Village soon develop similar symptoms.

*February:* Dr. Griggs determines that there is nothing physically wrong with the girls and suggests that the "evil hand" is upon them. Parris leads the community in prayer and fasting to cast off the evil spirits, but the afflictions persist. Mary Sibley gives Parris' servants Tituba and John Indian a recipe for a witch cake made with rye flour and the urine of the afflicted girls. According to Sibley, the cake, when fed to a dog, will reveal the identities of the guilty witches. Tituba and John Indian are caught making the cake. Pressured by adults, the girls accuse Tituba, Sarah Good, and Sarah Osborne of afflicting them. Warrants are issued for the three women.

*March:* Salem magistrates John Hathorne and Jonathan Corwin examine Tituba, Sarah Good, and Sarah Osborne. Good and Osborne deny the charges, but Tituba confesses to witchcraft and names the other two women as her accomplices. All three women are sent to prison. Martha Corey, Rebecca Nurse, Elizabeth Proctor, and Sarah Good's four-year-old daughter Dorcas are accused of witchcraft. Corey and Nurse are examined by magistrates.

*April:* The accusations and examinations continue as twenty-three more persons are jailed including: Nehemiah Abbott; Bridget, Sarah, and Edward Bishop; Mary Black; Giles Corey; Mary English; Abigail, Deliverance, and William Hobbs; John Proctor; Mary Warren; Sarah Wildes; and Rebecca Nurse's sisters Sarah Cloyce and Mary Estes.

*Early May:* Magistrates examine Lydia Dustin, Dorcas Hoar, Susannah Martin, Sarah Morey, and Reverend George Burroughs of Wells, Maine. George Jacobs and his granddaughter Margaret are also examined. Margaret confesses to witchcraft and testifies against her grandfather and Burroughs. Sarah Osborne dies in prison.

*Late May:* The new Governor of Massachusetts Sir William Phips arrives from England and establishes a seven-member Special Court to try the witchcraft cases.

*Early June:* The new court finds Bridget Bishop guilty of witchcraft, and she becomes the first person to be hanged as part of the witch trials. Spectral evidence, based on the seeing spectres and spirits, is legitimized by the court.

*Late June:* Sarah Good, Elizabeth Howe, Susannah Martin, Rebecca Nurse, and Sarah Wildes are tried and found guilty of witchcraft.

*July:* Good, Howe, Martin, Nurse, and Wildes are hanged on Gallows Hill.

*August:* George Burroughs, Martha Carrier, George Jacobs, John Proctor, and John Willard are tried, condemned, and executed for witchcraft. Proctor's pregnant wife Elizabeth is found guilty of witchcraft, but her sentence is postponed until after the birth of her infant.

*Early to mid-September:* Mary Bradbury, Martha Corey, Rebecca Eames, Mary Easty, Abigail Faulkner, Ann Foster, Dorcas Hoar, Abigail Hobbs, Mary Lacy, Alice and Mary Parker, Ann Pudeator, Wilmott Redd, Margaret Scott, and Samuel Wardwell are tried and condemned to death. Giles Corey refuses to enter a plea and is pressed to death.

*Late September:* Martha Corey, Mary Easty, Alice and Mary Parker, Ann Pudeator, Wilmott Redd, Margaret Scott, and Samuel Wardwell are the last persons to be hanged during the Salem witch trials.

*October:* Governor Phips orders spectral evidence inadmissible in the trials. By the end of the month, he dissolves the court.

*August 1706:* Salem Village's new pastor Reverend Green accepts Ann Putnam's confession into the church records.

## Vocabulary

*Conjure:* to summon a demon or spirit through a magic spell

*Fasting:* to go without food

*Bewitch:* to cast a spell on someone

*Curse:* to bring evil or injury on someone (Ann Putnam's family believed they were cursed because many of her young siblings died.)

*Poppet:* a doll

*Possessed:* controlled by an evil spirit

*Familiar:* an evil spirit that attends to the needs of a spell caster, often living in an animal such as a cat or a bird

*Magistrate:* a civil officer charged with administrating the law (In Salem, magistrates served as judges in the witch trials.)

*Examination:* questioning or interrogation

*Spectral evidence:* evidence that relies on the seeing of spirits or spectres

*Gallows Hill:* the spot where those convicted of witchcraft were hanged

*Salem Village:* the setting of the witch trials of 1692, now known as Danvers, Massachusetts

*Witch hunt:* to conduct a well-publicized and aggressive campaign against individuals who may be disloyal or subversive, based on minimal or questionable evidence

*Confession:* to admit to one's misdeed, fault, or crime

## Key Players in the Witch Trials of 1692

### Those Accused

GEORGE BURROUGHS was minister of Salem Village in 1660. His tenure in Salem was contentious and he soon moved to Wells, Maine. In 1683, Thomas and Ann Putnam filed a lawsuit against him. During the hysteria, Abigail Williams accused him of being the main instigator of the afflictions.

BRIDGET BISHOP was the wife of Edward Bishop of Salem Village. Her reputation for practicing witchcraft predated the hysteria. She was hanged on 10 June 1692.

GILES COREY testified against his wife Martha at her trial, and was later accused of witchcraft. He refused a trial to avoid having his property seized from his heirs upon his death. Corey was pressed to death on 19 September 1692 in an attempt to force a plea from him.

DORCAS (DORCY) GOOD was the four-year-old daughter of Sarah Good. Like her mother, she was accused of witchcraft. Because Dorcas pled guilty, she was not hanged. She was held in a dungeon for eight months and reportedly went insane.

SARAH GOOD's first husband died and left her in debt. She became a beggar woman. Her unnamed infant died in prison prior to Sarah's hanging on 19 July 1692.

TITUBA INDIAN was Reverend Samuel Parris' maidservant from Barbados. She was the first person accused of witchcraft. She eventually confessed and made accusations against Sarah Good and Sarah Osborne, adding fuel to the hysteria. She remained in prison during the trials and was later sold to another master.

REBECCA NURSE was the seventy-one-year-old ailing wife of a prosperous farmer, Frances Nurse. They had eight children and many grandchildren. Rebecca was highly regarded in Salem Village, and many of her neighbors spoke on her behalf during the trials. The grounds-swell of support temporarily prevented her death, but she was eventually hanged on 19 July 1692.

SARAH OSBORNE was one of the first three women to be accused of sorcery. Like George Burroughs, she had prior legal conflicts with the Putnams, and like Rebecca Nurse, she was ill by the time she was accused.

ELIZABETH PROCTOR, wife of John Proctor, was pregnant when her servant Mary Warren accused her of witchcraft. She was found guilty, but her sentence was postponed until after the birth of her infant. By then, the hysteria had died down.

JOHN PROCTOR was a successful farmer and businessman. Unlike Giles Corey, he spoke out against the witch hunt when it began and later defended his wife during her trial. He was accused of witchcraft and hanged on 19 August 1692.

## The Accusers

JOHN INDIAN, husband of Tituba, may have avoided being accused of witchcraft by becoming an accuser himself.

ELIZABETH HUBBARD was the servant and niece of Dr. Griggs, who first determined that the girls had been cursed. At the age of seventeen, she was in the circle of accusers.

MERCY LEWIS was the seventeen-year-old maidservant to the Putnams. Following the trials, she lived with an aunt and uncle in Greenland, New Hampshire.[1] There, she had an illegitimate child, and eventually married Charles Allen.

BETTY PARRIS, the nine-year-old-daughter of Samuel Parris, was one of the first girls to be afflicted. Before the trials began, she was sent to live with the Sewell family in Salem Town, where she quickly recovered from her afflictions.

ANN (CARR) PUTNAM was the wife of Thomas Putnam and mother of one of the chief accusers, Ann Putnam. Daughter of a wealthy entrepreneur, she became bitter over several inheritance proceedings that she felt unfairly left the bulk of family land and money to relatives. She gave birth to a number of stillborn children, adding to her sense of persecution. At the height of the hysteria, she joined the ranks of afflicted.

ANN PUTNAM, the twelve-year-old daughter of Ann and Thomas Putnam, was known as an honest and pious child. Her reputation made her an extremely effective accuser. In 1706, at the urging of Salem Village's new pastor Joseph Green, she wrote a confession apologizing for her role in the

---

[1]Francis Hill. 1995. *A Delusion of Satan: The Full Story of the Salem Witch Trials.* New York: Doubleday, p. 250.

trials. Her confession was accepted into the church records, and she died ten years later.

THOMAS PUTNAM, with his wife Ann, helped to bring Reverend Parris to Salem Village. Like his wife, Thomas felt cheated out of his inheritance. Many of the accused were involved with prior legal battles with Thomas Putnam.[2]

MARY WALCOTT was related to the Putnams. At the age of seventeen, she became one of the afflicted girls in March of 1692. She was seen knitting throughout most of the trials. She would stop knitting long enough to participate in the fits and then resume her needlework. In *Salem's Daughters*, Elizabeth Hubbard is given Mary's knitting habit.

MARY WARREN was the eighteen-year-old servant of the Proctors. She testified against Elizabeth Proctor, but recanted her testimony when John Proctor was also accused of witchcraft. She was herself accused by the other girls and imprisoned. Under tremendous pressure, Mary reverted back to her original charges and returned to the ranks of the accusers.

ABIGAIL WILLIAMS, the eleven-year-old niece of Samuel Parris, came to Salem Village with the Parris family. One of the first girls to be afflicted, she became a leading accuser of witchcraft.

### Religious and Political Leaders

JOHN HATHORNE, a prominent entrepreneur and the most zealous of the Salem magistrates, never apologized or admitted wrongdoing after the trials.

COTTON MATHER was the son of Harvard University president Increase Mather. His writings on witchcraft in the 1680s added fuel to the hysteria in Salem, and his advice was sought by prominent players in the trials.

SAMUEL PARRIS was a failed merchant from the West Indies. He came to Boston in 1680 and married Elizabeth Eldridge. Parris moved his family to Salem Village in 1688, where he began his first ministry a year later. Parris' appointment as pastor was extremely contentious as he made a number of demands on his parishioners. He relied on the Putnam family for support. His daughter and niece were the first girls in Salem Village to be afflicted.

SIR WILLIAM PHIPS arrived from England in May of 1692 with a long-awaited charter for the colony. As the newly appointed Governor of Massachusetts, Phips established the Court of Oyer and Terminer to oversee the witch trials. In October, bowing to public opinion, Phips banned the use of spectral evidence in the trials and dissolved the Court two weeks later.

---

[2]Paul Boyer and Stephen Nissenbaum. 1974. *Salem Possessed: The Social Origins of Witchcraft*. Cambridge, MA: Harvard University Press, pp. 110–33.

## Preperformance Lesson Plans

### Character Biographies

*Goal:* to explore life in Salem Village before, during, and after the witch trials

*Objectives*

1. to review what is known or believed about the Salem witch trials
2. to write fictional character biographies of Salem Villagers in 1692

*Method*

1. Ask the class to describe what life was like in Salem Village in 1692. What did people do for a living? What was life like for women and children? What did people eat? What role did the church play in their lives?

2. Discuss the effects of the witch trials on those villagers. Who benefited from the trials? Who was hurt? What would it be like to live in Salem Village after the trials? How did people feel about one another?

3. Divide the class in half. Ask members of one group to each write a fictional character biography of a relative of someone who was accused and/or hanged for witchcraft. Ask members of the other group to write biographies of relatives of people who did the accusing. These biographies should include:

   a. character name—first and last (*see the following list)

   b. occupation

   c. age

   d. relationship to the accuser or person accused

   e. family life

   f. summary of how the character's life was affected by the witch trials

4. Students read and discuss their biographies with the class.

---

*Here are some last names of persons living in Salem Village in 1692. Students may either choose a name from the following list or make up a new one. Students may also share the same last name: Willard, Easty, Peabody, Porter, Hobbs, Robinson, Nichols, Wilkins, Way, Elliot, Putnam, Nurse, Griggs, Preston, Cloyse, Jacobs, Hutchinson, Prescot, Trask, Rea, Bayley, Sibley, Herrick, Houlton, Haines, Watts, Bishop, Phelps, Small, Case, and Fuller.

*Poetic Point of View*

*Goal:* to deepen students' empathy for those involved in the trials

*Objectives*

1. to imagine the thoughts and feelings of those involved in the witch hysteria
2. to write a poem from the point of view of one person in the Salem trials

*Method*

1. Distribute copies of the Historical Timeline and Key Players sections of the study guide. Review the information with the students.
2. Each student picks one character from the Key Players.
3. From the perspective of their selected character, students list words or phrases that describe how they feel about themselves.
4. From the same perspective, students list words or phrases that describe how they feel about other people in Salem Village.
5. Each student picks three or four words or phrases from each list and writes a poem that incorporates them.
6. Share the poems with the class.

*Follow-up:* Ask each student to draw or paint a picture of a scene in the play through the eyes of their chosen person. What would that person have seen, thought, or felt?

## Postperformance Lesson Plans

### Interviewing Ann Putnam

*Goal:* to discover possible motives behind Ann Putnam's actions from 1692 to 1706

*Objectives*

1. to determine some of the influences on Ann Putnam
2. to discover how Ann's attitudes changed from the time of the trials to that of her confession

*Method*

1. Based on the Character Biographies in the preperformance lesson plans, divide the class into two camps (half of the students play characters whose family members were accused of witchcraft, the other half play characters whose family members did the accusing).

2. Set up the situation: The year is 1706. Students are in role as members of the congregation of Salem Village. Ann Putnam is now a woman. She wishes to confess that she was wrong in her accusations fourteen years ago. Ask for a volunteer to play Ann Putnam.

3. In role as Reverend Green, the teacher welcomes the congregation to the meeting and states that in a moment, Ann Putnam will come before them. The congregation is to decide whether to forgive Ann and allow her into the congregation, or if she is to remain an outcast, her soul forever barred from entering the kingdom of heaven.

4. The Reverend asks if there are any concerns among the congregation that members wish to express before Ann appears before them.

5. The Reverend introduces Ann Putnam to the congregation and asks them to listen to her confession with open minds.

6. Ann reads the confession (see final scene of *Salem's Daughters*).

7. Reverend Green acts as a mediator, fielding questions from the congregation to Ann Putnam. These questions can include those about her motivations, thoughts, and feelings during the trials or in seeking forgiveness today. In order to give the student playing Ann time to think, to heighten the language, and to make sure everyone hears the question, the teacher should restate each question.

8. Time permitting, several students could volunteer to play Ann on the hot seat.

9. When questions are through, Reverend Green leads a debate in which members of the congregation try to convince each other of their opinion on whether Ann should be forgiven and allowed into the congregation.

10. A vote is taken.

11. The Reverend picks a volunteer to inform Ann of their decision.

*Follow-up:* Ask students whether this exercise altered their opinion on whether to accept Ann into the congregation. If so, how? Might the outcome of the vote have been different if a secret ballot were taken?

## And That's the Way It Was

*Goal:* to explore the subjective nature of historical writing

*Objectives*

1. to explore how people can see and report on the same events in contrasting ways
2. to try to write a fair and balanced article, while holding strong sympathies for one side or the other

*Method*

1. Divide the class into two groups of journalists. Group A has sympathies with those who were arrested and/or hanged for witchcraft; Group B sympathizes with those who did the accusing.
2. Based on the previous exercise, *Interviewing Ann Putnam*, each student writes an article about exactly what happened in the meetinghouse (including the introduction by Reverend Green, Ann's confession, the questioning, the debate, the vote, and the presentation of the congregation's decision to Ann Putnam). While students have been assigned a strong sympathy to one side or the other, they should try to write a fair and balanced report of the events.
3. Collect the articles and collate them so that both group's articles are mixed in together.
4. Randomly pass out articles to the students. If someone ends up with their own article, ask them to switch with someone else. In role as modern day TV anchors, students read aloud the article that has been handed to them.
5. Discuss the variation in reporting. Can students detect the sympathies of each reporter? If so, how? What is the role of bias in reporting?

## What Were Ann's Options?

*Goal:* to explore the effects of outside pressure on decision making

*Objectives*

1. to examine the relationship between children and their parents in Puritan times
2. to determine whether Ann had any viable options for preventing the trials

*Method*

1. Students read the dialogue between Ann Putnam, Mercy, and Ann Senior in Act 4, Scene 1 of *Salem's Daughters*. Discuss Ann's dilemma in the scene.

2. Set up the following situation: Ann Putnam is about to testify against Tituba, but she has second thoughts.

3. Ask for one volunteer to play Ann, and another to play Ann's mother (or father, if a male student volunteers).

4. Students improvise the dialogue between Ann and her mother (or father), remaining true to what happens in the scene.

5. Freeze the scene at a high point. Ask the rest of the class:

   a. What's going on between these two people?

   b. At this point, what could Ann do to get out of testifying? Write these suggestions down on the board.

   c. What would you do if you were in her shoes? Write these suggestions down on the board.

6. Review the list of options. Ask the class which suggestion they would like to try first. Ask for two more volunteers to play Ann and her mother/father. Ann should try the suggested tactic. Ann's mother/father should remain true to their character's original intention. When the suggestion is played out, freeze the scene. Ask students to evaluate the effectiveness of the chosen tactic. Given the time period, was it a viable option for Ann? Students select another option from the list. Ask for two more volunteers and repeat the process.

## Point/Counterpoint

*Goal:* to explore the difference between reporting and editorializing

*Objectives*

1. to express strong opinions in a constructive manner
2. to debate questions in a news talk-show format

*Method*

1. Discuss the difference between reporting and editorializing. What is the role of each? What is a pundit? What qualities does an effective pundit have? What tactics do they use in persuading an audience?

2. Ask students to each write down three questions they have regarding the Salem trials.

3. Ask for one volunteer to play a pundit who is sympathetic to Ann Putnam and the other girls, and another pundit who is unsympathetic to them.

4. The volunteers sit facing each other in the center of the class, the teacher is off to the side.

5. In role as a talk show host, the teacher welcomes the studio audience to the show *Point/Counterpoint*. Announce that today's topic is the Salem witch trials, and that two specialists with opposing views are the guests.

6. In role as the studio audience, students raise their hand to ask a question (from method #2) concerning a person or an event from the witch hysteria. Either of the experts may respond first. At the teacher's direction, the other expert is given time for a rebuttal. The debate can continue so that each student speaks two or three times about the question.

7. Ask for two more volunteers and another question. Repeat the process.

8. Discuss what took place. Were the pundits able to focus on the questions? Did the debate get personal? What debate tactics were used? How effective was each tactic?

### The Examination of Mary Warren

*Goal:* to examine the effects of mass hysteria on the community in Salem Village

*Objectives*

1. to understand the role of peer pressure in the witch trials

2. to empathize with the underlying emotions of the characters involved in the trials

3. to utilize primary source documents for the purpose of character and story development

4. to gain an introductory understanding of legal documents and their significance

*Method*

1. Introduce the story of Mary Warren. Explain to students that they will be reading excerpts from *The Salem Witchcraft Papers* (Boyer and Nissenbaum, 1977), which contain the testimony of Mary

Warren. Mention that these are the court transcripts from the witch trials. Discuss what court transcripts consist of, and what purpose they serve. What do the students expect to discover from these documents?

2. If time allows, ask students to take turns reading aloud from the document. The transcripts are inherently dramatic and may provide students with creative inspiration for the next part of the lesson. Reading aloud will also give the teacher the opportunity to clarify the language for students. Discuss the students' first impressions of the transcripts.

3. Divide the students into small groups. Ask them to choose a moment in the testimony that they find particularly interesting or compelling. It can be from the examination itself or from one of the stories that Mary told (e.g., Mary's examination in the courtroom, while the other girls are accusing her; Mary's stories of the Proctors' witchcraft, such as the devil's book or the "poppets" they created; or Mary's examination in prison).

4. Ask students to create a tableau of their selected moment.

5. Students share their tableaux with the class. As each group presents their tableau, ask the rest of the class to share their impressions. It is important that they don't simply try to "figure out" what part of the story is being represented, but that they explore the underlying themes and relationships of the figures in the tableau. Once students have shared their ideas, the group can tell the rest of the class what moment they re-created.

6. After each group has presented their tableau, go around the room again and ask each group to reassume their pose. This time, explain that you will be tapping each character on the shoulder and asking them to say one sentence that their character might think or say at this moment. They are to say their sentence and then freeze again.

7. Discuss the ideas that came out of this activity. Did students gain any insight into the characters?

*Follow-up:* This lesson can be used as a springboard for students to script their own scene.

*Topics for Further Research and Discussion*

1. The role of race in the accusation of Tituba

2. The social status of the accused and their accusers and how it changed as the hysteria progressed

3. The social and economic circumstances that may have led to the accusations, such as land ownership and past grudges between accusers and the accused

4. A feminist perspective on the witch trials: The women who were accused were strong-willed and independent, and many were unconventional. Were they being punished for their outspoken behavior?

5. The accusation of witchcraft as a means of teenage rebellion in Puritan society

6. The fundamental beliefs of Puritanism, and how they contributed to the witch hysteria

7. The legal proceedings of the witch trials and how they compare to today's laws

8. Research on individual characters, such as Rebecca Nurse, Sarah Good, Sarah Osborne, Bridget Bishop, Samuel Parris, or Mary Warren

## Resources

Boyer, Paul S. 1993. *Salem Village Witchcraft: A Documentary Record of Local Conflict in Colonial New England*. Belmont, CA: Northeastern University Press.

Boyer, Paul, and Stephen Nissenbaum. 1974. *Salem Possessed: The Social Origins of Witchcraft*. Cambridge, MA: Harvard University Press.

———. 1977. *The Salem Witchcraft Papers*. New York: De Capo.

Brown, David C. 1984. *A Guide to the Salem Witchcraft Hysteria of 1692*. n.p.

Delbanco, Andrew. 1989. *The Puritan Ordeal*. Cambridge, MA: Harvard University Press.

Demos, John Putnam. 1982. *Entertaining Satan: Witchcraft and the Culture of Early New England*. New York and Oxford: Oxford University Press.

Fox, Stanford J. 1968. *The Massachusetts Witchcraft Trials*. Baltimore, MD: John Hopkins Press.

Gildrie, Richard P. 1975. *Salem Massachusetts, a Covenant Community*. Charlottesville, VA: University Press of Virginia.

Godbeer, Richard. 1992. *The Devil's Dominion: Magic and Religion in Early New England*. Cambridge: Cambridge University Press.

Hall, David D. 1991. *Witch-Hunting in Seventeenth Century New England*. Boston: Northeastern Press.

Hansen, Chadwick. 1969. *Witchcraft at Salem*. New York: George Brazilier.

Hill, Francis. 1995. *A Delusion of Satan: The Full Story of the Salem Witch Trials*. New York: Doubleday.

Karleen, Carol F. 1987. *The Devil in the Shape of a Woman: Witchcraft in Colonial New England*. New York and London: W.W. Norton & Co.

Kittredge, George Lyman. 1972. *Witchcraft in Old and New England*. New York: Athenum.

Morgan, Edmund S. 1963. *Visible Saints: The History of a Puritan Idea*. Ithaca, NY: Cornell University Press.

Morison, Samuel Eliot. 1956. *The Intellectual Life of Colonial New England*. New York: New York University Press.

Richardson, Katherine W. 1983. *The Salem Witchcraft Trials*. Salem, MA: The Essex Institute.

Rinaldi, Ann. 1992. *A Break with Charity: A Story About the Salem Witch Trials*. New York: Harcourt Brace and Company.

Simpson, Allen. 1955. *Puritanism in Old and New England*. Chicago: University of Chicago Press.

Starkey, Marion L. 1949. *The Devil in Massachusetts*. New York: Bantam Doubleday Dell Publishing Group, Inc.

————. 1973. *The Visionary Girls*. Boston: Little, Brown and Company.

Thomas, Keith. 1971. *Religion and the Decline of Magic*. New York: Charles Scribner's Sons.

*Three Sovereigns for Sarah*. 1985. Directed by Philip Leacock. 171 mins. PBS Home Video. Videocassette.

Trask, Richard. 1975. *Salem Village and the Witch Hysteria*. New York: Grossman.

# 2

## The Trial of Anthony Burns (1854)

## Overview

In 1999, Discovering Justice: The James D. St.Clair Court Education Project commissioned Theatre Espresso to write a new drama to be in residence at the Moakley U.S. Courthouse in Boston. The result was *The Trial of Anthony Burns*, the story of an escaped slave who was tried in Boston in 1854. Burns' arrest and subsequent return to slavery was a pivotal event in pre-Civil War America. Many Bostonians were furious that a man could be returned to bondage in a state that was considered to be the birthplace of liberty, and they stormed the courthouse in an attempt to free Burns. A guard was killed and as a result of the violence, the city of Boston was placed under martial law. Thousands of troops lined the streets of the city as Burns was placed on board a ship that brought him back to Virginia. Four years after the trial, Edward G. Loring, the judge who decided the case, was removed from the bench for his unpopular decision.

The case of Anthony Burns was selected for several reasons. First of all, the trial was complicated, involving prominent Boston lawyers and public figures, each with their own agenda. A meeting at Faneuil Hall erupted into a riot as Bostonians failed in their attempt to break into the Courthouse and free Burns. Historically, fervor over Burns' return to slavery bolstered the abolitionist movement and gave rise to the Republican Party. The case was also of interest to Judge Julian Houston, who initiated a traveling exhibit on the progress of black Americans titled: *The Long Road to Justice*.[1] The exhibit

---

1. Developed in cooperation with the Massachusetts Historical Society, the Justice Lewis Ruffin Society, Northeastern University, and the College of Criminal Justice.

was displayed in the Courthouse lobby in 2002, and was linked to the new play-in-residence.

While working with Theatre Espresso on *The Trial of Anthony Burns*, Discovering Justice also partnered with the Bostonian Society, whose collection of documents and artifacts served as a rich resource to the historical drama. Together, the two organizations created an exhibit containing documents and artifacts from the case of Anthony Burns. The exhibit, titled *The Price of Freedom: Anthony Burns and the Fugitive Slave Act,* set the stage for the drama by examining the historical context of the Burns case. It also presented tangible reminders of Burns' struggle, such as the handcuffs he wore while imprisoned. As students examined these artifacts, they were encouraged to think about what they would do if faced with the moral dilemma presented to the characters in the play.

In addition to the Moakley Courthouse, *The Trial of Anthony Burns* now tours to courthouses in Quincy, Worcester, and Springfield, and the Massachusetts Supreme Judicial Court. In 2004, the Orchard House (historic home of Louisa May Alcott and her family) provided a permanent residence for *Anthony Burns* at the Concord School of Philosophy, where Bronson Alcott and countless other abolitionists and thinkers fervently debated the issues of the nineteenth century. The play was also featured at Harvard Graduate School of Education's 2003 ASKWITH Forum on Arts and Civic Dialogue and The Greater Boston Federal Executive Board's 2004 Diversity Conference, held at the John F. Kennedy Library.

## Synopsis

The play focuses on the actions of Judge Loring. Acting both as Slave Bill Commissioner and Massachusetts State Judge, Loring sent Burns back into slavery for violating the Fugitive Slave Law of 1850. That law maintained that slaves were the property of their owners, and as such, had no legal rights. Although Loring based his decision on an established law, his judgment was extremely unpopular. In 1858, a partisan Massachusetts State Senate voted to remove him from office.

In the drama, students play members of the Massachusetts Senate in 1858. They explore questions surrounding Loring's actions: What else could he have done? If he had other options, what were they and why didn't he take them? After viewing the trial and surrounding events, they question various witnesses, participate in a debate, and then vote on Loring's fate. In doing so, students grapple with complicated issues of moral law versus human law, and decide when and if one should ever outweigh the other.

## Preparing the Students

Prior to Courthouse performances, teachers receive a copy of *The Trial of Anthony Burns* study guide (included in this chapter). At the start of each show, a Discovering Justice staff member informs the audience that the drama they are about to see has over forty characters, and that most actors will play several roles. They are also reminded that the drama is interactive, and they will be deciding on the fate of Judge Loring. Therefore, it is important that they carefully observe the actions of the characters. We have found that this brief introduction focuses the students' attention and prepares them for the fast-paced drama they are about to see.

## A Note to the Director

The play can be performed with as few as seven actors, or with a large ensemble. With a small cast, it is crucial that actors make distinct vocal and physical choices for each character. Chorus lines should be read with intention. To avoid sounding like a neutral narrator, chorus members should decide how they feel about the speaker they are announcing, or the historical information they are delivering. A sense of urgency is crucial throughout. The play is meant to be performed at a fast pace, so costume changes should be minimal (e.g., the addition or removal of a hat, a shawl, or a jacket can signal a character change). Also, the set should be simple: a podium and a couple of stools is enough. Scenes are meant to flow from one to another, without breaks for set or costume changes. As with *Justice at War*, Theatre Espresso company members rehearse the interactive portion of the drama (see Chapter 5, page 208).

## The Trial of Anthony Burns[*]

### by Bethany Dunakin and Wendy Lement

### *Characters*

*The Trial of Anthony Burns* premiered in 2000 with the following cast:

CHAIRMAN/FREEMAN/THOMAS/BUTMAN . . . . . . . .Nathaniel McIntyre
LORING/HIGGINSON/BOSTON POST REPORTER . . .Derek Stone Nelson

The Anthony Burns project was commissioned by the James D. St.Clair Court Public Education Project, and developed by Theatre Espresso. Copyright © 2000.
[*]CAUTION: All rights whatsoever in this play are strictly reserved. Requests to reproduce the text in whole or part, as well as applications for amateur or professional performance rights should be addressed to Wendy Lement, c/o Heinemann, 361 Hanover Street, Portsmouth, NH 03801.

ANTHONY BURNS . . . . . . . . . . . . . . . . . . . . . . . . . . . . . . . . . .Keith Mascoll
DANA/ALEXANDRIA GAZETTE REPORTER . . . . .Christopher Robin Cook
GRIMES/SHOPKEEPER/CHORUS . . . . . . . . . . . . . . . . . . . . .Jason Ridgley
PHILLIPS/SUTTLE/PIERCE/BATCHELDER . . . . . . . . . . . . .David Hanbury
PARKER/LIBERATOR REPORTER/ALCOTT/CHORUS . .Catherine Campbell

*Dramatis Personae:*
Chairman, facilitator of the drama
Judge Loring, presiding over the case
Richard Henry Dana, Burns' lawyer
Anthony Burns, fugitive slave
Reverend Grimes, abolitionist minister, pastor of Burns' church
Wendell Phillips, prominent abolitionist
Colonel Charles Suttle, claimant of Anthony Burns
Mrs. Parker, abolitionist
Thomas Higginson, prominent abolitionist
Marshal Freeman
Officer Batchelder, serving Marshal Freeman
Seth Thomas, lawyer to Colonel Suttle
Officer Butman
Boston Post Reporter
Judge Sprague
Mayor of Boston
Abolitionists One to Five
Shopkeeper
Rioters One and Two
Guard
Alexandria Gazette Reporter
President Franklin Pierce
Bailiff

*Donors:* James Williams, Hamilton Willis, Edwin Parker, Louisa May Alcott,
Daniel Elliott, and Elizabeth Powell Mason
Clerk
Guard at Courthouse

*Witnesses:* William Jones, George Drew, Stephen Maddox, James Whittimore,
John Favor, and Horace Brown
Peter Dunbar, Captain of the Guards
Liberator Reporter
Crowd/Protestors

*Chorus:* all cast members, except Anthony Burns, read chorus lines.

**Setting:** Boston, Massachusetts

**Time:** 1854 and 1858

*CHAIRMAN:* Good morning and welcome to this session of the Massachusetts State Senate. Before we begin, you must first take the oath of office. Please stand, raise your right hand, and repeat after me: "As a member of the Massachusetts State Senate . . . I do solemnly swear . . . that I will faithfully and impartially perform all the duties . . . incumbent on me as a senator . . . according to the best of my abilities and understanding . . . to the rules and regulations of the constitution . . . and the laws of this commonwealth. . . . " Thank you, Senators. You may be seated. We are here today to decide the fate of Judge Edward G. Loring. Many of you have called for the removal of Judge Loring from office for his actions during the trial of Anthony Burns. Still others in this chamber have solidly defended his conduct. Today we must make a decision. It is important, Senators, to remember that eight years ago in 1850, the United States Congress passed the Fugitive Slave Law, mandating the return of all runaway slaves, regardless of where they were captured. Many of us believed that this law would never be tested within the State of Massachusetts. But only four years later in 1854, Anthony Burns was arrested here, in the Bay State, and Judge Loring presided over that trial. Before we decide whether or not Judge Loring's actions were constitutional, we shall review the events, which led to the arrest and subsequent trial of Anthony Burns. We shall begin with day one: *The Arrest.* (*three hits of the gavel*)

*LORING:* In the name of the President of the United States of America, you are hereby commanded to apprehend Anthony Burns, a Negro man, charged with being a fugitive from labor, and with having escaped from service in the State of Virginia. If he may be found in your district you are further commanded to bring him before me, Edward G. Loring, Commissioner of the Circuit Court of the United States. (*one hit of the gavel*)

*CHORUS:* Shortly after six o'clock on the evening of Wednesday, the twenty-fourth of May, 1854, a Negro named Anthony Burns was arrested by a United States marshal near the corner of Brattle and Court Streets in the City of Boston, upon the charge of breaking into and robbing a silversmith's shop.

*CHORUS:* From *The Biography of Richard Henry Dana.* (*one drum beat*)

*DANA:* A gang of some six or seven men, who had been lurking in the immediate vicinity, rushed to the assistance of the officer.

*CHORUS:* From the *New York Tribune.* (*one drum beat*)

*BURNS:* When I was going home one night I heard someone running behind me. A hand was put on my shoulder and he said:

*BUTMAN:* Stop, stop; you're the fellow that broke into a silversmith's shop the other night.

BURNS: You've made a mistake.

DANA: Surrounding the prisoner they lifted him up bodily and, avoiding the sidewalk carried him rapidly down the middle of the street to the Courthouse.

POST REPORTER: (pompously) According to the Post . . .

CHORUS: (interrupts) One of the most extreme antiabolitionist papers in Boston.

POST REPORTER: (interrupts) . . . the arrest was made very quietly and he was gently escorted to an upper room in the Courthouse.

DANA: Burns was hauled up several flights of stairs to the jury room without pausing, or even allowing the prisoner's feet to touch the ground.

BURNS: In the Courthouse I waited for sometime, and as the silversmith did not come, I told them that I wanted to go home for supper.

CHORUS: A few minutes later the door opened, and Officer Butman entered the room accompanied by a slave agent, Mr. William Brent, and his boss Colonel Suttle—the claimant of Burns.

SUTTLE: (taking off his hat and bowing with mock politeness—Virginia dialect) How do you do Mr. Burns?

BURNS: (to audience) I called him as we do in Virginia. (to Suttle) Master.

SUTTLE: Why did you run away from me?

BURNS: (to audience) I didn't know what to say. (to Suttle) I fell asleep on board the vessel where I worked, and before I woke up she set sail and carried me off.

SUTTLE: Haven't I always treated you well, Tony? (no answer from Burns) Haven't I always given you money when you needed it?

BURNS: You have always given me twelve and a half cents once a year.

CHORUS: This conversation would later be very important because of the defense's attempt to claim that Burns was not the slave Suttle claimed him to be.

BURNS: I got no supper or sleep that night.

CHAIRMAN: Day two: Legal Counsel. (three hits of the gavel)

BURNS: The next morning they told me that my master said he had a legal right to me, and as I had called him "Master," having the fear of God before my eyes, I could not go from it.

CHORUS: From the "Testimony of Reverend Grimes." (one drum beat)

GRIMES: (to audience) I went to speak to Burns in the Courthouse, an officer objected to it, but then another officer who knew me gave me permission. (*to Burns*) Anthony, as your pastor, I'm asking you to have faith in those who would help you.

BURNS: Reverend, I appreciate what you're trying to do, but . . .

GRIMES: Listen to me. Abolitionists from all over the city have been spreading word of your arrest. I know at least four lawyers who are on their way to the Courthouse now.

CHORUS: From *The Journal of Richard Henry Dana*. (*one drum beat*)

DANA: Thursday morning, as I was going past the Courthouse, a gentleman told me that there was a fugitive slave in custody in the U.S. courtroom. I went up immediately and saw a Negro sitting in the usual place for prisoners, guarded by a large corps of officers. He was a piteous object, rather weak in mind and body, with a rather large scar on his cheek which looked much like a brand, a broken hand from which a large piece of bone projected, and another scar on his other hand. He seemed completely cowed and dispirited. I offered to act as his counsel.

BURNS: It is of no use. They will swear they own me and get me back. And if they do, I shall fare worse if I resist.

DANA: Listen Anthony, there may be some flaw in the papers or some mistake and I could get you off.

GUARD: You might as well get counsel. It won't cost you nothing.

DANA: (*to audience*) He looked completely helpless and could not say what he wished to do.

BUTMAN: You may ask him as many times as you have a mind to. You will never get him to have counsel, or to make any defense.

BURNS: If I must go back, I want to go back as easy as I can.

DANA: (*to audience*) I would not press upon him a defense under these circumstances.

CHORUS: Upon leaving the Courthouse, Richard Henry Dana was approached by fellow abolitionist, Wendell Phillips.

PHILLIPS: What will become of the man?

DANA: I suppose he will be sent back.

PHILLIPS: Where is he?

DANA: In the Courthouse. I just saw him.

PHILLIPS: Who is his counsel?

DANA: He has none.

PHILLIPS: Then what are you doing outside the Court? Go back in and ask Loring to delay the hearing.

The Trial of Anthony Burns, *(left to right) Christopher Robin Cook, Nathaniel McIntyre, Alan White (seated), and Derek Nelson, photo by Wendy Lement.*

*CHORUS:* Dana arrived in the courtroom shortly before nine o'clock, interrupting the proceedings.

*DANA:* Your Honor, time must be allowed for the prisoner to recover himself from the stupefaction of his sudden arrest.

*LORING:* Mr. Burns, do you understand what's happening here? (*no answer*) Do you need more time to decide whether or not to accept counsel? (*no answer*) So, you are saying that you would like more time, isn't that right?

*BURNS:* (*pause*) Yes.

*LORING:* Delay granted. He must have necessary time. The Court will reconvene on Saturday.

*DANA:* (*to audience*) Off the record, he told me I could take as much time as I needed.

*CHORUS:* From *The Biography of Wendell Phillips.* (*one drum beat*)

*PHILLIPS:* After being denied access to the prisoner, I went directly to Judge Loring to request written permission to speak to Burns. I had to convince him to accept legal counsel. Otherwise he'd have no hope of freedom.

LORING: (*official*) Permission granted. (*softer tone*) But Wendell. . . . You do realize that he will most likely be going back. Do you really want to stir up trouble?

PHILLIPS: (*to audience*) I knew then where Loring's sentiments lay.

LORING: (*to Phillips*) The law is the law.

PHILLIPS: (*to audience*) He had made up his mind before he even heard the case. Well, whether or not it was hopeless, I had to reassure Anthony that he wasn't alone. When I first saw him in the Courthouse, he was trembling, confused, astounded, friendless, not knowing what to say or where to look. But after a time, he began to tell me his story.

BURNS: I was stolen and made a slave as soon as I was born. When I learned about the North where men of my color could live without any man daring to say to them "you are my property," I determined by the blessing of God, one day to find my way there. Once in Boston, I didn't want to make myself known, so I didn't tell who I was, and I found work. And I worked hard, but I kept to myself and didn't tell anyone I was a slave. I made a living for myself, as I never could before.

PHILLIPS: (*to audience*) He was a much more intelligent and resolute man than we first supposed him to be. (*to Burns*) Look Anthony, Suttle claims that you want to go back to being his slave.

BURNS: I never said that.

PHILLIPS: Then will you let us defend you in court?

BURNS: Do you really think I have a chance?

LORING: (*echo*) The law is the law.

PHILLIPS: (*to audience*) What could I say?

BURNS: You know what they'll do to me, if I fight them.

LORING: (*echo*) Do you really want to stir up trouble?

PHILLIPS: (*to audience*) I had to think of the bigger picture.

BURNS: Master Suttle is a malicious man when he's crossed. I'll be taken to the first block and sold at the New Orleans Market.

LORING: (*echo*) He will most likely be going back.

PHILLIPS: (*to audience*) The abolitionists needed a martyr.

BURNS: Do you see this hand? The way it is now, I could never do the kind of work they'd be expecting.

PHILLIPS: (*to audience*) But is this fair to Anthony? (*decides*) No, this was our chance to light the world on fire and end the wretched institution of Slavery once and for all! (*to Anthony*) Anthony, you have to fight. We won't let them take you out of the State of Massachusetts. Right now people are

The Trial of Anthony Burns, *(left to right) Shelley Bolman and Alan White, photo by Wendy Lement.*

rallying to your defense. We'll storm the Courthouse if we have to. The city government is already on our side. The police have been ordered not to lift a finger to help that immoral kidnapper you call Master. We will overturn the vile Fugitive Slave law. We will be victorious!

BURNS: They say that in escaping, I disobeyed the law. No man has any right to steal me. The law which God wrote on the table of my heart inspires a love of freedom and leads me on. (*decides*) Tell Mr. Dana I'm ready to fight, if he's still willing.

PHILLIPS: (*to Burns*) You made the right decision, Tony. (*to audience*) Who was I trying to convince?

CHORUS: From *The Journal of Richard Henry Dana.* (*one drum beat*)

DANA: My first act as Burns' attorney was to ask Judge Sprague for a *writ de homine replegiando . . .*

CHORUS: In plain terms—to let him out on bail.

SPRAGUE: (*pompously*) It is not a writ known to this Court. It has never been issued to my knowledge by these Courts. And as I understand it, it is not issuable at the common law when the party is held under legal process.

CHORUS: In other words—no.

CHORUS: Upon learning of the arrest, Mrs. Theodore Parker issued the following announcement on her husband's behalf.

MRS. PARKER: Kidnapping again. A man was stolen last night by the Fugitive Slave Bill Commissioner. He will have his mock trial on Saturday, May twenty-seventh at nine o'clock in the kidnapper's "court" before the honorable slave bill commissioner in the Courthouse in Court Square. Shall Boston steal another man? (*one drum beat*)

CHORUS: (*sense of urgency*) As word spread throughout Massachusetts, Burns became an instant symbol of the abolitionist cause.

CHORUS: (*builds sense of urgency*) It is important to note that the Kansas-Nebraska act was passed on this day, allowing slavery in the territories of Kansas and Nebraska. This made the Burns trial even more heated.

CHORUS: (*builds sense of urgency*) The northern abolitionists were very fired up about slavery expansion and Burns' arrest only added to their sense of urgency.

CHORUS: (*builds sense of urgency*) Also, a crowd of abolitionists was arriving in Boston for their annual meeting.

CHAIRMAN: Day Three: *The Riot.* (*three hits of the gavel*)

BURNS: I was taken to the jury room with bracelets on my wrists—not such as you wear, ladies, of gold and silver—but iron and steel that wore into the bone.

CHORUS: From *The Journal of Richard Henry Dana.* (*one drum beat*)

DANA: I went up to see the fugitive. He was confined in a small room of the Courthouse with some six or seven men—of the rough, thief-catching order—smoking and playing cards. We withdrew to a window lest we be overheard. (*to Burns*) There's a strong feeling in favor of a rescue, and some of the abolitionists talk quite freely about it. Even the Mayor is with us.

MAYOR: (*thick Boston accent*) There has been a rumor that the city authorities will not take any measure to preserve public order. As mayor of the City of Boston, I assure you that this is the wrong impression. We are determined to exert every means to prevent rioting.

CHORUS: By four p.m. a radical group of abolitionists . . .

CHORUS: with members from the black community and the white . . .

CHORUS: assembled at Tremont Temple.

CHORUS: From *The Life of Thomas Wentworth Higginson.* (*one drum beat*)

HIGGINSON: Fellow freedom fighters, what we need today is a plan of action!

*ABOLITIONIST ONE:* I say we storm the Courthouse and carry him out tonight!

*ABOLITIONIST TWO:* We need a leader. We have no one to lead!

*HIGGINSON:* I have that plan.

*ABOLITIONIST THREE:* The only way to rescue him is by force!

*ABOLITIONIST FOUR:* I'm not risking my life!

*HIGGINSON:* Order! Order! Listen to . . .

*ABOLITIONIST FIVE:* We need a plan of action!

*CHORUS:* Frustrated with the disorganized crowd, Thomas Higginson decided to take matters into his own hands.

*HIGGINSON:* I'd like to buy one dozen axes.

*SHOPKEEPER:* Your name?

*HIGGINSON:* I'll pay cash.

*SHOPKEEPER:* Yes. But I still need your name.

*HIGGINSON:* Thomas . . . Tom . . . Higgins . . . Tom Higgins.

*SHOPKEEPER:* There you go, Mr. Higgins. Say what do you plan to do with all those axes?

*HIGGINSON:* You never know when you might need them. (*one drum beat*)

*MRS. PARKER:* (*an announcement*) A public meeting will be held at Faneuil Hall tonight at seven o'clock. Come secure justice for a man claimed as a slave by a Virginia kidnapper. He is now imprisoned in Boston Court house in defiance of the laws of Massachusetts. Shall he be plunged into the Hell of Virginia slavery?

*CHORUS:* That night, over two thousand people descended on Faneuil Hall. (*three drum beats*)

*ABOLITIONIST ONE:* Citizens of Boston, let me introduce our first speaker of the evening: Wendell Phillips. (*crowd cheers*)

*PHILLIPS:* You have called me to this platform for what? Do you wish to know what I want? I want that man set free in the streets of Boston. (*crowd cheers*)

I'm glad to hear your applause. This city government is on our side. If only they had been so earlier. Fellow citizens, tomorrow is to determine whether we are worthy of our city government. Whether we are ready to do the duty which they leave us to do. (*crowd cheers*) I am honored to introduce to you Mrs. Theodore Parker. (*crowd cheers*)

*MRS. PARKER:* Fellow subjects of Virginia.

*CROWD:* No, no, you must take that back. (*etc.*)

The Trial of Anthony Burns, *(left to right) Stacy Fisher, Shelley Bolman, Christopher Robin Cook, Cliff Odle, and Nathaniel McIntyre, photo by Wendy Lement.*

*MRS. PARKER:* Hear me. We are the vassals of Virginia. She reaches her arm over the graves of our mothers and kidnaps men in the city of the Puritans.

*CROWD:* Shame! Shame!

*MRS. PARKER:* Shame. So say I. But who is to blame? "There is no North," said Mr. Webster. The South goes clear up to the Canada line. There is no Boston today. Fellow citizens of Boston, there are two great laws in this country. One of them is the law of slavery. That law is declared to be a finality. Once the Constitution was formed to establish justice, promote tranquility, and secure the blessings of liberty. Now the constitution is to extend slavery into Nebraska. Slavery tramples on the Constitution. It treads down States' rights. But there is another law, my friends, that is the law of the people when they are sure they are right and determined to go ahead. (*cheers and confusion*) That which is not just, is not law. And that which is not law ought not to be obeyed. (*cheers, overheated*)

*ABOLITIONIST ONE:* Let us take him out.

*ABOLITIONIST TWO:* Let us go now.

*ABOLITIONIST THREE:* Bring your guns!

PHILLIPS: (*tries to calm the crowd*) You that are really ready to sacrifice something in behalf of this man, be not carried away by a momentary impulse. Let us go home tonight, fellow citizens. The zeal that will not keep till tomorrow will never free a slave. (*more cheers and confusion*)

HIGGINSON: (*enters from the back of the courtroom*) Mr. Phillips, I've just come from Court Square. A mob of Negroes is busting through the doors of the Courthouse, trying to free Burns. They need reinforcements. (*to audience*) To be honest, there was no mob of Negroes, but I had to say something to get them on their feet. (*to crowd*) Who will join me? Who will free Anthony Burns?!

CROWD: (*cheers and confusion*) I will. I'll join you. (*They run out leaving Phillips alone at the podium.*)

PHILLIPS: (*to crowd*) Wait . . . Higginson.

HIGGINSON: Join us, Phillips.

PHILLIPS: I will not be one of the tumultuous, aimless, purposeless mob!! (*mob cheers as they go out*) (*to audience*) He did not tell me of his plan. I stood there like a fool. I will never forgive him. (*alarm bell rings*)

CHORUS: The Courthouse bell rang in alarm at half past nine.

FREEMAN: (*to Batchelder*) Is that you there, Batchelder?

BATCHELDER: (*Irish dialect*) Yes, sir.

MARSHAL FREEMAN: You've helped us out before, haven't you?

BATCHELDER: Yes, sir.

FREEMAN: Would you see our Courthouse in flames?

BATCHELDER: Uh . . . no, Sir.

FREEMAN: Here's three dollars, son. Take this cutlass and guard the west door of the Courthouse with your life.

BATCHELDER: Three dollars. Yes, Sir!! I'll be ready for 'em, Marshal.

HIGGINSON: (*puts down his umbrella and mimes handing out axes*) My men led the charge armed with axes and a large battering ram.

RIOTER ONE: Pistols were heard in the crowd.

RIOTER TWO: We tried to force in the east door of the Court.

GUARDS: Blocked.

RIOTER ONE: He's over on that side.

RIOTER TWO: To the west door.

CHORUS: From the *Alexandria Gazette.* (*one drum beat*)

GAZETTE REPORTER: (*He speaks with a southern dialect, as the rioters mime using the battering arm in slow motion. A Chorus member hits the drum to punctuate their movements.*) The battering arm was manned by a dozen or fourteen men, white and colored, who plunged it against the door until it was stove in. Several brick-bats were thrown at the windows and glass rattled in all directions. Even the windows of the justices' chambers were riddled by bullets. Marshal Freeman displayed great courage in narrowly escaping pistol fire as he led his troops to defend the entrance.

RIOTERS: Rescue him! Bring him out! Where is he?!

FREEMAN: My men, with great heroism, seized and arrested several rioters with axes in their hands.

RIOTER ONE: Upon seeing the arrests, the mob fell back.

HIGGINSON: You cowards, will you desert us now? (*Higginson is struck by Batchelder. There are several drum beats as Batchelder is swallowed up by the crowd.*)

BATCHELDER: I am stabbed.

GAZETTE REPORTER: (*Southern dialect*) The saddest part of this outrage is that human life has been sacrificed.

CHORUS: Whether Batchelder was shot or stabbed is still debatable.

FREEMAN: We arrested nine or ten attackers.

RIOTER ONE: The crowd dispersed.

HIGGINSON: I retrieved my umbrella and somehow managed to escape.

CHORUS: From *The Journal of Richard Henry Dana*. (*one drum beat*)

DANA: Tonight, an attempt was made to rescue the slave. It was conducted by few and failed for want of numbers. The leader of this mob, I was surprised to learn in secrecy, was Reverend Higginson. I knew of his passion and courage, but I hardly expected a married man, a clergyman, and a man of education to lead the mob.

CHORUS: By twelve-thirty a.m., Courthouse Square was almost empty.

CHAIRMAN: Day four: *The Hearing.* (*three hits of the gavel*)

CHORUS: From *The Boston Post*. (*one drum beat*)

POST REPORTER: Today the hearing of the case of Anthony Burns before Judge Loring will afford an occasion for this community to decide whether law or anarchy is to prevail among us. We are confident of the results.

CHORUS: That morning Marshal Freeman sent the following telegram to the President of the United States.

FREEMAN: In consequence of an attack upon the Courthouse last night for the purpose of rescuing a fugitive slave, during which one of my own guards was killed, I now have under my control two troops of Marines from Fort Independence. Everything is now quiet.

CHORUS: President Franklin Pierce promptly replied.

PIERCE. Your conduct is approved. The law must be executed!

CHORUS: From *The Journal of Richard Henry Dana.* (*one drum beat*)

DANA: The Courthouse was filled with hireling soldiers, nearly all of whom were foreigners. The lazy hounds were lounging all day out of the windows and hanging over the stairs, but ready to shoot down good men at a word of command. The hearing began at ten o'clock.

BAILIFF: Oyez, Oyez, Oyez, the honorable Edward G. Loring is now sitting.

LORING: Let the hearing of Anthony Burns commence. (*one hit of the gavel*)

DANA: Your Honor, I move for a delay.

THOMAS: (*pompously*) I strongly protest any delay. My client, Mister Suttle, has been inconvenienced long enough. Ned, the law is clear. Mr. Suttle's property must be returned immediately to him.

DANA: Your Honor, I have only been appointed as legal counsel for the defendant for the period of one day. I have been denied adequate time with my client.

THOMAS: Ned, with all due respect, the delay which you granted two days ago resulted in a shameless display of violence and the tragic death of a brave guard. I see no reason to provide these criminals with yet another opportunity to trample upon the laws of this great nation.

DANA: Your Honor, first of all, my client was arrested for an entirely different charge than he is now facing. The owner of the silversmith shop has not stepped forward to identity my client. Furthermore, it has not been proved that the man before us is indeed, Anthony Burns.

THOMAS: A man knows his own property, Sir.

DANA: This man stands before you a free man, entitled to all the protection the laws can throw around him. I ask you to consider that this hearing is the only tribunal between this man and perpetual slavery. Shall we allow a man's right to freedom to be decided in haste? You, yourself need time to approach this case without bias. I humbly remind you that you serve both as judge and jury in this case and you ought to be able to say that you had given every chance for preparation and reflection. (*to audience*) I never spoke more to my satisfaction in all my life. I am quite mistaken if the general sentiment of the house was not with me.

LORING: In my opinion, Burns' status as a free man has yet to be established. I suggest you present this Court with concrete evidence as to his identity. A delay of two days is reasonable. This Court shall reconvene on Monday morning at eleven o'clock. (*one hit of the gavel*)

DANA: (*to audience*) I was hoping for two weeks at least.

*LORING:* Court adjourned. (*one hit of the gavel*)

*CHAIRMAN:* Day five: *The Sale of Anthony Burns.* (*three hits of the gavel*)

*CHORUS:* On Sunday, May twenty-eighth, Reverend Grimes approached Colonel Suttle of behalf of the prisoner.

*GRIMES:* Have you considered selling Anthony Burns, and thereby removing a need for a trial?

*SUTTLE:* Selling him?

*GRIMES:* If the case goes to trial, who knows what might happen? I'm prepared to pay your asking price for him today.

*SUTTLE:* I sorely doubt you could afford my asking price, son.

*GRIMES:* Try me, Sir.

*SUTTLE:* Well, let's see. He's got a strong build. And even though he's got a lame hand, he's a hard worker. I hardly need to tell him what to do. He knows his work.

*GRIMES:* How much?

*SUTTLE:* Well, I think twelve hundred dollars is about right for Tony.

*GRIMES:* Twelve hundred dollars?!

*SUTTLE:* Like I said, it's more than you can get your hands on.

*GRIMES:* But if I do . . . if I raise twelve hundred dollars by nine o'clock this evening, do you agree to sell Anthony Burns?

*SUTTLE:* You get the money. I'll draw up the papers, son.

*GRIMES:* Don't worry. You'll have your money. Meet me at Judge Loring's house at nine o'clock this evening.

*SUTTLE:* (*starts to write bill of sale and then hands it to Grimes*) All right, but this offer is only good for today.

*GRIMES:* I understand. (*starts to leave*)

*SUTTLE:* (*stops him*) Now, I wouldn't want anyone to get the idea that I am in any way trying to side step the law.

*GRIMES:* Of course not.

*SUTTLE:* Well, all right then, nine o'clock.

*CHORUS:* From *The Journal of Richard Henry Dana.* (*one drum beat*)

*DANA:* Anthony told me that his life had been insured for eight hundred dollars in Richmond, from which he supposed that he was probably worth about a thousand dollars. It was a new language to hear a man estimating his own value.

*CHORUS:* From the "Bill of Sale of Anthony Burns." (*one drum beat*)

*GRIMES:* (*reads*) "It being understood that the slave named Anthony Burns, now and here claimed as a fugitive, will be sold by his master, for the sum of twelve hundred dollars. We the undersigned promise to pay the following amount."

JAMES WILLIAMS: James Williams: fifty dollars. (*one drum beat*)

HAMILTON WILLIS: Hamilton Willis: three hundred dollars.

GRIMES: Thank you. (*one drum beat*)

EDWIN PARKER: Edwin Parker: four hundred dollars. (*one drum beat*)

LOUISA MAY ALCOTT: I refuse to sign anything that refers to Mr. Burns as a "slave."

GRIMES: (*taking a pen to the document*) I can just . . . cross that word out.

LOUISA MAY ALCOTT: That's better. Louisa May, for the Alcott family: twenty-five dollars.

GRIMES: (*He expected more.*) Thank you, Miss Alcott. (*one drum beat*)

DANIEL ELLIOT: Daniel Elliot: two hundred dollars. (*one drum beat*)

ELIZABETH POWELL MASON: I can't decide. Buying a slave . . . it just doesn't seem right.

GRIMES: Mrs. Powell, think of it as buying his freedom.

ELIZABETH POWELL MASON: Oh . . . I suppose if you put it that way . . . Elizabeth Powell Mason: sixty dollars. (*three drum beats*)

CHORUS: From *Fugitive Slaves and American Courts*. (*one drum beat*)

GRIMES: After raising the money, I met Loring at his house.

LORING: I hear you've been busy, Reverend.

GRIMES: If Suttle will only keep his word.

LORING: He seems like a man of honor.

GRIMES: I won't believe it till this business is signed and sealed.

LORING: Stop worrying, Leonard. There's no reason to think that that sale will fall through. And even if it does, he'll have a trial. Assuming there's enough evidence in his favor, Burns will walk out of that courtroom a free man.

GRIMES: It's almost ten o'clock. Where's Suttle?

THOMAS: By the time Colonel Suttle arrived at Judge Loring's, I had advised him against the sale.

SUTTLE: Ned, is it true that I am putting myself in jeopardy of arrest, if I sell a slave in the state of Massachusetts?

LORING: Well, technically, yes. But I really can't imagine that happening.

GRIMES: I am fully prepared to assume all responsibility in this matter, Colonel.

SUTTLE: Well, be that as it may, this is Sunday, and I never sign anything on the Lord's day.

GRIMES: But the trial is scheduled for eleven o'clock tomorrow.

LORING: Calm down, Leonard. Meet me in my chambers at eight o'clock and we can complete the sale and avoid a trial.

SUTTLE: Good evening, gentlemen.

MRS. PARKER: (*announcement*) Negotiation successful! The alleged fugitive to be bought and liberated tomorrow morning! (*one drum beat*)

CHAIRMAN: Day six: *Monday Morning*. (*three hits of the gavel*)

CHORUS: Outside the chamber of Judge Loring. (*one drum beat*)

GRIMES: Excuse me, has the Judge come in yet? I've been waiting for over an hour.

GUARD: I've told you before. He's not here.

GRIMES: Sorry, have you seen Colonel Suttle? We both had an appointment with the Judge at eight o'clock.

GUARD: No, no and no!! You people just don't give up.

CHORUS: At the Revere Hotel. (*one drum beat*)

GRIMES: Could you at least tell me what time Colonel Suttle left the hotel?

CLERK. I'm not in a position to disclose that sort of information.

CHORUS: In front of the Courthouse. (*one drum beat*)

GRIMES: (*calls out*) Colonel Suttle, where were you? I waited inside the Courthouse for over an hour. Forget that. I have the money. All I need is your signature on the final sales agreement.

SUTTLE: (*smoking a pipe*) Now I believe I told you my offer was only good on Sunday.

GRIMES: But I have the paper that you signed, agreeing to sell Burns.

SUTTLE: Mr. Grimes, does this look like Sunday to you? Our business is through for today. (*tears up the agreement*) Now, if you wish to purchase Tony once I get him back to Virginia, well . . . that's a conversation for another day.

GRIMES: (*to audience*) I never did find Judge Loring before the trial started. And he never spoke to me about the sale of Anthony Burns again.

CHORUS: The Trial of Anthony Burns. (*one drum beat*)

FREEMAN: For the first time in Boston history, the Courthouse is closed to the public.

BAILIFF: Let the record show that on this day, May the twenty-ninth, 1854, the Trial of Anthony Burns commenced. The honorable Judge Edward Loring presiding. (*three hits of the gavel*)

LORING: Counsel, are you ready to present your case?

DANA: (*interrupts*) Your Honor, we cannot proceed with this examination under the present circumstances. This room has been packed with armed men. Every part of this building is overrun with military guards, making it impossible for the defendant's supporters to gain access.

LORING: The examination will proceed.

FREEMAN: (*interrupts*) I'll have you know that those "supporters" are the very same thugs and murderers that attacked the Courthouse three days ago!

LORING: Marshal Freeman, there is no motion before the court to remove the guards. Therefore, we will proceed with the trial.

FREEMAN: (*defensive*) I understand that, Ned. But he has just openly charged us with unlawfully filling this courtroom and stuffing the passageways with armed men. And such language if uttered here should be replied to. I'll have you know that those guards are here with the consent of the President of the United States. By what power, Mr. Dana, do you propose to have them removed?

LORING: Marshal, if anyone should be concerned with this point, it would be me. So, without further interruption, Mr. Thomas, will you present your case?

GRIMES: I'd like proof that you actually have jurisdiction in this case.

LORING: I have been in this post for fifteen years, Reverend Grimes. Mr. Thomas, I order you to proceed with you case.

THOMAS: Gladly, Your Honor. I call Colonel Suttle to the stand.

BAILIFF: Do you swear to tell the truth, the whole truth and nothing but the truth, so help you God?

SUTTLE: I do.

BAILIFF: Please be seated.

THOMAS: Colonel, what is your profession?

SUTTLE: I keep a dry goods store in Stafford County, Virginia, Sir.

THOMAS: Do you recognize the man before you as the slave Anthony Burns?

DANA: Your Honor, I vehemently object to the term "slave" being used to describe my client. There is no evidence that the prisoner is indeed a slave.

LORING: It is the opinion of this Court that no man can be called a slave without corroborative legal evidence. Mr. Thomas, you will find a more appropriate word.

THOMAS: Colonel, is this *gentleman* before you Anthony Burns?

*SUTTLE:* He most certainly is. I've known him since he was born.

*THOMAS:* When was the last time you saw Burns in Virginia?

*SUTTLE:* Well, he went missing on March twenty-fourth. I saw him that Sunday before. It must have been March nineteenth.

*THOMAS:* Have you seen him since then, Colonel?

*SUTTLE:* Yes, I did. I saw him in the Courthouse last Wednesday, the night he was captured. And I spoke with him.

*DANA:* Objection.

*LORING:* Overruled.

*THOMAS:* And did Burns recognize you?

*DANA:* Objection. Section six of the Fugitive Slave Law states that the testimony of the alleged fugitive is inadmissible in a court of law. It is the height of cruelty to the prisoner to take advantage of the only power he has under this law.

*LORING:* The word "testimony," as understood by this court, must be regarded as evidence given by a witness and not confessions or admissions. But I don't wish to prejudice the liberty of the prisoner. Objection sustained.

*THOMAS:* Your Honor, might I still ask the questions, so that we may take down the answers for future use?

*LORING:* I'll consent, Mr. Thomas (*Dana reacts with outrage.*), but be advised that the answers may be struck at a later date. Colonel Suttle, you may answer the question.

*THOMAS:* Did Burns recognize you?

*SUTTLE:* Of course he did. Burns manifested a desire to return home.

*All but* SUTTLE *and* BURNS *turn their backs in slow motion to signal the flashback.* SUTTLE *and* BURNS *move toward each other. The scene from the top of the play is shown again, from* SUTTLE'*s perspective. It is played melodramatically.*

*SUTTLE:* Have you not always received kind treatment from me?

*BURNS:* Yes.

*SUTTLE:* Have I not always permitted you to go where, and work for whom you pleased?

*BURNS:* Yes.

*SUTTLE:* When you were sick, did I not give up my own bed that you might be made as comfortable as possible?

BURNS: (*affected to tears*) You did, Master; you did, kind Master.

SUTTLE: Do you want to go back to Virginia?

BURNS: I do.

SUTTLE: Will you go back?

BURNS: I will. I want to go back today. (*big smile*) I'm a good deal happier at home.

*As the other actors turn back around in slow motion,* BURNS *backs up to his original position and the smile fades from his face. He is horrified by* SUT-TLE's *account of the conversation.*

SUTTLE: (*to Thomas*) His only object in leaving at all appears to have been a species of curiosity, which being thoroughly gratified, he desired to return.

THOMAS: Your Honor, at this time I would like to submit Exhibit A: Mr. William Brent's signed deposition verifying the conversation between Colonel Suttle and the defendant.

DANA: Objection, Your Honor. Mr. Brent works as a slave agent for Colonel Suttle.

LORING: Overruled. I will review Mr. Brent's statement. Proceed, Mr. Thomas.

THOMAS: Are you absolutely positive that this man is Anthony Burns?

SUTTLE: No doubt in my mind. That's him, all right.

THOMAS: No further questions.

LORING: Court is adjourned until eleven o'clock tomorrow morning. (*one hit of the gavel*)

CHAIRMAN: Day seven: *The Trial Continues.* (*three hits of the gavel*)

LORING: Mr. Dana, are you ready to present your defense?

DANA: I am, Your Honor.

LORING: Proceed.

DANA: According to the Fugitive Slave Law of 1850, in order for an alleged owner to retrieve his "property," he must prove both the identity of the fugitive and his intent to escape. Now, yesterday we heard Colonel Suttle testify that Anthony Burns "went missing" on March twenty-fourth. I shall now present concrete evidence which proves that the man before you today has resided in the city of Boston since at least March first. Therefore, you can only conclude that the prisoner is not Anthony Burns.

CHORUS: The testimony of William Jones. (*one drum beat*)

*JONES:* I met the defendant on March first and employed him in my Matta-pan factory as a window washer.

*CHORUS:* The testimony of George Drew. (*one drum beat*)

*DREW:* As bookkeeper of the Mattapan Works, I can confirm that the prisoner was employed at the beginning of March. I paid him myself.

*CHORUS:* The testimony of Stephen Maddox. (*one drum beat*)

*MADDOX:* The defendant came into my clothing store 'round the end of February looking for work. But no jobs were available at that time. But I remember noticing that big scar on his face.

*CHORUS:* The testimony of City Councilor James Whittimore. (*one drum beat*)

*WHITTIMORE:* I saw him cleaning windows at the Mattapan Works on the eighth or ninth of March.

*CHORUS:* The testimony of John Favor. (*one drum beat*)

*FAVOR:* The prisoner stopped by my shop around the first of March and asked if he could help with carpentry. I wondered how he could hold a hammer with that bad hand of his.

*CHORUS:* The testimony of Officer Horace Brown. (*one drum beat*)

*BROWN:* Before I became a police officer, I worked as a carpenter at the Mattapan factory. I left work there on the tenth of March and remember saying good-bye to the prisoner before I left. I have no doubt that this is the same man.

*CHORUS:* (*to audience*) By the end of the day, nine witnesses testified that they had seen the defendant in Boston three weeks prior to when he supposedly escaped.

*THOMAS:* I am surprised that a respected lawyer, such as Richard Henry Dana, would bring before this Court witnesses of such low character and credibility. They obviously have strong ties with the abolitionist movement, and therefore, their testimony must be disregarded.

*DANA:* Your Honor, each of these men will testify that he has no affiliation with any abolitionist organization.

*LORING:* That won't be necessary, Mr. Dana. Court is adjourned until eleven o'clock tomorrow morning. (*one hit of the gavel*)

*CHORUS:* That evening Peter Dunbar, Captain of the Guard, called up to Burns who was being held in the jury room of the Courthouse.

*DUNBAR:* Hey Anthony, why didn't you come ride with me today?

*BURNS:* Oh, they couldn't spare us both at one time. If I went, you'd have had to stay behind in my place.

*DUNBAR:* Sensible to the last. Is that a cigar you're smoking?

BURNS: A gift from the guards. Even though they're angry with me just now. I won't join in their poker game.

DUNBAR: You had a good day today. On my way out of the Courthouse some of the guards told me they're hoping you get off. And I hear they have a surprise for you tomorrow.

BURNS: A new pair of handcuffs?

DUNBAR: Good-luck tomorrow, Anthony.

CHAIRMAN: Day eight: *Closing Arguments.* (*three gavel hits*)

CHORUS: From the *Boston Post.* (*one drum beat*)

POST REPORTER: (*pompously*) Last night a U.S. officer started the generous project of procuring an entire new suit of clothes for Burns. And in a very short time, the officers had contributed some forty dollars with which a handsome suit was purchased. This morning, Burns appeared in the courtroom dressed in a new and serviceable apparel. He expressed his warmest thanks to the officers for their generous and unexpected gift.

LORING: Mr. Dana, will you present your closing argument?

DANA: Yes, Your Honor.

LORING: Proceed.

DANA: Sir Matthew Hale said it was better that nine guilty men should escape, than that one innocent man should suffer. This maxim was first applied to a case of murder, where one man's life was on one side and the interest of an entire community on the other. How much more should it be applied to a case like this, where on the one side is something dearer than life—and on the other no public interest whatsoever, but only the value of a few hundred pieces of silver. We have a right then to expect from Your Honor a strict adherence to the rule that this man is free until proven a slave beyond every reasonable doubt.

Colonel Suttle says that he owned a slave in Virginia named Anthony Burns who escaped to Massachusetts, and that the prisoner at the bar is that Anthony Burns. Let him prove it all! Let him fail in one point, and the man goes free.

The prosecution has presented only one witness: Colonel Suttle. His testimony can only be viewed as biased. The defense, on the other hand, has proved that this man lived in the state of Massachusetts at least three weeks prior to the date that Anthony Burns allegedly escaped.

You see before you a free man. The eyes of many millions are upon you, sir. Your decision will hold its place in the history of America—in the history of the progress of the human race. May your judgment be for liberty and not for slavery. For happiness and not for wretchedness. For hope, and not for despair. The defense rests.

*LORING:* Mr. Thomas, are you ready with your closing argument?

*THOMAS:* I am.

*LORING:* Proceed.

*THOMAS:* The claimant in this case, Charles F. Suttle, is from Virginia, and under the laws of that state, he held to service and labor one Anthony Burns, a colored man. He claims that on or about the twenty-fourth day of March, Anthony escaped from the State of Virginia, and that he is now here in court. He prays you to consider his proofs in support of his claim, and, certify to him, under your hand and seal, the right to transport Anthony Burns back to Virginia. This is his whole case; this is all that he asks you to do.

The defense claims that Suttle is wrong in testifying that he saw the fugitive on March nineteenth. The date is not material. Suttle may possibly be mistaken in the date, but as to the identity of the person, he is not.

I take leave of the case, confident in the proofs presented, confident in the majesty of the law, and confident that the determination here will be just.

*LORING:* Upon hearing the closing arguments, this court will adjourn until nine o'clock tomorrow morning, when I will render my decision. (*one hit of the gavel*)

*CHAIRMAN:* Day nine: *The Decision of Judge Edward G. Loring.* (*three hits of the gavel*)

*CHORUS:* From the *Liberator.*

*LIBERATOR REPORTER:* June first, 1854. As early as six o'clock this morning, a crowd assembled in Court Square to hear the decision of Judge Loring. The bell on the Courthouse tolled at nine o'clock. The excitement and the crowd in the square increased by the moment. The northerly side of the street was thronged with people, among whom were many females of every shade of complexion anxiously awaiting to hear the announcement of the Judge. (*one hit of the gavel*)

*LORING:* It occurs to this Court, that the Fugitive Slave Law has already been deemed as constitutional by the unanimous opinion of the Judges of the Massachusetts Supreme Court. It remains for me now to apply the law to the facts of this case. The facts to be proved by the claimant are three:

1. That Anthony Burns owed him service in Virginia.

2. That Anthony Burns escaped from that service.

These facts have been proved by the record. The third fact is that of the identity of the fugitive. That is the only fact I have a right to consider.

The claimant has presented only one witness whose testimony in the case could easily be viewed as biased. The defense has offered nine witnesses, many of whom are known and respected members of the community. There is a complete and irreconcilable conflict between these two sides. Therefore, I must look to other evidence to settle this question. I find that evidence in the conversation between Burns and the claimant on the night of the arrest, as corroborated by Mr. Brent. Therefore, the third fact of identity has been proven by the claimant.

DANA: (*tries to interrupt*) Your Honor . . .

LORING: Based on the law and facts of the case, I hereby order that the defendant, Anthony Burns, be immediately returned to servitude in the State of Virginia.

DANA: (*tries to interrupt*) Your Honor . . .

LORING: This case is closed. (*one hit of the gavel*)

LIBERATOR REPORTER: As soon as the decision was announced, the police cleared the square of all persons.

CHORUS: From *The Journal of Richard Henry Dana*. (*one drum beat*)

DANA: The decision was a grievous disappointment to us all, and chiefly to the poor prisoner. He looked the image of despair.

CHAIRMAN: Day ten: *Anthony Burns Is Carried Back to Virginia*. (*three hits of the gavel*)

CHORUS: Friday morning June second, Reverend Grimes and Richard Henry Dana were denied private consultation with the prisoner in the Courthouse.

DANA: As they will not let me speak to you in confidence, I can only say my good-bye.

BURNS: I know that you did everything you possibly could.

GRIMES: Anthony, they're only sending you back to make an example of you. Please believe me when I say that we will get you back here as soon as the ship hits the dock in Virginia. Trust in God.

BURNS: But what am I to do in the meantime?

CHORUS: They were interrupted by the arrival of Colonel Suttle.

BURNS: Master Charles, what are you going to do to me?

SUTTLE: What do you think I *ought* to do with you, Tony?

BURNS: I expect you will sell me.

SUTTLE: Well, you have caused me great expense. My lawyers fees alone have been four hundred dollars. (*Suttle makes a threatening gesture toward Burns and then leads him off stage.*)

CHORUS: Preparations were made for the return of Burns to Virginia.

*FREEMAN:* To prevent further violence during the transport of the prisoner to the ship, I placed the city of Boston under martial law. Over two thousand armed men lined the streets of the city to keep the public order.

*CHORUS:* From the *Liberator*. (*one drum beat*)

*LIBERATOR REPORTER:* Burns was escorted from the Courthouse by Marshal Freeman and some half-dozen aids who surrounded them as they passed through the crowds of protesters.

*PROTESTERS:* (*chant the following under the following speech*) Shame! Shame! Shame! Shame!

*LIBERATOR REPORTER:* Over fifty thousand people lined the streets to hiss, boo, or cheer, or just to catch a glimpse of the fugitive. As the procession moved down Court Street, several occupants displayed folds of black fabric on the outside of their stores. The officers slowed as they passed the Commonwealth Press where three American flags dressed in mourning were hung and lines of crape were stretched across the street. Suddenly, the procession was doused with cayenne pepper or some other noxious substance, thrown from one of the windows. A vial of sulfuric acid was hurled from the building and narrowly missed an officer. Just after the military passed down State Street, a coffin was lowered out of a window with the inscription: "Liberty" written upon it. The procession turned at the head of Long Wharf and proceeded to T Wharf where the steamer *John Taylor* was waiting. Burns was marched directly aboard and taken to the cabin and out of sight of the crowd.

*CHORUS:* From the *Alexandria Gazette*. (*one drum beat*)

*GAZETTE REPORTER:* (*Southern dialect*) We rejoice at the recapture of Burns, but a few more such victories and the South is undone.

*CHORUS:* In challenging the decision of Judge Loring, Anthony Burns declared:

*BURNS:* Why did you not execute God's law on the man who stole me from my mother's arms? How is it that you trample down God's law against the oppressor and wrest it to condemn me the innocent and oppressed? (*All the actors clear the stage except for the Chairman.*)

*CHAIRMAN:* (*three hits of the gavel*) Senators of the Massachusetts Legislature, you have just witnessed the Trial of Anthony Burns. Now, it is your job to review the actions of Judge Edward G. Loring, and to decide whether or not he upheld the laws of this State and of the Nation. To help in this decision, I will ask the following men to come before you, so that they may present their opinions on the matter. Wendell Phillips,

Richard Henry Dana, the Reverend Leonard Grimes, Judge Edward G. Loring. In a moment, you will have an opportunity to question each man, to argue for or against Judge Loring, and to vote on his fate. First we shall hear from Wendell Phillips.

PHILLIPS: Thank you, Chairman. Honored senators of the state of Massachusetts, I come before you today to insist that Judge Loring went out of his way on every occasion to oppress the man that was before him. When I first spoke to him on the matter of Burns, it was clear the case was decided before we ever entered the courtroom. He flaunted his immoral allegiance to slaveholding tyranny throughout the trial. Today we must right the grievous wrongs of the past. We must let the people of the Commonwealth know that we stand for liberty and justice for all men.

CHAIRMAN: Thank you, Mr. Phillips. We shall now hear from Richard Henry Dana.

DANA: Senators, the conduct of Judge Loring was considerate and humane. If a man is willing to execute the law and be an instrument of sending back a man into slavery, he could not act better in his office than Judge Loring. I think we owe it to the manner in which he addressed Burns and urged him to accept counsel, that there was any defense at all. Though he committed a serious error on a fundamental question of human rights, I am concerned that the removal of Judge Loring sets a dangerous precedent. Loring was following an established law, and we cannot remove him solely because we disagree with his decision.

CHAIRMAN: Thank you, Mr. Dana. We shall now hear from the Reverend Leonard Grimes.

GRIMES: Honored senators, up until my dealings with the Judge on Sunday, I too believed we had a fair and just commissioner. But I was deceived. Judge Loring was not abiding by any strong moral principle. On Sunday, he assured me that he was behind the sale of Burns as a means of securing his freedom. But once he was pressured by Suttle's lawyers, he withdrew support. He was spineless before the powerful, and a tyrant to the weak. Now it is your duty to remove the slave commissioner from his office.

CHAIRMAN: Thank you, Reverend Grimes. We shall now hear from Judge Loring.

LORING: Honored members of the Senate, I respectfully ask you to consider the following. Magistrates do not make the laws, and it is not for them to usurp or infringe upon that high power; therefore, if they are honest, they administer the laws as they are committed to them. On this depends the security of everything the law protects; and that security will be lost when magistrates shape their official action by their own personal feelings or that of popular opinion. In returning Anthony Burns to his owner, I upheld the law as my position required me to do.

CHAIRMAN: Thank you Judge Loring. Senators you now have an opportunity to question any of the witnesses before you. All I ask is that you raise your hand, so that I may call on you. Has anyone a question for any of these men? (*if there are no questions*) Remember, in a few moments you will need to decide on the fate of Judge Loring. I urge you to discover as much information as possible before you vote. Who will ask a question? (*questions*)

At this time I will ask the witnesses to step into the outer chamber, while we debate the issue at hand. Senators, in a few moments we will decide the fate of Judge Loring. Should we allow him to maintain his position, or should he be removed from office?

If there are any among you that wish to convince your fellow senators of your opinion, now is the time to speak. Would anyone care to argue for one side or the other? Yes, Senator _____, please rise and state your opinion clearly so that all may hear. (*debate*)

Senators, it is now time to vote. When I call the question, I will ask you to rise and remain standing until I have completed the count, and only to vote once. All those in favor of allowing Judge Loring to maintain his position, please rise. (*the count is taken*) All those who wish to remove Judge Loring from office, please rise. (*the count is taken*) Senators of Massachusetts, by a vote of _____to_____ you have decided to _____.

Senator _____, would you tell Judge Loring of our decision when he enters the chamber? (*calls*) Gentlemen, please step forth so you might hear our decision. (*They do.*) Senator _____, please inform Judge Loring of our decision. (*He/She does.*) Senators, you have completed the difficult task before you. Your arguments were well spoken and the decision of the legislature shall stand. This session of the Massachusetts Legislature is adjourned.

# *The Trial of Anthony Burns* Study Guide

## *Learning Goals*

1. to explore the tension between human and moral law
2. to examine the evolutionary nature of the U.S. justice system
3. to determine what role the abolitionists played in the events leading up to the Civil War
4. to explore the abolitionists' goals and strategies in defending Anthony Burns

## *What Happened in History*

Massachusetts was at the center of the abolitionist movement in pre-Civil War America. However, escaping from slavery was illegal, and state judges were compelled by the Fugitive Slave Act of 1850 to return runaway slaves to their owners in the South. In 1854, a slave named Anthony Burns escaped to Boston where he lived as a free man until he was captured and placed on trial. Before the trial, local residents—including twenty-two-year-old Louisa May Alcott—descended upon Faneuil Hall for a freedom rally that erupted into a violent riot outside the Courthouse where Burns was held.

During the trial, Richard Henry Dana and a team of prominent Boston lawyers fiercely defended Burns' right to freedom. Citing the Fugitive Slave Law, Judge Edward G. Loring rejected their arguments and returned Burns to his Southern master. This action galvanized abolitionists and converted conservative citizens into militant freedom fighters. Indignation over the Burns case helped give birth to the Republican Party, propelled Abraham Lincoln to the White House, and eventually led to the Civil War. In 1858, a partisan Massachusetts Legislature voted to remove Loring as judge of probate for his unpopular verdict in the Burns case.

## *Historical Timeline*

*September 1850:* The Fugitive Slave Law passes as part of the Compromise of 1850.

*March 1854:* Anthony Burns, an escaped slave from Virginia, arrives in Boston, Massachusetts.

*Wednesday, 24 May:* Burns is arrested as a suspect in a jewelry store robbery. At the Courthouse, Burns is confronted by his owner,

Charles Suttle, and Suttle's slave agent William Brent. Burns acknowledges Suttle by calling him "master."

*Thursday, 25 May:* At the Courthouse, Richard Henry Dana, a prominent lawyer and supporter of the abolitionist cause, approaches Burns. Wary of his fate at the hands of an angry Colonel Suttle, Burns feels it is best not to resist. Despite Burns' reluctance, the Reverend Theodore Parker convinces him to allow Dana and other lawyers to defend him. Dana, now acting as Burns' lawyer, requests a delay in the trial. He is granted two days.

*Friday, 26 May:* Over two thousand abolitionists meet at Faneuil Hall. The crowd reaches a fevered pitch when Reverend Thomas Higginson bursts in and announces that a mob of angry Negroes is storming the Courthouse. The crowd surges out of the meeting and proceeds to the Courthouse. The group is disorganized and out of control, and numbers dwindle by the time they reach their destination. Marshal Freeman's guards are given advanced warning and prepare for the arrival of the abolitionists. The angry mob breaks a door down and a guard named James Batchelder is killed. Nine or ten attackers are arrested.

*Saturday, 27 May:* At Burns' hearing, crowds on both sides of the issue gather outside the Courthouse. The mayor orders U.S. troops to guard the Courthouse, making it very difficult for even the lawyers to make their way into the courtroom. Burns' lawyers request and are granted a delay until Monday. Marshal Freeman wires President Franklin Pierce, who supports the Fugitive Slave Act, to approve his use of U.S. troops. Pierce instructs him to use whatever means necessary to maintain order. That evening, Reverend Grimes tries to collect money to purchase Burns from Suttle, based on Suttle's verbal agreement to sell him.

*Monday, 29 May:* Suttle's lawyer advises his client that it is against the law to sell or purchase a slave in Massachusetts. Suttle backs out of the sales agreement with Grimes. The court proceedings officially begin, and for the first time in Boston history, the Courthouse is closed to the public.

*Monday–Wednesday, 29–31 May:* The evidence against Burns rests on two important facts. First, William Brent, Suttle's slave agent testifies that Burns disappeared on 24 March. Second, Burns' statements to Suttle after his arrest on 24 May help to confirm his identity.

Burns' lawyers use a loophole in the Fugitive Slave Law and attempt to prove that Burns is not the same man who escaped from Colonel Suttle. To support their claim, the defense presents nine witnesses who testify that they saw Burns before 24 March, the day that Suttle claims he escaped. By the end of the day on 30 May, the public believes that Burns will likely be released.

*Thursday, 1 June:* Judge Edward G. Loring renders his decision. Based on Burns' conversation with Colonel Suttle, his identity is deemed irrefutable and therefore Burns is to be returned to Virginia.

*Friday, 2 June:* Burns is brought by procession to a ship that will take him back to Virginia. The city is placed under martial law for most of the day.

## Vocabulary

*Abolition Movement:* a social movement made up of people trying to end slavery in the United States

*Abolitionist:* someone fighting to end slavery

*Compromise of 1850:* an agreement reached by the U.S. Senate that established many controversial policies related to slavery

*Fugitive Slave Law:* This law was part of the "Compromise of 1850" in which antislavery advocates gained the admission of California as a free state, and the prohibition of slave-trading in the District of Columbia. The slavery party received concessions with regard to slaveholding in Texas. Passage of this law was so hated by abolitionists that its existence played a pivotal role in ending slavery. This law also spurred the continued operation of the fabled Underground Railroad, a network of over three thousand homes and other "stations" that helped escaping slaves travel from the southern slave-holding states to the northern states and Canada.

*Kansas-Nebraska Act:* Passed in 1854, this law permitted slavery in the territories of Kansas and Nebraska, marking a turning point in slave ownership in the United States.

*Martial Law:* a temporary rule by military authorities over the civilian population, such as in an area of military operations in time of war, or when civil authority has broken down

*Massachusetts Personal Liberty Act* (1855): As a result of the uproar over the Fugitive Slave Law of 1850, and the capture and extradition of Anthony Burns in 1854, Massachusetts passed so-called "personal liberty" acts aimed at thwarting federal requirements. The state laws guaranteed the writ of *habeas corpus*, the right to a jury trial, and other procedural devices that protected runaways. The laws also made it difficult and costly for slave owners to prove their case in court. A key provision called for the removal of any state official who aided in the return of runaway slaves. The personal liberty laws, while anathema in the South, reflected the growing opposition of mainstream northern society to the "peculiar institution."

## Key Players *in* The Trial of Anthony Burns

ANTHONY BURNS was a fugitive slave who escaped from Virginia to Boston, Massachusetts in 1854.

RICHARD HENRY DANA was the leading abolitionist lawyer for Burns. Though he opposed the Fugitive Slave Law, he believed in the sanctity of the law and respect for those who must uphold it. After Burns' trial, he supported Judge Loring and opposed the State Senate's decision to remove him from his position.

REVEREND LEONARD GRIMES was a leader of the black abolitionist movement in Boston and pastor of the Twelfth Baptist Church of Boston, known as the fugitive slave church.

THOMAS WENTWORTH HIGGINSON was a minister and abolitionist from Worcester, Massachusetts. Higginson fervently opposed the Fugitive Slave Law and believed in defending the freedom of escaped slaves at any cost. He was one of the major organizers of the attempt to rescue Burns from the Boston Courthouse.

JUDGE EDWARD G. LORING was both a Judge of Probate and the Commissioner presiding over fugitive slave cases in Massachusetts.

COLONEL CHARLES F. SUTTLE was the owner of the slave Anthony Burns.

OFFICER JAMES BATCHELDER was a Marshal's guard who was killed during the storming of the Boston Courthouse.

WENDELL PHILLIPS was a prominent abolitionist lawyer and orator. He was put on trial for his role in the failed attempt to rescue Burns.

LOUISA MAY ALCOTT was from a prominent family in Concord, Massachusetts, who was active in the abolitionist movement. Author of *Little Women*, Alcott became a famous writer.

## Pre-Lesson Plans

### The Fugitive Slave Law of 1850—Part One

*Goals*

1. to examine the goals and rationale behind the Fugitive Slave Law of 1850
2. to acquaint students with the idea of working in role

*Objectives*

1. to briefly review major conflicts of pre-Civil War America
2. to interpret selected text from the Fugitive Slave Law
3. to speculate on the objectives of legislators who drafted the Fugitive Slave Law

*Method*

1. Discuss the role of historians in society. What do they do? What are some of their goals? Methods? How do they interpret the past? What are their limitations?
2. In pairs, ask students to discuss what they think was happening in pre-Civil War America—around 1850. Ask each pair to share their thoughts with the class and list them on the blackboard. In groups of five or six, instruct students to go up to the board and put a question mark next to any item that they are not sure of (their own or someone else's). At this point, don't worry about misconceptions.
3. Explain to the students that they will be playing present-day historians faced with interpreting a document from 1850.
4. In role as the president of the National Historical Society, the teacher welcomes fellow historians (the students) to this special conference on important historic documents. Explain that the purpose of this conference is to interpret a newly discovered draft of the Fugitive Slave Law. Divide the historians into their previous groups. Hand out copies of the edited law (available online at *www.nationalcenter.org/FugitiveSlaveAct.html*).
5. Ask the groups to read the document out loud. Tell them the Society wishes to publish a pamphlet that helps people understand the Fugitive Slave Law. The main questions that need to be answered

are: What is this document trying to accomplish? Why would such a law be drafted? Who would be interested in seeing this law passed? Allow time for group discussions.

6. Ask groups to report their findings. Write the major points on the board. After each group has finished their report, lead a discussion about the major points. Is there a consensus around any of the interpretations? Are there differences in opinion?

### The Fugitive Slave Law of 1850—Part Two

*Goal:* to explore the effects of the Fugitive Slave Law of 1850 on specific populations in pre-Civil War America

*Objectives*

1. to brainstorm possible consequences of the Fugitive Slave Law
2. to express an intellectual understanding of the Fugitive Slave Law in an emotional and physical context

*Method*

1. Review the comments written on the board in step two of the previous lesson plan. Ask the students to add any new thoughts they have about pre-Civil War America. They can add new question marks or erase any old ones that they made personally. They can also erase their own comments if they have changed their minds. Remind students not to erase anything written by another student.

2. Discuss the following questions:

   a. What might the effect of the Fugitive Slave Law be on the following populations: southern slaves, northern abolitionists, escaped slaves, slave owners?

   b. Under what conditions might the Fugitive Slave Law be overturned?

3. In groups of six, ask students to create a tableau (frozen picture) of the effect of the Fugitive Slave Law on the populations discussed in step two. The tableau may be realistic or abstract, but it should represent two or more of these populations.

4. Ask each group to create a second tableau of the same populations after the Fugitive Slave Law has been overturned. Again, the tableau may be realistic or abstract.

5. On a count of ten (teacher counting out loud), ask students to transform from their first tableau into their second one. Remind students to take the full ten seconds to make the transformation.

You can say "freeze" to mark the end point. Let them practice the transformation a second time.

6. Ask each group to share their transformation from one tableau to the other with the class, counting to ten for each group. After each presentation, ask the student observers for words or phrases that express the emotions of the piece.

## Post-Lesson Plans

### Tracing the Lives of the Characters

*Goals*

1. to trace the effect of the trial of Anthony Burns on the lives of those involved
2. to develop writing skills through drama

*Objectives*

1. to conduct research on what happened to the characters in the play following the trial
2. to conduct character interviews
3. to write eulogies of selected historical figures

*Method*

1. Based on the list of historical characters, ask each student to select a character to research. Several students may research the same character. Students should focus primarily on what happened to their character after the trial of Anthony Burns in 1854. Suggested resource materials appear at the end of the chapter.
2. Ask each student to write an "autobiography" (first person account) of their character's life. These can be collected or shared with the class.
3. Divide the students into pairs (A and B) so that no pair has researched the same character. A takes on the role of the historical character they researched. They should play that character toward the end of their life. B is in role as a reporter. B interviews A, writing down all important information. Switch, so that B takes on their character and A interviews them.
4. Ask students to write a eulogy of the person they interviewed focusing on what happened to that person after the trial.

*Follow-up:* Improvise two-person scenes between the researched characters several years after the trial. Decide where they might meet. What would they say to each other?

### Free Anthony Burns

*Goal:* to explore the goals and methods of three groups of abolitionists in attempting to free Anthony Burns

*Objectives*

1. to identify and discuss tactics taken by abolitionists in the case
2. to determine the pros and cons inherent in each strategy
3. to debate and determine which course of action will produce the best results

*Method*

1. Ask students to identify tactics used by the abolitionists to try to free Anthony Burns. The following objectives were explored in the play:
   a. break him out of prison
   b. buy him
   c. put him on trial
   Students may come up with additional ideas.
2. Divide students into three or more groups (depending on the number of tactics identified). Ask each group to take on the role of abolitionists in 1854. Assign a tactic from step one to each group. Groups should identify a leader to head the discussion and a secretary to write down important points. Ask each group to brainstorm the pros and cons of their tactic.
3. Each group presents their findings to the class.
4. Hold an emergency meeting of abolitionists. Let students know that they can argue for or against any of the tactics brought forth. In role as Wendell Phillips, the teacher welcomes fellow abolitionists to the meeting. Tell the crowd that Anthony Burns has just been arrested and is being held in the Courthouse. Ask for suggestions for what steps should be taken. Lead a debate on each suggestion and then vote on what action(s) to take.

*Follow-up:* As reporters in 1854, ask students to write an editorial about the outcome of the emergency meeting of abolitionists. Students can share the highlights of their editorial with the class.

## Personal Liberty Act

### Goals

1. to examine how the Anthony Burns case affected American history, specifically the antislavery movement
2. to participate in a mock legislative process

### Objectives

1. to explore the difficult issues of law and morality raised during the drama
2. to develop oratory and presentation skills
3. to determine possible solutions to the struggles faced by those opposed to the Fugitive Slave Law
4. to work collaboratively to devise a law that prevents the disorder and derision experienced in Massachusetts when Anthony Burns was returned to slavery

### Method

1. Discuss the issues raised during the Anthony Burns trial. Why did Judge Loring feel that he had to return Anthony Burns to slavery? Did the citizens of Massachusetts agree with his decision? Could Loring have maintained Burns' freedom without violating the Fugitive Slave Law? What could the State Legislature do to prevent fugitive slaves from being returned to their owners in the future? Discuss the conflict between State law and Federal law. How are these conflicts resolved?
2. Review the Fugitive Slave Law. Ask students to assume the role of State Legislators. In role, they must create a law that will counteract the Fugitive Slave Law.
3. Divide students into small groups. Ask them to write down the major points to be included in this new law. Then, bring the class back together and ask groups to present their ideas. Keep a list of all items on the board. Ask the students if they have any suggested modifications for any of the ideas listed. Once all the ideas are on the board, ask the class to vote on whether each one should be included in its new law.

Follow-up: Discuss the passing of the Personal Liberty Act (available online at http://usinfo.state.gov/usa/infousa/facts/democrac/20.htm). This Act and the resulting Personal Liberty Laws were written in response to Massachusetts citizens' reaction to the Fugitive Slave Law, particularly the Burns case.

### Moral Law versus Human Law

*Goals*

1. to explore the tension between moral law and human law
2. to draw connections between issues raised in the drama and similar modern-day legal struggles

*Objectives*

1. to review the tension between moral law and human law as it relates to the trial of Anthony Burns
2. to identify modern examples when the tension between moral law and human law has been debated in the courts
3. to conduct research on selected modern court cases
4. to argue the merits of their selected court case

*Method*

1. Lead a discussion about the tension between moral law and human law as it was portrayed in the performance of *The Trial of Anthony Burns*.
2. Ask students for examples in other times in history when this tension has existed (e.g., the Japanese Internment Camps). Ask for examples from recent events (e.g., holding aliens in prison without trial following the attack on the World Trade Center). Write these suggestions on the board. Come to a consensus (or vote) on a specific case that the class would like to explore.
3. Divide the class in half. Ask each half of the class to research one side of the issue (use newspapers, magazines, and information on the Web).
4. Set up a mock trial where one-half of the class becomes the plaintiff and the other half becomes the defense. Members of each group assume the roles of witnesses and lawyers. Allow the groups enough preparation time. Bring in a "judge" from outside the class to preside over the trial.

# Resources

## Publications

Adams, Charles Francis. [1890] 1968. *Richard Henry Dana: A Biography.* Detroit, MI: Gale.

*The Boston Slave Riot and the Trial of Anthony Burns.* 1854. Boston: Fetridge and Company.

Dana, Richard Henry. 1968. *The Journal of Richard Henry Dana, Jr., Volume II.* Edited by Robert F. Lucid. Cambridge, MA: Belknap-Harvard University Press.

Edelstein, Tilden. 1968. *Strange Enthusiasm: A Life of Thomas Wentworth Higginson.* New Haven, CT: Yale University Press.

Finkelman, Paul. 1988. *Fugitive Slaves and American Courts.* Volume 3. *Slavery, Race and the American Legal System.* New York: Garland.

———. 1981. *An Imperfect Union: Slavery, Federalism, and Comity.* Chapel Hill, NC: University of North Carolina Press.

"The Fugitive Slave Case in Boston." *Alexandria Gazette.* 30 May 1854: 2.

Hamilton, Virginia. 1988. *Anthony Burns: The Defeat and Triumph of a Fugitive Slave.* New York: Knopf.

Higginson, Thomas Wentworth. 1921. *Letters and Journals of Thomas Wentworth Higginson.* Edited by Mary Thacher Higginson. Boston: Houghton Mifflin.

*Liberator* 2 June 1854: 2–3.

Morris, Thomas D. 1974. *Free Men All: The Personal Liberty Laws of the North, 1780–1861.* Baltimore: Johns Hopkins University Press.

Parker, Theodore. [1855] 1970. *The Trial of Theodore Parker.* New York: Negro University Press-Greenwood.

Pease, Jane H., and William H. Pease. 1975. *The Fugitive Slave Law and Anthony Burns: A Problem in Law Enforcement.* Philadelphia, PA: Lippincott.

Tuttleton, James W. 1978. *Thomas Wentworth Higginson.* Boston: Twayne-G.K. Hall.

Von Frank, Albert J. 1998. *The Trials of Anthony Burns: Freedom and Slavery in Emerson's Boston.* Cambridge, MA: Harvard University Press.

## Websites

The African-American Mosaic: A Library of Congress Resource Guide for the Study of Black History and Culture: *http://lcweb.loc.gov/exhibits/African/afam001.html.*

Africans in America: *www.pbs.org/wgbh/aia.*

# 3

## Justice at War

### The Story of the Japanese American Internment Camps (1944)

## Overview

*Justice at War* is a TIE piece written by members of Theatre Espresso in 1993 to address a topic that we felt was not adequately covered in the teaching of American history. The play, which examines the case of *Mitsuye Endo v. Milton-Eisenhower* (1944), has toured to schools and courthouses throughout Massachusetts for more than a decade. Over the years, we've noticed that national and international events affect the participation of students in *Justice at War*. Following national tragedies, such as the Oklahoma City bombing, a hostage crisis, or the attack on the World Trade Center, students demonstrate a keen awareness of the tension between national security and civil liberties. In the case of American soldiers being held hostage in a foreign country, students tend to ask more questions about the conditions in which the Japanese Americans are being held.

## Synopsis

Mitsuye Endo of Sacramento, California, has petitioned that her detention at the Topaz Relocation Camp in Utah is unconstitutional. The Supreme Court has decided to hear the case. In role as Supreme Court Justices, students preside over the trial. Students are introduced to Chief Justice Stone who briefs them on the Endo case. Opening statements are delivered by James Purcell of the American Civil Liberties Union (Endo's lawyer), and by Solicitor General Fahey (attorney for the defense). Purcell places Endo's detention in legal terms, arguing that the War Relocation Authority had no right to detain innocent citizens and that the camps are racially motivated. Fahey points out the legal basis for the camps, citing executive order 9066, signed by President Roosevelt to protect American borders from sabotage during the war.

Endo gives her testimony, a personal account of her ordeal, from the racial tensions in her neighborhood before the bombing of Pearl Harbor, to the imposed curfews and loss of her home and job as a civil servant. Endo describes her life in a cold and bleak compound surrounded by barbed wire. She is then cross-examined by the defense lawyer. General DeWitt, who was in charge of the relocation effort, gives testimony and is cross-examined by James Purcell. The General maintains that the relocation was required for military security.

Chief Justice Stone reminds the justices (students) that they must have as much information as possible before making a decision on the case. They are encouraged to ask questions of the lawyers and their witnesses. Following the questions, the justices go into deliberation. A majority and a minority opinion are formed. The justices present their opinions to the plaintiff and the defense.

## Preparing the Students

As with *The Trial of Anthony Burns*, teachers receive a study guide (provided at the end of this chapter) prior to Theatre Espresso's performance. Teachers explain to their students that one of the evacuees, Mitsuye Endo, has filed suit against the War Relocation Authority, claiming that she has been imprisoned in an internment camp even though she has not been charged or convicted of a crime. Her case is now before the Supreme Court. Teachers also explain that the students will be playing Supreme Court Justices during World War II, and that they should pay attention to the arguments on both sides of the case in order to make an informed decision.

## A Note to the Director

The play was devised to be performed by professional actors for school groups, but it may also be performed by high school students for their peers. In either case, the actors need to be well versed in the history of the camps in order to participate in the interactive portion of the drama. The play may also be read in the classroom and serve as a springboard for discussion and further research. Since the play offers few occasions for movement, directors should encourage the cast to take advantage of any opportunities that arise, such as standing to make an objection or answer a question from the audience. Also, be aware of the rhythms and dramatic builds within the testimony, especially Purcell's second examination of DeWitt. Cue pickup is extremely important in maintaining the dramatic tension. Period costumes, and props such as the map and the photos, help to make the production visually interesting, but the play relies primarily on the vocal choices of the actors.

# Justice at War*
# The Story of the Japanese American Internment Camps

Mimi Jo Katano, Wendy Lement, and Jordan Winer

## Characters

*Justice of War* premiered in 1994 with the following cast:

PAPER BOY (*or GIRL*)/BAILIFF . . . . . . . . . . . . . . . . . . . . . . . . . . . .Aimee Bel
NEWSCASTER/GENERAL JOHN L. DEWITT . . . . . . . . . . . . . . .Jay Bragan
FIRST PERSON/JAMES PURCELL
      (*male or female—JANET PURCELL*) . . . . . . . . . . . . . . . .Wendy Lement
SECOND PERSON/ SOLICITOR GENERAL FAHEY
      (*male or female*) . . . . . . . . . . . . . . . . . . . . . . . . . . . . . . .Nancy Gahagan
CHIEF JUSTICE STONE (*male or female*) . . . . . . . . . . . . .Jeremy Solomons
MITSUYE ENDO . . . . . . . . . . . . . . . . . . . . . . . . . . . . . . . . . .Mimi Jo Katano

PROLOGUE

SOUND CUE: *Andrews Sisters singing "Don't Sit Under the Apple Tree," interrupted by sound of falling bombs.*

PAPER BOY: (*enters with newspaper and shouts over sound of bombs*) Extra! Extra! Read all about it! Oahu bombed by Japanese planes! We are at war!!
NEWSCASTER: (*from off*) Washington, December 7, 1941. The Japanese attacked Pearl Harbor from the air. Civilian casualties mounting. Blackout ordered for Oahu. Japanese parachutists land on island. Police have been instructed to shoot on sight.

*SOUND CUE: President Roosevelt's speech—recorded: "Yesterday, December 7, 1941, a date that will live in infamy, the United States was suddenly and ruthlessly attacked by naval and air forces from the empire of Japan." During the preceding speech,* MITSUYE ENDO *enters reading a newspaper, which hides her face.* FIRST PERSON *and* SECOND PERSON *also enter and stand next to each other. All freeze once on stage, creating a tableau.*

FIRST PERSON: I heard Mrs. Smith's boy, Philip, was on the Arizona.

SECOND PERSON: Thousands of planes came out of nowhere. They haven't heard from him.

FIRST PERSON: We've never been attacked before.

SECOND PERSON: I have a Japanese family living *right next door.* Are we safe?

FIRST PERSON: Something has to be done! (*They exit.*)

PAPER BOY: Latest casualty count; over four hundred killed! Three hundred injured on Oahu, alone! (*exits*)

NEWSCASTER: (*from off*) March 1, 1942. All Japanese Americans on the west coast ordered to report to relocation camps.

*SOUND CUE: Fade up, Andrews Sisters singing "Boogie Woogie Bugle Boy." During this,* MITSUYE *lowers her paper slowly. We see her face for the first time. She exits quickly. The music fades.*

*End Prologue*

BAILIFF: The Honorable, the Chief Justice and the Associate Justices of the Supreme Court of the United States. Oyez. Oyez. Oyez. All persons having business before the honorable Supreme Court of the United States are admonished to draw near and give their attention, for the Court is now sitting. God save the United States and this honorable court.

STONE: Welcome, Justices, to the new session of the Supreme Court. My name is Chief Justice Stone. Before we begin, you must first take the judicial oath of office. Please stand, raise your right hand, and repeat after me: "I do solemnly swear . . . that I will administer justice . . . without respect to persons, . . . and do equal right to the poor and to the rich, . . . and that I will faithfully and impartially discharge . . . and perform all the duties incumbent upon me . . . as a Justice of the Supreme Court . . . under the Constitution and laws of the United States." Thank you. You may be seated. Now, as the Chief Justice, my job is to outline our task today. Your job as newly sworn in justices of the Supreme

Court is to hear the evidence in this case and to pass judgment on how we see the law. We have just sworn to uphold the Constitution and to judge each case based on the facts and not to let our personal feelings interfere in our judgment.

Our case today is that of Mitsuye Endo versus the United States. We must bear in mind that the country is still in shock over the bombing of Pearl Harbor, three years ago, in 1941, and we are still at war with Japan. The Constitution lays down that "No state shall deprive a person of life, liberty or property without due process of law." (*FYI, due process is mentioned in the Fifth and Fourteenth Amendments.*) However, the Constitution also suggests that in times of national emergency, or if the country is invaded, personal freedoms can be suspended. (*FYI, Article 1, Section 9 alludes to this.*)

The questions before you are these: 1. Did the War Relocation Authority have the right to take Miss Endo from her home and move her to an internment camp? 2. Was the security of the country at risk from Miss Endo?

Usually in our court, we receive the evidence from other courts that have already tried the case and hear only from lawyers. Today is an exception. Today we will hear from both lawyers *and* witnesses. On the brief for the government we will hear from Solicitor General Fahey and her witness General John L. DeWitt. On the brief for the other side in this case is Mr. James Purcell of the American Civil Liberties Union and his witness, Mitsuye Endo, currently a resident at the Topaz Internment Camp in Utah. (*The lawyers and their witnesses enter as their names are called.*) This court is now in session. You may be seated. Solicitor General Fahey, are you ready with your opening Statement?

FAHEY: Thank you, Your Honor. Justices of the Supreme Court, as we speak, our nation is gripped in a great war. On two different continents American men and women are risking their lives to preserve our liberty. There is no more serious matter than war. War changes everything. Even in a strong and stable society such as ours. Families are torn apart, the future is put on hold, the comfort of individuals becomes *less* important than the survival of us as a *nation*. When the Japanese bombed the American base at Pearl Harbor, our nation was thrown into a panic and looked to its elected officials to take leadership.

Job number one was protecting *all* U.S. citizens, regardless of ethnic origin, and weeding out any traitors. To this end, and in order to protect our citizens of Japanese origin from hostility, we protect, feed, and house them in specially built facilities. There are countless Japanese

Americans who have proven their loyalty and are able to leave of their own free will. Justices of the court, I submit to you that General DeWitt and the War Relocation Authority acted under orders of the President of the United States and the freely elected Congress. We are confident, that in all respects, General DeWitt's actions were necessary to maintain the security of the United States. Thank you.

*STONE:* Mr. Purcell, are you ready with your opening statement?

*PURCELL:* Thank you, Your Honor. Honored Justices of the Supreme Court, imagine this. One day strange men come to your home, or to your job. They tell you that you are no longer free to live or do as you wish. They tell you that "for your own protection" you must report to an assembly center. So you move, with your entire family, and you go to live in a stall that was once used for horses. Your new "home" is surrounded by barbed wire, and guards, armed with machine guns, watch your every move. And now imagine that *not once* during this entire nightmare, were you ever charged with committing any crime.

What would you, as American citizens, do if all this happened to you? Wouldn't you call on the Government? Wouldn't you say that as an American citizen you have the right *not* to be held without a fair trial? Wouldn't you *insist* that under the Fifth Amendment of the Constitution that no one shall deprive you of life, liberty or property without due process of law?

I submit to you today that all this happened to Mitsuye Endo, and thousands of other American citizens like her. The only reason for their imprisonment is their Japanese ancestry. This court exists in order to guard the Constitution, the highest law of the land. Mitsuye Endo's liberty was taken away because she committed the crime of having Japanese blood. I call upon you today to restore Miss Endo's liberty. In so doing you will restore our greatest hope for freedom and democracy in the future of our civilization. Thank you.

*STONE:* Solicitor General Fahey, will you please call your witness to the stand.

*FAHEY:* Thank you, Your Honor. I would like to call General John L. DeWitt to the stand?

*BAILIFF:* Please raise your right hand and put your left hand on the bible. Do you swear to tell the truth, the whole truth and nothing but the truth, so help you God?

*DEWITT:* I do.

*BAILIFF:* You may be seated.

*FAHEY:* Please state your name for the Justices.

*DEWITT:* General John L. DeWitt.

*FAHEY:* You are a General in the United States Army?

*DEWITT:* Yes, Sir.

*FAHEY:* General, what is your command?

*DEWITT:* I am commander of the Western Defense.

*FAHEY:* What, exactly, does that entail?

*DEWITT:* I am in charge of the security of our west coast against acts of espionage and sabotage.

*FAHEY:* Under peacetime conditions, would you be given such a command?

*DEWITT:* No Sir.

*FAHEY:* Then this is a special assignment?

*DEWITT:* Yes Sir, we are at war with Japan.

*FAHEY:* General DeWitt, did you order the evacuation of Japanese Americans from the west coast, including Miss Endo?

*DEWITT:* I did.

*FAHEY:* Now, under whose authority did you execute the evacuation?

*DEWITT:* Under the authority of the President of the United States. Executive Order 9066 calls for the identification of security zones along our west coast. If I may? (*The bailiff holds a large mounted world map. The General refers to the map with a pointer.*) The Japanese have already attacked us here at Pearl Harbor. Following the attack on Pearl Harbor, U.S. intelligence picked up numerous radio transmissions emanating from our west coast. The exact location of these transmissions, what was transmitted and who received these transmissions has yet to be identified. We at the War Department consider this a serious threat to national security. For, we believe the Japanese, their next target will be somewhere here along our west coast and then eventually all the way to Washington. Executive Order 9066 calls for the identification of Security Zones along our west coast and the evacuation of persons who may be dangerous to the security of those areas. (*The Bailiff hangs the map up on the set.*)

*FAHEY:* Does Executive Order 9066 call for the relocation of the evacuees to relocation camps?

*DEWITT:* No. Following the notice of evacuation, several Japanese Americans took it upon themselves to relocate to the interior of the country. These relocations were unsupervised. Once in their new locations, these Japanese were the victims of racist attacks. It became clear to us that the unsupervised relocation of 110,000 Japanese from the west coast would cause a great disturbance to public order.

*FAHEY:* What actions were taken, General, to prevent this disturbance?

*DEWITT:* Public Law 503 was passed to establish the War Relocation Authority. Our goals were to move the Japanese Americans out of the security zones and into relocation centers, to separate the loyal from the disloyal, and to protect the Japanese against further racist attacks.

*FAHEY:* In your professional opinion, General, has the relocation been successful?

*DEWITT:* Yes Sir, very successful.

*FAHEY:* No further questions, Your Honor.

*STONE:* Mr. Purcell, do you wish to cross-examine the witness?

*PURCELL:* Yes, thank you, Your Honor. General DeWitt, you stated that Public Law 503 established the War Relocation Authority in order to "separate," as you say, the loyal from the disloyal.

*DEWITT:* That is correct.

*PURCELL:* General, I have read Public Law 503, and nowhere in it do I find authority given to place American citizens in prison camps.

*DEWITT:* They are not prison camps. They are relocation centers.

*PURCELL:* Are the detainees free to come and go at their will?

*DEWITT:* Yes, if certain requirements are met.

*PURCELL:* But if these "requirements" are not met, then they *are* prisoners.

*FAHEY:* Objection.

*PURCELL:* I'll rephrase the question. General DeWitt, does Public Law 503 *explicitly* call for the internment of Japanese Americans?

*DEWITT:* Not explicitly. But Congress and the President are fully aware of the measures taken.

*PURCELL: (He is thrown by this answer.)* I have no further questions.

*STONE:* General, you may stand down. Mr. Purcell, are you ready with your witness?

*PURCELL:* Yes, Your Honor, at this time I would like to call the appellant Mitsuye Endo to the stand.

*STONE:* Proceed.

*BAILIFF:* Please raise your right hand and put your left hand on the bible. Do you swear to tell the truth, the whole truth and nothing but the truth, so help you God?

*ENDO:* I do.

*BAILIFF:* You may be seated.

*PURCELL:* Please state your name for the court.

*ENDO:* Mitsuye Endo.

*PURCELL:* Miss Endo, where were you born?

Justice at War, *(left to right) Christopher Robin Cook and Bernice Luison Sim, photo by Wendy Lement.*

*ENDO:* Sacramento, California.

*PURCELL:* Miss Endo, how old are you?

*ENDO:* Twenty-four.

*PURCELL:* Are you a citizen of Japan?

*ENDO:* No, I'm a citizen of the United States.

*PURCELL:* Did you attend school in Japan?

*ENDO:* No, I went to school in Sacramento.

*PURCELL:* While in school, did you learn to read or write Japanese?

*ENDO:* No.

*PURCELL:* Do you speak Japanese?

*ENDO:* No, I only speak English.

*PURCELL:* Have you ever been to Japan?

*ENDO:* Never.

*PURCELL:* Have you ever contacted anyone in Japan?

*ENDO:* No. I don't even know anyone there.

*PURCELL:* Miss Endo, what religion are you?

*ENDO:* I'm Catholic.

*PURCELL:* Were you employed in Sacramento prior to the evacuation?

*ENDO:* Yes.

*PURCELL:* In what profession?

*ENDO:* I was a clerk for the Department of Motor Vehicles.

*PURCELL:* You were an employee of the State of California?

*ENDO:* Yes.

*PURCELL:* Do you still hold that position?

*ENDO:* No.

*PURCELL:* Were you fired?

*ENDO:* No.

*PURCELL:* Did you leave your job voluntarily?

*ENDO:* No.

*PURCELL:* Miss Endo, please tell the court under what circumstances you left your job.

*ENDO:* Following the attack on Pearl Harbor, all of the State employees of Japanese descent were given a questionnaire to fill out.

*PURCELL:* Please describe that questionnaire for the court?

*ENDO:* It was seven pages long, and it asked about our citizenship, how long we had been in the United States, if we were loyal to Japan, questions like that.

*PURCELL:* How did you answer these questions?

*ENDO:* I wrote that I am a loyal citizen of the United States.

*PURCELL:* Miss Endo, prior to this time, had your superiors ever complained about your work?

*ENDO:* Never.

*PURCELL:* After filling out this questionnaire, what happened to you?

*ENDO:* I received a notice of charges from my employer.

*PURCELL:* Charges? What were these charges?

*ENDO:* That I am a dual citizen of Japan; that I read and write Japanese; that I belong to Japanese societies; and that I am a threat to the security of the United States.

*PURCELL:* Miss Endo, are you, in any way, a threat to the security of the United States?

*ENDO:* No.

*PURCELL:* Why, then, did your employer single you out for these charges?

ENDO: I wasn't singled out. Everyone of Japanese descent received the exact same charges.

PURCELL: Were you given an opportunity to respond to these charges and return to work?

ENDO: No. All Japanese Americans on the west coast were ordered to report to relocation centers. We had to sell or give away everything we owned, except for what we could carry.

PURCELL: What about your home?

ENDO: There wasn't time for my father to sell it, so we lost it to the bank. My mother had to give away all our furniture. Someone bought the china my grandmother had brought from Japan, for *five dollars*.

PURCELL: Up to this point, Miss Endo, were you ever charged with committing any crime?

ENDO: No.

PURCELL: What happened when you reported to the relocation center?

ENDO: One of the guards put a tag on me and my two pieces of luggage. The tag said "Tanforan," which was the name of the detention center I was to be bussed to.

PURCELL: Were you told why you were being sent to a detention center?

ENDO: They said it was for our protection.

PURCELL: Would you please describe Tanforan, for the court?

ENDO: It was a racetrack, which had been converted to a prison.

PURCELL: Why do you call it a prison Miss Endo? You were never charged with committing any crime.

ENDO: It was surrounded by barbed wire and there were guards who were ordered to shoot anyone who tried to leave.

PURCELL: Please describe the living conditions.

FAHEY: Objection.

STONE: Overruled. Answer the question, Miss Endo.

ENDO: The barracks were horse stalls that had been converted to living quarters. Each family had a single stall. The walls didn't reach the ceiling so you could hear everything that went on in the stalls on either side. There was no privacy between families. They put a covering over the floor but the dirt still came through and it smelled as if the horses were still there. The only furniture was some cots. We were lucky. We arrived early and were able to get mattresses. Once they ran out, people had to sleep on the springs.

PURCELL: Did each family have their own bathroom?

*FAHEY:* Objection.

*STONE:* Overruled.

*ENDO:* No, there were bathrooms in the middle of the compound but there weren't enough for everyone. There were always long lines and once you got in . . . it was very embarrassing . . . there were no doors or separation between the toilets.

*PURCELL:* Did each family have their own kitchen?

*FAHEY:* Objection. I fail to see the relevance of this line of questioning. The conditions of the camps are not on trial here. Tanforan was a temporary facility, which has since been closed.

*PURCELL:* Your Honor, I think it is important that the justices understand exactly how *American citizens* were being treated in these camps.

*STONE:* To the best of my knowledge none of the justices have had an opportunity to visit the camps. Therefore it is in our best interest to have as much information as possible. Objection overruled. Please answer the question Miss Endo.

*ENDO:* No. There was a mess hall where hundreds of people ate. Again there were long lines and it was impossible to have any privacy.

*PURCELL:* How was the food?

*ENDO:* It was quite awful.

*PURCELL:* Miss Endo, do you still reside at the Tanforan Center?

*ENDO:* No, I was there for six months. Then I was moved to the Topaz Detention Center in Utah, in the middle of the desert.

*PURCELL:* In the middle of the desert. That is where you live now?

*ENDO:* Yes, I was only allowed to leave in order to testify here today. Then I will be returned.

*PURCELL:* Miss Endo, how do you feel about the Japanese attack on Pearl Harbor?

*ENDO:* I believe that the war is wrong.

*PURCELL:* Is it your wish to see Japan invade the United States?

*ENDO:* No! This is my country! I have a brother fighting in the war.

*PURCELL:* Your brother is in the Japanese army?

*ENDO:* No, he's a soldier in the United States army, in Europe.

*PURCELL:* So, while your brother is fighting for America, you are being held in what amounts to a prison.

*FAHEY:* Objection. Counsel is leading the witness.

*STONE:* Sustained.

PURCELL: I'll rephrase the question. Miss Endo, your brother is a soldier, fighting in the United States Army, and you are being held, against your will, in a camp. How does this make you feel?

ENDO: Confused by what has happened. I am an American. I speak only English and I have friends of all races. In school I was taught that everyone is equal under the law. I am proud to be an American. I was a girl scout! I knew there were some people who didn't like me because my ancestors came from Japan. But I always thought I could show them that I am a good citizen. Then everything changed. Suddenly I was the enemy. I started to think maybe I had done something wrong, but I couldn't think what. I don't understand why people would do this to me. It makes me a little angry.

PURCELL: Miss Endo, have you, at any time, resisted orders of General DeWitt or the War Relocation Authority?

ENDO: No. I always did what I was told.

PURCELL: But you just said you were angry.

ENDO: I believe that I must prove that I am a loyal citizen of the United States. I was raised to not question authority. By not resisting I feel I can obey the law and be a good citizen.

PURCELL: Miss Endo, please rise and tell the court why you came here today.

ENDO: I am a loyal citizen of the United States. I have been imprisoned even though I was never charged or convicted of committing any crime. I am unable to go to work because I have been moved two hundred miles from my home to a camp. I am not a threat to the United States and I will continue to defend her honor.

PURCELL: Thank you, Miss Endo. I have no further questions, Your Honor.

STONE: Solicitor General Fahey, do you wish to cross-examine the witness?

FAHEY: I do, Your Honor, thank you.

STONE: Proceed.

FAHEY: Miss Endo, you paint a very bleak picture of the relocation camps. One might think you *are* imprisoned in a concentration camp.

ENDO: I believe I *am* in a concentration camp, Sir.

FAHEY: Miss Endo, I have here pictures taken from the Topaz center. (*Bailiff brings on pictures and holds the first one up.*) Do you recognize these pictures?

ENDO: I do.

FAHEY: Can you describe them for the Justices?

*ENDO:* It's of a volleyball game at Topaz.

*FAHEY:* A volleyball game? At a concentration camp? Would you agree, Miss Endo, that the participants are smiling?

*PURCELL:* Objection.

*FAHEY:* It is a simple question, Your Honor, they are either smiling or they are not.

*STONE:* Overruled. Answer the question.

*ENDO:* It looks like they might be smiling.

*FAHEY:* Having a good time, aren't they?

*PURCELL:* Objection. Your Honor, it is impossible for my client to discern, from a photograph, whether or not people are "having a good time."

*STONE:* Sustained.

*FAHEY:* Miss Endo, please describe this next picture for the Justices. (*The bailiff holds it up.*)

*ENDO:* It is of a music concert.

*FAHEY:* A music concert? In this "prison" you told us about?

*ENDO:* It is important for the Japanese Americans to make life as normal as possible. (*The bailiff hangs both pictures upon the set.*)

*FAHEY:* In fact, Miss Endo, there are schools, gardens, musical concerts, sporting events. . . . Not exactly the dismal conditions you described earlier.

*ENDO:* We worked very hard to make the best of a terrible situation.

*FAHEY:* Indeed, war is a terrible situation. Miss Endo, you claim that you are unable to leave the Topaz Relocation Camp.

*ENDO:* Yes.

*FAHEY:* Are you sure?

*ENDO:* Yes.

*FAHEY:* You testified that you read English.

*ENDO:* I do.

*FAHEY:* Then please explain to the Justices why you were unaware of the leave forms given to each detainee. Many loyal Japanese Americans went through the channels provided by the WRA. They have been moved from the camps and are now living and working, even attending college in communities around the country.

*ENDO:* I did fill out one of those forms requesting leave.

*FAHEY:* And you were denied?

*ENDO:* No.

*FAHEY:* Then you could leave if you *wanted* to?

*ENDO:* It's very complicated.

*FAHEY:* I bet it is.

*ENDO:* I was offered a deal by the government, that if I dropped this case I would be allowed to leave. I felt that pursuing this case was more important than my freedom.

*FAHEY:* So you were motivated by political reasons?

*PURCELL:* Objection.

*STONE:* Overruled.

*FAHEY:* (*stepping between Endo and Purcell to block their nonverbal communication*) Miss Endo, are you motivated by political reasons?

*ENDO:* (*pause*) Yes.

*FAHEY:* Thank you. I have no further questions.

*STONE:* Miss Endo, you may stand down. At this time, Justices, you will have an opportunity to ask . . .

*PURCELL:* Your Honor? Forgive the interruption. However, at this time I ask the court's permission to recall General DeWitt to the stand.

*FAHEY:* Objection!

*STONE:* You've had an opportunity to question the witness, Mr. Purcell.

*PURCELL:* Yes, Sir. (*searching*) However, the Sol. General's line of questioning raised certain points which need clarification by Gen. Dewitt. Therefore, it is imperative to my case that I have the opportunity to requestion him.

*STONE:* As this is an unusual case, I will allow it.

*FAHEY:* Your Honor, I strongly protest this action.

*STONE:* Protest noted. Mr. Purcell, this had better be brief.

*PURCELL:* Yes, Sir.

*STONE:* General, please retake the stand? (*There is a pause before DeWitt starts to move. Stone speaks again as DeWitt approaches the stand.*) The court reminds the General that he is still under oath. (*Dewitt stops briefly, and then sits. He is annoyed.*)

*PURCELL:* General, would you tell the court how many Japanese Americans have been convicted of sabotage or espionage against the United States?

*DEWITT:* They bombed Pearl Harbor!

*PURCELL:* That's not what I asked, General. Please answer the question. How many American citizens, of Japanese ancestry, *living in the United States*, have been convicted of sabotage or espionage?

*DEWITT:* None.

*PURCELL:* Not one?

*DEWITT:* No. As you can see, the War Relocation Authority has done and excellent job of protecting our borders. By removing the Japanese from the coast, we have removed the threat of such attacks.

*PURCELL:* But there was a period of several months between the attack on Pearl Harbor and the relocation of the Japanese Americans.

*DEWITT:* Approximately four months.

*PURCELL:* And during those four months, *not one* act of sabotage or espionage was committed by a Japanese American citizen?

*DEWITT:* No.

*PURCELL:* Why, then, did you feel it was necessary to tear families from their homes and place them in "relocation camps?"

*DEWITT:* Precautionary measures, Mr. Purcell. The Japanese surprised us at Pearl Harbor. We had no intention of letting that happen again. The fact that no sabotage had taken place was a clear indication that it would happen.

*PURCELL:* I see. General, have you ever disagreed with a policy of the United States?

*DEWITT:* No, as a soldier I comply with all orders given by Congress and the President.

*PURCELL:* General, on a personal level, have you ever openly disagreed with a policy of the United States?

*DEWITT:* Yes, on occasion.

*PURCELL:* Would you consider yourself a traitor?

*DEWITT:* I am a United States General, Sir!

*PURCELL:* But you *openly disagreed* with the government of the United States.

*DEWITT:* It isn't a crime to disagree with the government. As long as I follow orders.

*PURCELL:* "*It isn't a crime to disagree with the government.*" In fact, freedom of speech is protected under the Constitution. General, in order to "separate the loyal from the disloyal," did you ask Japanese Americans whether or not they disagreed with the government?

*DEWITT:* We did.

*PURCELL:* And if they said they disagreed, what happened to them?

*DEWITT:* They were labeled as traitors and sent to a maximum-security camp.

*PURCELL:* Exactly what crime had been committed?

*DEWITT:* I said they were traitors, and I am under orders to protect this country.

*PURCELL:* Yes, but what had they actually done since, in your own words, "it isn't a crime to disagree with the government?"

*DEWITT:* You're twisting my words.

*PURCELL:* General, you testified that the camps were necessary to protect Japanese Americans from racist attacks.

*DEWITT:* Yes sir.

*PURCELL:* I'm a bit confused, General. If you were the victim of a racist attack, would you be put in prison?

*DEWITT:* Of course not.

*PURCELL:* Most likely the perpetrator of the crime would be prosecuted, wouldn't you say?

*DEWITT:* Yes.

*PURCELL:* Why, then, in the case of these Japanese American victims, were they imprisoned instead of their attackers?

*DEWITT:* If you haven't noticed, we are at war with Japan.

*PURCELL:* General, where are your ancestors from?

*FAHEY:* Objection! Relevancy!

*PURCELL:* Your Honor, I am trying to establish what it means to be an American, in the eyes of the General. His opinion on this issue is central to our case.

*STONE:* You are trying the court's patience, Mr. Purcell. I will allow this. However, you had better come to your point quickly.

*PURCELL:* Thank you, Your Honor.

*STONE:* Answer the question, General.

*DEWITT:* My father is of Dutch ancestry and my mother is German.

*PURCELL:* Aren't we at war with Germany, sir?

*DEWITT:* Congratulations on read this morning's paper, Mr. Purcell. Every idiot knows we are!

*PURCELL:* Then if someone attacked you because they hated Germans, should you and all the German Americans living on the east coast be put in prison?

*DEWITT:* No.

*PURCELL:* Isn't that exactly what happened to the Japanese Americans?

*DEWITT:* That's different.

*PURCELL:* How is that different, General?!

*DEWITT:* They attacked us! They bombed Pearl Harbor! You can't blame Americans whose sons are dying in a war with Japan for being upset when hundreds of Japanese start moving into their neighborhoods. Of course there was violence. We at the War Relocation Authority do not condone that violence, but it is a fact. We have taken every step necessary to protect our Japanese American citizens from danger.

*PURCELL:* General DeWitt, was any attempt made to relocate the German American population living on the east coast?

*DEWITT:* No, but . . .

*PURCELL:* I have here, General, reports listing dozens of cases of *convicted* German American spies. How were these cases handled?

*DEWITT:* On an individual basis.

*PURCELL:* So, if someone *did* start rounding up all the German Americans, you would be in prison *right now.* Isn't that right, General?

*DEWITT:* How dare you . . .

*FAHEY:* Objection! Counsel is badgering the witness!

*STONE:* Mr. Purcell, control yourself!

*PURCELL:* Withdrawn. No further questions.

*STONE:* Solicitor General Fahey, do you wish to re-direct?

*FAHEY:* Thank you, Your Honor. General, please tell the court how many Americans were killed in the bombing of Pearl Harbor.

*PURCELL:* Objection! My client is not a Japanese citizen. She is an American citizen. She is *not* responsible for the bombing of Pearl Harbor.

*STONE:* Overruled. You opened this line of questioning, Mr. Purcell.

*FAHEY:* General?

*DEWITT:* Two thousand, four hundred and three, including innocent women and children.

*FAHEY:* So this attack was a serious threat to the security of the United States?

*DEWITT:* Eighty percent of U.S. Naval warships in the Pacific were lost. Let me remind you that we had never been attacked on American soil before this time. Under the circumstances, we had to take immediate steps toward the protection of *all* citizens.

*FAHEY:* In your expert opinion, General, is Miss Endo's internment justified?

*DEWITT:* I realize that Miss Endo's comfort has been compromised during this national emergency. However, during times of emergency, and especially during times of war, the comforts of the few must be superseded by the needs of a nation.

*FAHEY:* Thank you. No further questions.

*STONE:* If there are no further interruptions, Justices, you now have the opportunity to ask any questions you may have. You may ask questions of either witness or their lawyers. Are there any questions at this time? (*if there are no questions*) Justices, I remind you that you will be called upon to vote on the fate of Miss Endo and thousands of Japanese American citizens. If you need clarification on any of the testimony given thus far, now is the time to ask. Has anyone a question? (*assuming someone raises their hand*) Yes, Justice, please rise and state your question.

(*Stone fields questions, asking each student to stand. Stone repeats each question—heightening the language, giving the other actors time to think of a response and making sure that everyone else heard the question. Stone also determines who the question is directed to.*) I believe our time for questions is through. I will now ask the lawyers and their witnesses to wait in the outer chamber while we reach our decision. (*Endo, Purcell, Fahey, and Dewitt exit.*) Justices, in a few moments we will vote on whether or not the camps are constitutional. To help us in this decision, we shall review the facts on both sides of the case. We shall begin with the government. What were the important arguments brought forth by Solicitor General Fahey and his witness defending their actions? (*The bailiff writes each argument down on a large sheet of paper. Again, Stone asks each student to stand and he repeats each statement, but this time he also condenses the language so that it can be written down quickly.*) Good. Now, what were the important arguments brought forth by Mr. Purcell and his witness as to why the camps are unconstitutional? (*Repeat the aforementioned process.*) Justices, it is now time to vote. When I call the question, I will ask you to rise and remain standing until I have completed the count, and only to vote once. All those who believe that the government was justified in placing Miss Endo in an internment camp, please rise (*count is taken*). All those who believe that Miss Endo's constitutional rights were violated, please rise. (*count is taken*) Justices of the Supreme Court, by a vote of ____ to ____, you have decided that: (*the camps are unconstitutional and shall be closed—or—the government was justified in establishing the camps and they shall remain open.*) Bailiff, please ask the witnesses and their attorneys to return to the courtroom. (*as the actors enter*) I will now ask for two volunteers to read our findings. (*He picks one person to read the arguments from one side and one person to read the arguments for the other side. The Bailiff holds up the sheet of paper for each student.*) By a vote of ____ to ____, the Justices have decided that _____. (*The lawyers and their witnesses react to the decision.*) Honored Justices, you have completed the difficult task before you. Your arguments were well spoken and the decision of the court shall stand.

# *Justice at War* Study Guide

## *Learning Goals*

1. to explore the meaning of democracy through the eyes of those who had their freedom taken away
2. to learn tolerance and respect for all ethnic groups
3. to vocalize thoughts and feelings toward injustice
4. to examine the root causes of prejudice against Japanese Americans before, during, and after World War II
5. to explore the plight of 110,000 Japanese Americans who were sent to internment camps following the bombing of Pearl Harbor

## *What Happened in History*

On 7 December 1941, the day that the Japanese bombed the U.S. naval base at Pearl Harbor, President Roosevelt issued Proclamation No. 2525 restricting travel for Japanese Americans, and authorizing the detention of any alien enemy who appeared dangerous. Two months later, the President issued Executive Order 9066, establishing military zones along the West Coast. The order set the stage for the exclusion of Japanese Americans from the zones, but it did not authorize the detention of those who were forced to leave. General John L. Dewitt, Commander of the Western Defense, used Executive Order 9066 to justify the evacuation and internment of over 110,000 Japanese Americans in ten permanent camps. No Japanese American was ever convicted of sabotage or espionage against the United States. Still, men, women, and children were forced from their homes and kept in harsh conditions for the remainder of the war. Mitsuye Endo's case against the government was the fourth such case to be brought before the Supreme Court, and the first to be decided in favor of the plaintiff. The narrow decision in *Endo* v. *Milton-Eisenhower* led to the eventual closing of the camps.

## *Historical Timeline*

*1869:* The first Japanese to settle on the U.S. mainland arrive at Gold Hill near Sacramento, California.

*1870:* The U.S. Congress grants naturalization rights to free whites and people of African descent, omitting mention of Asian races.

*1886:* The Japanese government lifts its ban on emigration, allowing its citizens for the first time to make permanent moves to other countries.

*1911:* The U.S. Bureau of Immigration and Naturalization orders that declarations of intent to file for citizenship can only be received from whites and from people of African descent, thus allowing courts to refuse naturalization to the Japanese.

*1913:* The Alien Land Bill prevents Japanese aliens from owning land in California.

*1924:* Congress passes an Immigration Act stating that no alien ineligible for citizenship shall be admitted to the United States. This stops all immigration from Japan.

*7 December 1941:* Japan launches a surprise attack on Pearl Harbor.

*19 February 1942:* President Roosevelt signs Executive Order 9066, giving the War Department authority to define military areas in the western states and to exclude from them anyone who might threaten the war effort.

*12 August 1942:* The evacuation is completed; 110,000 people of Japanese ancestry are removed from the West Coast and placed in ten inland camps.

*18 December 1944:* The U.S. Supreme Court rules that loyal citizens cannot be held in detention camps against their will—the first major step toward closing the camps.

*14 August 1945:* Japan surrenders, ending World War II.

*20 March 1946:* The last remaining detention center closes.

*June 1952:* Congress passes Public Law 414, granting Japanese aliens the right to become naturalized citizens.

## Vocabulary

*U.S.S. Arizona:* U.S. battleship that sank after being bombed by Japanese forces in Pearl Harbor killing 1102 crewmen

*Relocation Camps:* temporary homes in remote areas of the United States administered by the War Relocation Authority for the Japanese Americans who were evacuated from their homes on the West Coast

*Pearl Harbor:* U.S. naval base bombed by Japanese forces on 7 December 1941, inciting the United States to join World War II

*War Relocation Authority (WRA):* government agency created by President Franklin D. Roosevelt in March 1942 to oversee the orderly evacuation of Japanese Americans from the West Coast

*Internment Camp:* another term for the relocation camps previously defined, particularly used by those who consider the term *relocation* inaccurate as it implies that Japanese Americans moved there voluntarily

*Fifth Amendment:* guarantees that no American citizen may be "deprived of life, liberty, or property without due process"

*Executive Order 9066:* Signed by President Roosevelt on 19 February 1942, it gave the Secretary of War the authority to designate certain areas of the United States as "military areas . . . from which any or all persons may be excluded."

*Public Law 503:* In March 1942, President Roosevelt signed this law, making it a federal offense to violate any order issued by a designated military commander under authority of Executive Order No. 9066.

*Prison Camp:* a camp for prisoners of war, or a low-security prison where prisoners are put to work

*Dual Citizen:* a person who holds citizenship in two countries

*Relocation Center:* a temporary processing center for Japanese Americans who were being moved to relocation camps

*Tanforan:* a race track taken over by the U.S. Army and used as an assembly center for Japanese and other people who were evacuated from the Pacific Coast

*Topaz Detention Center:* a camp in Utah for Japanese American detainees that opened in September 1942

*Concentration Camp:* a prison camp in which political dissidents, members of the minority, ethnic groups, or prisoners of war are confined—usually under harsh conditions

*Espionage:* spying or a government's use of spies to learn another government's military plans

*Sabotage:* the willful destruction of property or obstruction of public services

*Issei:* first generation Japanese immigrants born in Japan

*Nisei:* second generation Japanese Americans born to Issei parents

## *Key Players in the Japanese American Internment Camps*

JOHN L. DEWITT, a lifelong army man, was commander of the Western Defense during World War II. In March 1942, General Dewitt ordered the evacuation of more than 110,000 Japanese Americans from the Pacific Coast and southern areas of Arizona. Throughout the War, he affirmed his mistrust of, and hatred toward, Japanese Americans.

MITSUYE ENDO was ordered to leave her home in Sacramento and sent to the Tule Lake Assembly Center in Modoc County, California, and later to the Topaz Relocation Center in Utah. (Note: In *Justice at War,* Endo reports that she was sent to the Tanforan Assembly Center, which processed more detainees than Tule Lake.) Because of her status as a model American citizen—she had worked for the State of California prior to the war and her brother was fighting in the U.S. Army in Europe—Endo was recruited by the American Civil Liberties Union to be the appellant in a test case against the Government. She filed a Writ of Habeas Corpus in July 1942. Her case was forwarded to the U.S. Supreme Court by the Ninth Court of Appeals. In December 1944, the Supreme Court decided by a five to four majority that the War Relocation Authority could not detain loyal citizens. The decision in her case led to the closing of the camps in 1945.

CHARLES FAHEY, Solicitor General of Washington D.C., defended the War Relocation Authority in the Endo case.

GORDON K. HIRABAYASHI was convicted of knowingly disregarding a curfew in California imposed by a military commander as authorized by an Executive Order of the President. His conviction was reaffirmed by the U.S. Supreme Court, which refused to address the issue of constitutionality raised in the case.

TOYOSABURO (FRED) KOREMATSU was arrested and convicted for failing to report to an assembly center and for remaining in San Leandro, California, a military area, contrary to the Civilian Exclusion Order No. 34 of the Western Defense Command. In December 1944, the U.S. Supreme Court upheld Executive Order 9066 and the evacuation in his case.

JAMES PURCELL was a young American Civil Liberties attorney who recruited Mitsuye Endo as the appellant, and took her case all the way to the U.S. Supreme Court.

FRANKLIN DELANO ROOSEVELT was the thirty-second U.S. President (1933–1945). Following the attack on Pearl Harbor, Roosevelt signed Executive Order 9066, authorizing Secretary of War Stimson to define military areas from which any and all persons could be excluded.

HARLAN FISKE STONE was the U.S. Attorney General under President Calvin Coolidge. In 1925, he resigned to serve as an Associate Justice of the Supreme Court. Franklin D. Roosevelt appointed him Chief Justice of the Supreme Court in 1941. He held that office until his death in 1946.

MINORI YASUI, like Hirabayashi, was convicted of knowingly disregarding a curfew order in California. The U.S. Supreme Court reaffirmed his conviction.

## Preperformance Lesson Plans

### Picturing Pearl Harbor

*Goal:* to help students understand the circumstances that led to the internment of Japanese Americans

### Objectives

1. to review the facts surrounding the bombing of Pearl Harbor
2. to re-create and reflect on the terror felt by Americans during and immediately following the attack on Pearl Harbor

### Method

1. Ask students to read a brief historical account of the bombing of Pearl Harbor. If photos of the attack are available, they can be included in this activity (see the *Resources* section at the end of this chapter).
2. Discuss the reading in class. Which moments make strong impressions on the students?
3. Split the class into small groups of four or five. Ask students to choose a moment that is described in the reading and re-create it as a tableau.
4. Each group shares their tableau with the class. After each group presents, ask the rest of the students to share their observations. What do they think is happening in each tableau?
5. Discuss the activity with the class. What emotions were represented in these tableaux? Can the students recall a moment in their own lives when they felt similar emotions?

*Follow-up:* Explain to students that in the 1940s news did not travel as quickly as it does today. It took weeks for people across the country to learn details of the attack on Pearl Harbor. Ask each student to imagine that they are relative of an American who is stationed at Pearl Harbor. Several days have passed since the bombing, and they have not heard from their loved one. Ask them to write a letter to their relative expressing their concern.

## The Shell Collection

*Goal:* to put a human face on the plight of Japanese Americans during World War II

*Objectives*

1. to imagine what it was like to be a young Japanese American facing internment
2. to create scenes based on the ordeal of a fictional Japanese American girl

*Method*

1. Hand out handwritten copies of Ikuko's letter (follows). Tell students that the letter was found in the former home of a Japanese American girl named Ikuko, who was interned during World War II. Ask for a volunteer to read the letter to the class.

Dear Janice,

My mother says we have to leave tomorrow. I wasn't going to write because of what you said, but Mrs. Powell told me to. She promised to give this to you in class. I don't know if you can write to me where I'm going.

I can only take one suitcase, so I have to leave my photo album with the Halls. I took out the picture of you and me at the beach, the one where we are both buried in sand up to our necks. I laugh every time I look at it. I'm taking it with me.

Anyway, I'm not trying to start a war and I hope you are still my friend. I'm giving Mrs. Powell my shell collection. I told her you can keep it till I come back.

Ikuko

2. Ask students what they know about Ikuko from the letter. Next, ask students what they think might be true about Ikuko. Finally, ask students what questions they have about Ikuko and her situation. Write these questions on the board.
3. Divide the class into groups of three or four. Ask each group to select a question to explore. It's okay to have more than one group exploring the same question.
4. Ask students to make a list of characters they would like to interview in order to help answer their questions. From the list, select

the top three or four choices (depending on how many students are in that group).

5. Each member of the group selects a character to play. The remaining members of the group interview each character, rotating until all characters have had an opportunity to speak. If a group finishes early, they can interview additional characters from the list.

6. Each group shares what they discovered with the rest of the class.

7. Based on the information learned in the interviews, students create a short scene that explores the question.

8. Students perform their scenes for the class.

9. Discuss what has been discovered about Ikuko from the scenes.

*Follow-up*

1. Tell students that Ikuko and her family were ordered to go to a bus station. There, they were given tags to put on themselves and their luggage. The tags read "Tanforan," which was the name of the detention center where they and other Japanese Americans were being sent.

2. In a large open space, ask students to stand in a semicircle. Ask students what Ikuko might have seen when she arrived at the train station. Ask if anyone has an idea for a tableau of the scene. The student may use as many people as she needs to create the tableau. Once the scene is set, ask the student to stand back and look at it, and make any adjustments to the picture.

3. Now ask the student to place Ikuko into the picture. Tell students to relax.

4. Repeat the previous sequence with another student sculpting the tableau. This time, after the students relax, tell them that in a moment you will ask them to re-create that tableau. But this time, you will walk around the room and tap each of them on the shoulder. When they are tapped, they should speak one or two lines of their character's thoughts.

5. Discuss what occurred.

## Postperformance Lesson Plans

### Redress for Japanese Americans

*Goal:* to explore the controversial subject of compensation to groups who suffered economic loss because of actions taken by the U.S. government

*Objectives*

> 1. to examine different sides of the debate over redress for Japanese Americans
> 2. to develop arguments for or against redress
> 3. to debate the issues around redress in a clear and constructive manner

*Method*

> 1. Set up the following situation for the students. The year is 1983, almost forty years since the internment camps closed. The following proposal will be submitted to Congress for redress for Japanese American survivors of the internment camps during World War II.

**Commission on Wartime Relocation and Internment of Civilians Proposal for Redress Presented to the Congress of the United States June 1983 Recommendations**

> - Congressional acknowledgment and public apology for wrongs done in 1942
> - Presidential pardon for those who resisted relocation
> - Benefits and status change for Japanese Americans who were dishonorably discharged after the bombing of Pearl Harbor because of wartime prejudice
> - Establishment of a foundation to sponsor research and education about the internment camps so that similar events can be prevented in the future
> - A one-time, tax-free compensation of twenty thousand dollars to each survivor of the camps.
> 2. Divide the students into four groups. Each group is given one of the following identities:
>   a. a Japanese American who is presenting the proposal to Congress (Her aging grandmother was in the camps.)
>   b. a woman whose grandfather died in the attack on Pearl Harbor (Her grandmother suffered emotional and financial hardship. She wonders why Japanese Americans should be awarded compensation, when her grandmother didn't receive anything. She suggests that the Japanese government pay them, as Japan started the war. As a taxpayer, she doesn't want her money going to reimburse Japanese Americans.)

    c. a member of the House Budget Committee (He is concerned that if the Japanese Americans receive redress, then the door will be open to African Americans, American Indians, Chinese Americans who worked on the railroads, and so on. Paying sixty thousand Japanese American survivors twenty thousand dollars each would cost U.S. taxpayers $1.2 billion. If other groups start asking for redress, the country would go bankrupt. Who is to say who deserves it more?)

    d. a Rabbi from the World Jewish Congress (He helped Jews in Germany obtain redress after World War II, and believes that the Japanese Americans deserve more than the twenty thousand dollars proposed.)

3. Provide each group with background materials and ask them to prepare their arguments. Their goal is to convince a Congressional committee to vote according to the views of their character. They should prepare a brief opening statement and a list of arguments. Ask each group to select a representative to present the opening statement.

4. Invite another class or colleagues to play the Congressional committee. Direct each of the groups in a, b, c, and d as listed in step two to stand in one corner of the room. The teacher, in role as the chair of the Congressional committee, invites representatives from each group to make their opening statement.

5. Under the supervision of the chairperson, students participate in an open forum debate on the proposal. Any group member playing a character can ask another character a question. The question can be answered by any member of the group playing that character. Colored dots on the floor will mark where each character should stand when they speak.

6. The chairperson then encourages members of the Congressional committee to ask questions of the characters. Again, any member of a group can respond as that character.

7. The chairperson then leads the committee in a vote and the decision is announced.

8. Postdrama questions:

    a. Are we responsible for wrongs done in the past?

    b. Can we compensate a group who has been wronged in the past? How?

    c. How does what happened to the Japanese Americans compare with what happened to Native American Indians, African-Americans, or other groups?

    d. Should these groups be redressed? If so, how? Who is going to pay for it?

    e. Why was one group of people suddenly denied their constitutional rights?

    f. Could this kind of thing happen again? If so, what steps could be taken to prevent it?

*Follow-up:* In role as Japanese Americans recently released from the camps, students write a letter to President Roosevelt expressing their feelings and opinions about what happened to them. If students wish to be compensated for their losses, they must give reasons to support their claim.

### Write an Essay

*Goal:* to explore modern-day parallels to the internment of Japanese Americans during World War II

*Objectives*

    1. to utilize and strengthen research skills

    2. to write a persuasive essay

*Method*

    1. Ask students if they can remember a modern-day incident when ethnic or racial groups claimed that they had been subjected to civil liberties violations (see number 6 in the next section, *Topics for Further Research and Discussion,* below). Make a list on the board.

    2. Ask students to choose one of these examples and conduct further research into the background of the alleged civil rights violation, if it was challenged, and the end result.

    3. Ask students to write a persuasive essay that addresses whether the civil rights of the ethnic or racial group were indeed violated.

*Topics for Further Research and Discussion*

    1. conditions in the relocation camps

    2. scope of the wartime relocation camps (number, location, and capacity of U.S. camps and those in Mexico and Canada)

    3. 442$^{nd}$ division of Japanese American soldiers fighting in Europe

4. root causes of prejudice against Japanese Americans before, during, and after World War II

5. fate of Japanese Americans after the camps were closed

   a. economic hardships

   b. loss of property and possessions

   c. those who returned to the West Coast

   d. those who remained in the camps

   e. those who settled in other parts of the United States

   f. those who repatriated to Japan

   g. continued prejudice

   h. establishment of societies to help Japanese Americans return to civilian life

   i. fight for redress

6. other times in history when ethnic or racial groups have been subjected to civil liberties violations

   a. Palmer Raids after World War I

   b. Korean War (the McCarran Act)

   c. Vietnam War Era (repression of Civil Rights activists)

   d. Oklahoma City bombing

   e. attack on the World Trade Center (11 September 2001)

7. process by which a court case reaches the U.S. Supreme Court

8. U.S. Supreme Court cases (other than Mitsuye Endo's) that dealt with the treatment of Japanese Americans during World War II

   a. Hirabayashi

   b. Yasui

   c. Korematsu

## Resources

Armor, John, and Peter Wright. 1989. *Manzanar*. New York: Vintage.

*Come See the Paradise*. 1990. Directed by Alan Parker. 139 min. Fox Studios. Videocassette.

Dower, John W. 1986. *War Without Mercy: Race and Power in the Pacific War*. New York: Pantheon.

*Farewell to Manzanar*. 1976. Directed by John Korty. 120 min. Universal Studios. Videocassette.

Fine, Sidney. 1984. *Frank Murphy*. Ann Arbor, MI: University of Michigan Press.

Guterson, David. 1990. *Snow Falling on Cedars*. New York: Vintage.

Hiraoka, Leona, and Ken Masugi. 1994. *Japanese American Internment: The Bill of Rights in Crisis*. Amawalk, NY: Jackdaw Publication Division of Golden Owl.

Houston, Jane Wakatsuki, and James D. Houston 1973. *Farewell to Manzanar*. New York: Random House.

Irons, Peter. 1983. *Justice at War: The Story of Japanese American Internment Cases*. Berkley, CA: University of California Press.

McEvoy, J. P. 1943. "Our 110,000 New Boarders." *The Reader's Digest* (March): 5–68.

Mochizuki, Ken. 1993. *Baseball Saved Us*. New York: Lee & Low.

Natkiel, Richard, and Robin L. Sommer. 1985. *Atlas of World War II*. New York: Barnes and Noble, Inc.

Okimoto, D. J. 1970. *American in Disguise*. New York: Walker/Weatherhill.

Otsuka, Julie. 2002. *When the Emperor Was Divine*. New York: Random House.

Robinson, Gerald H. 2002. *Elusive Truth: Four Photographers at Manzanar*. Nevada City, CA: Carl Mautz.

Sides, Hampton. 2001. *Ghost Soldiers*. New York: Doubleday.

Slackman, Michael, ed. 1986. *Pearl Harbor in Perspective*. Honolulu, HI: Arizona Memorial Museum Association.

*Snow Falling on Cedars*. 1999. Directed by Scott Hicks. 125 min. Universal Studios. Videocassette.

Takahashi, Kazuyuki. 1944. "The Nisei and Selective Service." *The New Republic* (March): 382.

Tateishi, John. 1984. *And Justice for All: An Oral History of the Japanese American Detention Camps*. New York: Random House.

Weglin, Michi. 1976. *The Untold Story of America's Concentration Camps*. New York: Morrow.

Yarborough, Tinsley E. 1988. *Mister Justice Black and His Critics*. Durham, NC: Duke University Press.

## Websites

*www.askasia.org/teachers/Instructional_Resources/Lesson_Plans/Asian_American/LP_asianam_1.htm*

*www.parentseyes.arizona.edu/wracamps/index.html*

*www.topazmuseum.org/*

# 4

## *Voicings*

### The Story of the Rosenberg Case (1951)

*The collaboration of theatre and history provides rich possibilities for teaching and learning that are both humanistic and personal. A common ground of the two disciplines is the telling of human stories; yet personal stories have been underutilized as a teaching resource. The process of interviewing a historical informant brings history to life and deepens a theatre student's experience of performance. In developing the script, students become both historians and story-tellers, actively engaged in preserving and transmitting the history of ordinary women's lives.[1]*

## Overview

*Voicings* was developed during an Oral History and Performance course co-taught by Wendy and historian Susan Zeiger at Regis College in Weston, Massachusetts. The course, modeled on one piloted in 1986 by then Emerson College Professors Ron Jenkins (Theatre) and Blanche Linden-Ward (History), focuses on the process of creating a documentary theatre script; combining oral histories of women with research on a specified historical event and theatrical period. Students explore methods and gain practical experience in documenting personal stories and translating those stories into a performance piece. They are asked to consider how ordinary women shaped—and were in turn shaped by—historical events.

1. Written by Dr. Susan Zeiger, as part of the 1996 *Oral History and Performance* course proposal at Regis College.

The first cycle of the course was held in fall 1997. The course topic was radical women of the 1930s and 1940s, and the target theatre genre was epic theatre. *Voicings* was performed the following semester both for the community at large and for the women who were interviewed during the course. *Voicings* was Regis College's first multimedia production, incorporating film, slides, and a voice collage compiled by eight Regis College students.

## Voicings: The Story of the Rosenberg Case*

Based on Oral Histories of Radical Women of the
1930s, 1940s and 1950s and Their Daughters

By Wendy Lement with contributions by Kristy Kanhai,
Tammy King, Meghan Lee, Naomi Letendre, Ruth-Anne Macauley,
Christine Proulx, Kristen Sargent, and Valentina Walczak

### Characters

*Voicings* premiered in 1998 at Regis College with the following cast:

| | |
|---|---|
| LAURA ROSS | Meghan Buckley |
| MARY BETH/ANNOUNCER/PIANIST | Jessica Clancy |
| ANN TIMPSON/PRINCIPAL | Kali Walker |
| JOAN SOKOLOFF | Catherine Jordan |
| YOUNG JOAN/CAROL** | Kaitlin Varoski |
| KIM | Jeanne Fischetti |
| YOUNG KIM | Julie Blank |
| YUMIKO KASHU | Yumiko Mochizuki |
| JUDITH WOODRIFF | Kristen Pulsifer |
| YOUNG JUDITH WOODRIFF | Julie Keefe |
| SARA SUE KORITZ | Anna Perez |
| JEAN/NORA** | Catherine Kamp |
| LUCY RICARDO/ETHEL ROSENBERG | Erin Conroy |

**The characters of Nora and Carol are based on the oral history of Sara Sue Koritz.

JULIUS ROSENBERG . . . . . . . . . . . . . . . . . . . . . . . . . . . . . .Lawrence Bull
MRS. BELIOT . . . . . . . . . . . . . . . . . . . . . . . . . . . . . . . .Allyson DiGregory
RABBI/KATZINSKY** . . . . . . . . . . . . . . . . . . . . . . . . . . . .Nina Schiarizzi
RICKY RICARDO/SPORTSCASTER . . . . . . . . . . . . . . . . . . . .Ron Heneghan
FBI AGENT . . . . . . . . . . . . . . . . . . . . . . . . . . . . . . . . . . . . .David Smailes
ENSEMBLE/DANCER . . . . . . . . . . . . . . . . . . . . . . . . . . . .Christine Proulx
ENSEMBLE/PERCUSSION . . . . . . . . . . . . . . . . . . . . . . . . .Jennifer Savoie

All cast members also play a variety of smaller roles including reporters, various officials, students, and men and women on the street.

The musical score was composed by Peter Stewart. The musical director was Miranda Henry Russell. The choreographer was Mimi Katano. Costumes were designed by Jeff Burrows and Andrew Poleszak.

*The set consists of a series of platforms of different sizes and heights. Downstage center is a flat cleared area. Set changes are very minimal, a stool or benches come on and off as needed. Props and costume changes are suggestive. Three large screens hang on which slides are projected. The play begins with a voice collage of the women who were interviewed and a slide collage.*

**Setting:** Boston, New York, and various locations

**Date:** 1905–1997

SCENE ONE: THE 1905 REVOLUTION

*Setting: 1997, Boston in a living room of an old lady named Laura Ross. The setting changes as* LAURA *tells her story of the 1905 Revolution. From the little living room in her Boston apartment, the story moves into a synagogue in a Jewish Ghetto in Russia. The flashback takes place in three separate acting areas, the* STUDENTS *in one, the synagogue in another, and the* SOLDIERS *in a third space. When the story brings the* STUDENTS *and then the* SOLDIERS *into the synagogue, each group reacts as if they were in the same space, but physically they remain in their own distinct area.*

LAURA: (*Laura is sitting in a rocker swaying back and forth as she tells her story.*) It's a long, long struggle for us to maintain the Constitution and the Bill of Rights. We have to learn our history. Not just the history fed to us by people who are trying to take it away, for expansionist purposes, for big profits. We have as much right in this world as anybody else.

---

**The character of Katzinsky is based on an interview with Aaron Katz.

Right? We're in the struggle. It's not done for. We are in a situation where you need to know what side you're on. Like that song. We want a world where we all have chance. Right? And our families, and the people who come from other countries. You have to resurrect all the people who . . . that were pawned through the centuries. You know. (*The company quietly sings "Hine Ma Tov," a Jewish prayer, as they enter with benches and set up the synagogue.*) My mother and father came from Velnagambania, they lived in a Jewish Ghetto. My first husband's grandmother and her husband were the keepers of the synagogue. What they would call the janitors, or the . . . I don't know what you would call them. (*Laura gets up and becomes one of the members of the synagogue and sits on the bench, and holds her grandmother's hand.*) But anyway, one day, during the 1905 Revolution, which was the Russian Scholars against the Czar. This particular day, in the middle of service . . .

*WOMAN ONE (LAURA'S GRANDMOTHER):* The place was all filled, and people were sitting on benches.

*STUDENT ONE:* (*Students run into their space.*) The Czar's troops raided the University . . .

*STUDENT TWO:* Running . . . (*We hear barking off stage.*)

*STUDENT THREE.* And chased us . . .

*STUDENTS ONE & TWO.* Running . . .

*STUDENT FOUR.* Until we came to the synagogue.

*STUDENTS ONE, TWO, & THREE.* Hearts pounding . . .

*WOMAN TWO:* The students came right into the synagogue.

*ALL STUDENTS:* Pounding . . .

*WOMAN THREE:* And we knew they'd be killed . . .

*STUDENT ONE:* . . . if we're caught.

*WOMAN FOUR.* So . . . we hid them . . . under the benches. (*The students are hid.*)

*ALL:* We were terrified.

*RABBI:* But I kept going on with the service. (*Rabbi sings throughout. He stands behind the rest of the members of the synagogue.*)

*SOLDIER ONE:* (*A commander and two soldiers enter, barking. The commander holds the two soldiers on leashes attached to collars.*) We tracked the students to the next village.

*SOLDIER TWO:* (*to the Commander*) Hey, they could be in there.

*COMMANDER:* So I gave the command. (*The soldiers enter. The Commander lets the two soldiers off of their leashes and one breaks to the left, the other to the right as the Commander stands and watches.*)

LAURA: They came right into my grandmother's synagogue. They were looking for these students.

ALL STUDENTS: (*quietly*) Pounding.

WOMAN ONE: And the place was filled with people.

ALL STUDENTS & WOMEN: (*whispering*) Nobody moved.

SOLDIERS ONE & TWO: (*sniffing*) As we inspected the place.

ALL STUDENTS & WOMEN: (*quietly*) Pounding.

WOMAN TWO: And then . . . they left. (*All sigh.*)

LAURA: And that was the 1905 Revolution. (*Laura begins to move from the bench in her husband's great grandmother's synagogue to her living room, into her chair.*) And the Jews didn't have a plate to eat in but they were supporting these Russian college students. Isn't that something? So this goes all the way back. You know, people's rights or capitalism. Well, they didn't get any of the students. I hope they lived to the second revolution. They won in 1917. So that was 1905 Revolution. And that was my first husband's grandmother who sat there. (*laughs*) It sounds like a crazy tale but we have a lot of family tales. You know. (*Laura stands and sings "Which Side Are You On." The company joins in as the benches are moved for the next scene.*)

SCENE TWO: THE STRIKE

*The company sits on stage miming a weaving motion to the beat of a drum. The person beating the drum walks throughout the space, representing the foreman. ANN sits in front.*

ANN: I was a union organizer for the textile industry. I was nineteen years old and barely making ten dollars a week. We knew that the workers needed to organize in order to improve working conditions and get more pay. I was in Pawtucket, PA and we were organizing a strike at a textile mill. Well, we got all the men outside and there was an excited murmur over the crowd. We were going to stand up against our oppressors. We were going to get more pay. We were going to fight. (*chants*) We're going to fight. We're going to fight. (*louder*) We're going to fight.

ALL: (*Other actors join in standing one at a time.*) We're going to fight. We're going to fight. We're going to fight. (*louder*). WE'RE GOING TO FIGHT! WE'RE GOING TO FIGHT! WE'RE GOING TO FIGHT! WE'RE GOING TO FIGHT! WE'RE GOING TO FIGHT! WE'RE GOING TO FIGHT! WE'RE GOING TO FIGHT! (*softer*) We're going to fight. We're going to fight. We're going to fight. (*very tired, moving down to ground*) We're going to fight. We're going to fight. We're going to fight.

ANN: I looked around. The men had all gotten really tired and discouraged. They were almost ready to give up. So I took it upon myself to rally them back up. (*She stands on a chair.*) Come on men. We're doing good. Remember what we are fighting for. We need more money to feed our families. And we are not animals. The owners of this mill must take notice of us. We need better working conditions. We've gotta fight! (*She begins to sing "Solidarity Forever." The workers join in the chorus as they rise. Ann leads the workers around the stage where they pick up sticks, which they hold as picket signs. The workers march into the final tableau. A priest now stands above and the workers remain frozen through Ann's speech.*) Now during the Lawrence strike while all the mills were shut down, I was sent there to help. The workers in Lawrence, in the Lawrence mills, mostly were Italians and mostly were foreign born that come here for a better life and so forth, and a lot of them, when they were still noncitizens worked in the Lawrence mills. Many Americans, their offspring, many of their sons and their daughters worked in the mills too. Well, there was this Catholic priest. I'm not necessarily picking them out as against any other kind of minister. But during one of the big strikes, this particular priest was urging the workers. He says . . .

PRIEST: (*Deflated, the workers sit down one at a time during this speech.*) You should be thankful that you have jobs. You're foreigners you have come here from another country and the employers were good enough to give you jobs. You should be thankful to them for doing this.

ANN: And, uh, and at the same time—oh, and he says, by the way . . .

PRIEST: You should have nothing to do with that woman . . .

ANN: He was speaking about me.

PRIEST: . . . because she is the Red Flame from Hell!

ANN: And that became my nickname.

NEWSPAPER MAN ONE: Red Flame sets Lawrence ablaze!

ANN: Wherever I went, the newspapers picked it up—described me as the Red Flame.

NEWSPAPER MAN TWO: Why do they call you the Red Flame?

ANN: (*laughs, to audience*) I didn't have red hair. Well, uh, now I'm kind of gray.

NEWSPAPER MAN THREE: So, it's not the hair?

ANN: (*to the reporter*) No. (*to the audience*) Anyway, the publicity didn't have the effect that they thought among the workers, because the workers knew that the speeches I made talked about their wages, their working conditions, why the mills were beginning to move south.

NEWSPAPER MAN ONE: Red Flame sets Georgia ablaze!

ANN: (rolls her eyes at the reporter, then continues) Workers from Atlanta appealed to me to come and help them organize, because they were worse off than the northern workers. And cause I was quite good at it. I went to Georgia, one of the worst antilabor states in America, to organize a strike. (company hums "Solidarity Forever" and moves into a strike tableau) Now Georgia had this law that said:

PUBLIC OFFICIAL: Anyone who provokes, through either speech or writing, riots in the streets will be in violation of the antiinsurrection law.

ANN: "Riots" meant even peaceful demonstrations. So, I was arrested. (Two actors become police and pull Ann downright. One actor stands above as the judge, while the workers look on.)

JUDGE: And the punishment for violating the antiinsurrection law is . . . the death penalty.

REPORTER TWO: Red Flame to burn in the electric chair.

ANN: So there I was, eighteen or nineteen years old, and sentenced to death. They kept me in jail for seven weeks. My lawyers fought and argued, and finally forced the court to let me out on bail, even though it was a capital punishment case. So I made bail . . . and went on a national tour. (Ann sings "The Popular Wobbly" and the workers join in.) I went around and talked about labor unions and antiinsurrection laws and the working conditions of the textile industry.

SUPREME COURT JUSTICE: Eventually, the case came to the U.S. Supreme Court, and the antiinsurrection law was declared unconstitutional.

ANN: And my conviction was overturned. That is why I am still here today, and why I'm still going to:

ALL: FIGHT! (Musical reprieve of "The Popular Wobbly" takes us into the next scene.)


SCENE THREE: THE BOOK

JOAN: When I was a little kid, I went on picket lines with my parents. (Lights up on actors in a picket line. Young Joan is among them.) I remember picketing this store called Dutton's in what we now call the South End and they wouldn't hire, well then they were called Negroes, they wouldn't hire Negroes, so we picketed to get them to employ black people, and I remember the people walking by saying . . .

*PEOPLE ON THE STREET:* Go back to Russia!

*JOAN:* This had to be 1948, and I remember friends of mine on my street saying . . .

*GIRL ONE:* I can't play with you because Negroes go to your house.

*JOAN:* And when my mother was called before commissions. Her name was in the paper. She was named by the FBI. That was in the paper, too. And I remember kids saying . . .

*GIRL TWO:* I can't play with you, your mom's a Communist.

*JOAN:* I remember other kids saying . . .

*GIRL THREE:* Well, even though your mom's a Communist, my mom says she's nice, so I can play with you.

*JOAN:* I remember feeling that we were doing the right thing. I do remember always feeling her values were right. If I didn't do something that she wanted me to do, I felt really guilty. Once, on my way to school she said . . .

*MOTHER:* (*Lights up on Young Joan and her mother.*) I want you to take this book of Langston Hughes poetry and give it to your teacher. Tell her she should read from this every day during Negro History Month.

*YOUNG JOAN:* (*tentatively*) Okay.

*JOAN:* (*to audience*) What could I do? It was totally absurd of her to ask me to do this but she was my mother. I couldn't say, no. (*Young Joan and the other actors set up the classroom.*) So I got to school and put the book in my desk and thought about it every day. Maybe it wasn't *such* a bad idea. (*Lighting and sound effects indicate that this is a fantasy.*)

*YOUNG JOAN:* (*to the teacher as she enters*) Here, Mrs. Jones, I brought this book in for Negro History Month. My mother says you should read from it every day.

*MRS. JONES:* (*taking book*) Why, thank you, dear. What a wonderful idea. Children, see what Joan has brought in? Let's thank her. (*children clap*) You get an A+ for the year. (*The fantasy ends.*)

*JOAN:* (*To audience*) But the longer I sat there, the more it seemed like the worst idea ever. (*Lights and sound signal the second fantasy.*)

*YOUNG JOAN:* (*to Mrs. Jones*) Here, I brought this book in for Negro History Month. My mother says you should read from it every day.

*MRS. JONES:* (*backing away*) That's very nice, dear. (*to children, pointing at Young Joan*) COMMUNIST! Children, she's part of a Communist plot! (*Children scream and the fantasy ends.*)

*JOAN:* So, I put the book in my desk and it sat there for months. I was scared. One day, I went home and my mother asked . . .

*MOTHER:* Well, did your teacher read from the book?

*YOUNG JOAN:* No. I showed it to her. She said she couldn't do it because . . . she didn't have enough time.

*MOTHER:* Hmph!

*JOAN:* I felt so guilty. I should have done it. Why didn't I? I was nine years old. I had these very bigoted Boston schoolteachers. There were a number of things of that sort. (*Joan's Mother reads "Freedom 2" from Langston Hughes' book.*)


Scene Four: Accused

*KIM:* (*Piano music from "Strange Fruit" plays under Kim's monologue. Behind her actors set up a living room, sit and read. Young Kim is among them.*) I grew up with lots of books in our house. So, even though the outside world seemed to think the country was on the right track, there were hints that all was not right. My mother had this book with pictures of black children living under the most terrible conditions, sleeping on dirt floors. These people were so...neglected, and when you compared how they were forced to live with people I knew, you couldn't help but think, well, something has to be done. I mean, there were pictures of black men being lynched. Oh, and that song my mother used to sing, Strange Fruit. (*A cast member sings a verse of "Strange Fruit" as Kim listens. The piano continues under the following, as the actors begin stuffing envelopes.*) I was surrounded by adults who I felt would do anything to change the world and make it better. And I was allowed to sit in on night meetings when they were held at our house. There were lots of leaflets and petitions, and I would often join my mother on the picket line. I remember growing up to believe that you should speak out. It was a very open feeling. (*The actors begin leaving the living room in secrecy, one by one, throughout the following.*) My first sense that things were changing came when my parents told me not to let anyone in the house and not to talk to strangers. This was very different. Now, I was supposed to learn *not* to trust anyone, including my neighbors who were being questioned about my family's political activities. It was such a shock.

Once a musician named Paul Robeson gave a major concert at the State Park. (*voiceover of Robeson's opening speech at the concert*) Violence broke out, due to Robeson's presumably Communist beliefs. (*Recording of Robeson singing "Every Time I Feel the Spirit" plays while actors move in a slow motion riot. They freeze and Kim continues speaking while the music plays low under.*) I actually saw the film footage. The thing was that the police, who were supposedly there to keep order, were allowing the riot to happen. They just stood by and watched. And my stepfather was there. (*Actors move into a bus formation taking on the roles of people in Kim's story.*) He was on a bus that arrived at the concert when the crowd started throwing stones. The bus driver ducked to avoid the rocks, and my stepfather grabbed the wheel. I thought that was such a heroic thing to do. One rock hit him in the neck, but he kept hold of the wheel. Sometimes it's everyday folks who perform the most remarkable acts of bravery. This was a very big event in my life. (*music ends*)

Then, when I was eleven, my stepfather died and a lot of our friends came to his funeral. (*Slides of headlines about the Smith Act Trials are projected. Actors move into a funeral arrangement.*) Later, during the Smith Act Trials, the fact these people attended his funeral would be used as evidence against them. (*Several actors move apart from the group.*) My mother and I went to the trials. These were people we knew, good human beings, being put on trial for their beliefs. I began to view the country as a place of danger. (*The separated actors run off in different directions.*) Friends of mine were stopped by FBI agents, who tried to trick and even torture them into implicating their parents. I knew I could never stand up to that kind of interrogation so I felt the best way to keep my family safe was for me to *not* know as much as possible. (*One by one the slides go out during the following lines, and the remaining actors run off in various groupings.*) I stopped reading newspapers and watching newsreels. I stopped listening to conversations. I separated myself from the world in which I lived. I felt this was the best way to protect the people I loved. If I didn't know anything, I couldn't give anything away. My six-year-old brother was so terrified, he devised a plan to escape our house using the fire escape, so he could never be trapped by people who came to question him. It was his way of coping.

Then my mother was blacklisted. Of course they don't tell you, but one day they cut her character from the T.V. series she was in, and suddenly no one in New York would hire her. So she moved to Chicago to find work. I was sent to boarding school, where I had a mini-persecution of my own. (*In shadow we see a tableau of a student whispering to the principal.*) And what frightened me most about the incident was not the accusation, though I did nothing, it was the fact that it was all done in secret.

YOUNG KIM: (*stopping a girl in the hall*) Lori . . .

LORI: (*evasive*) Hi, Kim. Look, I'm late for gym. . . . See you . . . sometime.

YOUNG KIM: But I just . . . (*stops another girl*) Hey, Agnes, wait up.

AGNES: I can't.

YOUNG KIM: Please, just for a second. What is going on?

AGNES: I'm sorry, but I can't be . . .

YOUNG KIM: What!?

AGNES: I . . . I'm not supposed to talk to you.

YOUNG KIM: Why? God, just tell me.

AGNES: Well . . .

YOUNG KIM: Please.

AGNES: (*pause*) Okay, but let's get out of the hallway.

YOUNG KIM: (*They move.*) Now tell me.

AGNES: It's the thing with Mary Beth Johnson . . .

YOUNG KIM: What thing?

AGNES: Whatever you said to her, that, you know . . .

YOUNG KIM: No, I don't know.

AGNES: Well, I don't know either. But what ever you said, it drove her to commit suicide.

YOUNG KIM: What!? I just saw her go into the office.

AGNES: Well, she tried to kill herself. Anyway, we all had to go and tell her what we knew.

YOUNG KIM: About Mary Beth, everyone knows she's . . .

AGNES: About you.

YOUNG KIM: Me?

AGNES: You know . . . your political . . . whatever.

YOUNG KIM: But no one has asked me about any of this.

AGNES: Whatever it was, you shouldn't have said it to Mary Beth.

YOUNG KIM: But I didn't! Look, when was this supposed to have happened? That I said . . . whatever it was.

AGNES: Saturday afternoon. There were some girls in the lounge talking.

YOUNG KIM: Saturday afternoon . . . I wasn't even in the lounge then. People must know I wasn't there.

AGNES: She says you were, and now they're going to expel you.

YOUNG KIM: Expel? This is crazy. They haven't asked me anything. Nobody has said a word.

AGNES: Well, they figure cause your mom's . . . you know, that you must have done it.

KIM: (*to the audience*) That was enough. If they weren't going to confront me, I was going to them. I became my own advocate. After waiting for what felt like an eternity, I was finally called in to defend my case. (*Young Kim moves to the office. The principal stands above.*) Inside the office were the principal and . . . all of my teachers. (*Teachers march in wearing sportslike banners with either a L (for Left) or R (for Right). They take their positions Left and Right. Throughout the following scene, score is kept on the projection screens.*)

SPORTSCASTER: (*with a microphone*) Ladies and gentlemen we're here at the Meadow Creek School for the final face off between suspected Communist sympathizer: Kim Becker on the left . . .

TEACHERS ON LEFT: (*cheer*) Go Kim. Go Kim. Go Kim. Go!

SPORTSCASTER: And today's challenger: Mary Beth Johnson on the right.

TEACHERS ON RIGHT: (*cheer*) Go Mary Beth! Go Mary Beth! (*Teachers chant low under the following.*)

SPORTSCASTER: Kim looks scared, but determined. While everyone knows that Mary Beth has a history of being unstable . . . today she's poised and ready for a fight. Here comes the Principal, Mrs. Wetling. Let the battle begin.

PRINCIPAL: (*She tries her best to make everyone happy and hates confrontation.*) Now Kim, I hear you've been causing some trouble here at Meadow Creek.

KIM: No. I haven't done anything wrong.

PRINCIPAL: (*relieved*) Oh . . . well, good. I guess that settles that.

TEACHERS ON RIGHT: (*chant*) Kick Kim out. Kick her out.

PRINCIPAL: (*changes to a stern tone*) It has been brought to my attention that you made several inappropriate comments to Mary Beth Johnson last Saturday afternoon.

KIM: But . . .

TEACHERS ON RIGHT: Boo!

PRINCIPAL: Perhaps we should hear from Mary Beth.

TEACHERS ON RIGHT: (*chant*) Go Mary Beth. Go Mary Beth. (*Teachers continue low under the following.*)

SPORTSCASTER: The tension in this room is not to be believed. Mary Beth looks confident as she steps up to speak.

MARY BETH: (*glows with anticipation, then suddenly whimpers as she speaks*) Well, we were all talking in the lounge. And then Kim says, out of the blue, she says, "Your daddy is a dirty capitalist pig." And then she says, "people are starving and it's your daddy's fault, cause he's an invest-ment banker." (*Teachers on the Right hiss at Kim.*)

SPORTSCASTER: This round is not going well for Kim. She looks frightened and confused.

MARY BETH: And I felt so bad . . . that I . . . that I . . . that I . . . swallowed this whole bottle of aspirin. (*holds up bottle and then sinks into tears*)

TEACHERS ON LEFT: (*shaking their heads*) T-t-t-t-t-t-t-t.

TEACHERS ON RIGHT: (*chant*) Expel Kim! Expel Kim! (*During this Mary Beth stands and smiles triumphantly.*)

SPORTSCASTER: It looks like it's all over for Kim.

PRINCIPAL: (*blows whistle*) In light of this accusation, Kim, I have no other choice, but to . . .

YOUNG KIM: (*shouts*) WAIT!

ALL TEACHERS: (*murmur*)

SPORTCASTER: All eyes are on Kim as she steps up to speak. What will she say?!

YOUNG KIM: (*Young Kim makes a sign for them to stop.*) I wasn't in the lounge on Saturday. I was at the movies. Look, here's my ticket. (*She holds up the ticket.*)

TEACHERS ON LEFT: (*cheer wildly*) No more witch-hunts! No more witch-hunts!

SPORTSCASTER: Holy, moly! Look at that comeback!

PRINCIPAL: Well, I guess it was just one big . . . misunderstanding. Let's all go to the cafeteria.

TEACHERS ON RIGHT: (*chant*) Go Mary Beth. Go Mary Beth! (*Mary Beth slowly stands as if recovering from a punch and gets ready to take a swing.*)

SPORTSCASTER: Oh my Lord. Would you look at this. Mary Beth is com-ing back for more. She looks more determined than ever.

MARY BETH: Just one minute! Kim brainwashed the foreign students with her Communist crap.

PRINCIPAL: (*whines*) Oh no. (*back in control*) Kim, is this true?

YOUNG KIM: No . . . I . . . I volunteered to help a student with her history homework. That's all.

MARY BETH: She twists the readings to reflect her Communist ideas.

ADULT KIM: (*Everyone freezes as Adult Kim enters and speaks to the audi-ence.*) This made me furious. I specifically made the decision to focus strictly on vocabulary. I would never have let her know my beliefs. I felt that was unfair because she couldn't speak English very well.

*MARY BETH:* Just ask Yumiko Kashu.

*TEACHERS ON RIGHT:* (*running in circles around the stage while they chant*) Find Yumiko! Find Yumiko! (*Teachers on the Left go into a huddle formation.*)

*SPORTSCASTER:* (*over the chant*) The teachers on the Right are turning the school upside down looking for Yumiko Kashu. Will they find her in time? (*pause*) Yes! She's being dragged to the principal's office. What a fight! The principal is having trouble containing the crowd. I wouldn't want to be in her shoes. (*Yumiko stands frozen center stage.*)

*PRINCIPAL:* (*yells*) Quiet! (*calmer*) Now, Yumiko. Does Kim help you with your homework?

*YUMIKO:* Yes. Kim is very nice.

*TEACHERS ON RIGHT:* (*chant*) Kick Kim out! Kick her out!

*PRINCIPAL:* (*makes a sign to quiet them, and it works*) Shhh! And when Kim helps you, does she . . . change things?

*YUMIKO:* I'm sorry?

*PRINCIPAL:* Does she, say . . . negative things about . . . the United States?

*YUMIKO:* I don't understand. Maybe Kim can explain it to me. (*Teachers on the Left giggle.*)

*PRINCIPAL:* Look, Yumiko, does Kim tell you things . . . about the Soviet Union?

*YUMIKO:* No . . . we study Greece now. Do you want Kim to tell me about the Soviet Union, too?

*PRINCIPAL:* No!! (*takes a deep breath*) Yumiko, how does Kim help you study?

*YUMIKO:* Oh. She tells me what the words mean.

*PRINCIPAL:* That's all she does?

*YUMIKO:* Yes. She . . . translates the words for me. She is very nice.

*SPORTSCASTER:* There is a hush in the crowd, ladies and gentlemen. (*All teachers say "hush."*) After what's happened here so far. It's anybody's guess how this battle will end.

*PRINCIPAL:* I see. Well, Kim, I'll ask you to step outside the office, so that we can . . . figure it out. (*The company turn their backs and freeze during the following.*)

*ADULT KIM:* (*to audience*) Apparently, I had created quite a stir. While half the faculty assumed I must be guilty of something, the other half was afraid of getting caught up in a witch-hunt. They argued for what seemed to be forever. Then I was finally called back in.

SPORTSCASTER: This is it, folks. Kim's fate is about to be decided. Which side are you on? Let's listen in.

PRINCIPAL: Kim, after considering all that has been said today, and everyone's thoughts and feelings, and of course, what's best for the future of Meadow Creek . . . We've . . . I've . . . that is . . . you can stay at the school.

TEACHERS ON LEFT: (cheer wildly)

PRINCIPAL: On the condition that you and I meet once a week to discuss your "ideas." Is it agreed?

YOUNG KIM: Yes, Mrs. Wetling. (Teachers on the Left turn into circle formation and yell, "YES!!" Teachers on the Right move into a defensive huddle.)

SPORTSCASTER: That winds up the final match between Kim Becker and Mary Beth Johnson. For more accusations, stay tuned for the Smith Act Trials. So long for now. (Dream music starts as the actors move into their positions in the minefield.)

SCENE FIVE: THE MINEFIELD

KIM speaks slowly. Dream music with sounds of war plays under the following. As each character speaks, the actress playing her younger counterpart slowly moves from behind her into the minefield. The rest of the actors serve as obstacles in the minefield, moving almost imperceptibly.

KIM: (as Young Kim walks cautiously through the mist) My entire sense of the McCarthy era is of walking in a minefield—that sense of the wrong action hurting, not only yourself, but many people. My memories are like those of someone who has lived through a war, but I never have.

JOAN: (as Young Joan enters the fog) I was scared of losing my mother. Of being abandoned. Wicked separation problems. Never went to summer camp. Went once and they had to come get me. I was terrified something would happen while I was gone. I was terrified. People were in prison, people went underground. I had to be there to make sure everything's okay. Financial disaster, being blacklisted, my father's health, all that stuff. I was just a worried little kid. The FBI sat in front of our house and it was scary. Not in a physical sense, but emotionally, it was terrifying.

JUDITH: (as Young Judith enters the space) I would ask myself questions. I heard how many people who had gone underground had poison, so if they were found, they could kill themselves. Then they wouldn't have to be tortured or reveal the names of people they loved. So I thought about that, and I thought I would probably just kill myself and that . . . that was the solution.

*KIM:* I used to dream of walking in a minefield and never knowing where to step.

*ALL:* Never feeling safe. (*The company freezes then moves quickly off while the music plays under.*)

SCENE SIX: THE ARREST

YOUNG JOAN *and her mother* ELAINE *sit on a corner of the stage.* ELAINE *is reading to her daughter from the Langston Hughes book.* ELAINE *is in a nightgown. Her bathrobe covers* YOUNG JOAN. *They share the lines from "I Dream a World" as if reading a goodnight story.*

*JOAN:* There was a little satellite McCarthy committee here. I think it was run by a guy named Powers. But it was a mini, little McCarthy, H.U.A.C. thing. And my mother was called before that state investigating committee, and I remember one night the police came. (*Three actresses sing "Who's Going to Investigate the Man Who Investigates the Man Who Investigates Me," Andrews Sisters' style while the following action takes place. All movements are done as a dance: Police officers enter and knock on the door. Joan's mother gets up to answer the door. She peeks her head out. The officers enter violently. Under the direction of a head officer, they begin taking dozens of books off the shelves. Elaine is held back by two officers. Young Joan looks on in terror. The officers leave with their mimed boxes of books. Young Joan runs to hug her mother. The officers throw her off. She returns and puts the bathrobe over her mother's shoulders. They drag Elaine out of the apartment. Young Joan watches as her mother disappears from sight. The song continues as the police office is set up.*)

*JOAN:* Not only had they arrested my mother, they arrested our books—big piles of "subversive" books. She was in jail overnight, and this kind of funny anecdote happened. Women appreciate this.

*This scene is conducted in front of giant shadows. Lights up on* ELAINE *in the police station. She is being interrogated. The police shove imaginary book after book at her.*

*ELAINE:* I want to speak to my lawyer.

*OFFICER ONE:* We know you have ties to the Communist Party.

*ELAINE:* I have rights.

*OFFICER ONE:* Just tell us who's in your little circle of friends and you can go home tonight.

*ELAINE:* I want to speak . . .

*OFFICER ONE:* . . . to your lawyer. Yeah, I know. Frank, search her.

*OFFICER TWO:* Me? Shouldn't we get a woman?

*OFFICER ONE:* I said, search her. (*yells*) And can anybody get some coffee in here. We're going to be up all night with this one.

*ELAINE:* I want to speak to my . . .

*OFFICER ONE:* Would you shut up with the lawyer, already. Frank, I told you to search the broad.

*OFFICER TWO:* I . . . I feel weird.

*OFFICER ONE:* For Christ sake! I'll search her myself. (*The officer begins the search. Elaine protests.*) What the hell are you getting paid for, Frank? Huh? Unbelievable. (*feels something*) Wait a minute. What have we here? (*He pulls an imaginary tampon from Elaine's bathrobe pocket, then speaks to Elaine.*) And what might this be?

*ELAINE:* It's a . . . tampon.

*OFFICER ONE:* (*laughs smugly*) A tampon. Right. (*pause*) Frank, what's a tampon?

*OFFICER TWO:* (*too embarrassed to say*) Ahhh . . .

*OFFICER ONE:* Call in the squad.

*OFFICER TWO:* But . . .

*OFFICER ONE:* I said call the bomb squad. Now! (*Officer Two runs out.*) I bet the CIA will be very interested in this little device. What other weapons has the KGB planted on you? I asked you a question! (*Elaine tries to control her urge to laugh. Suddenly alarms are sounded, lights flash and a squad of men rush in with protective headgear. Officers One and Two and Joan are shoved aside, as the squad dissects the tampon.*)

*SQUAD LEADER:* (*removing his hood*) It's safe now. We've managed to deactivate the device. (*He calls to a janitor who is sweeping.*) You there.

*JANITOR:* Me?

*SQUAD LEADER:* Bring this device to the lab. (*The Janitor crosses and picks up the tampon. As he runs out, he drops it.*) Be careful, you idiot!

*JANITOR:* (*starts to leave then turns*) But it's a tampon. (*The Squad Leader looks confused. The Janitor shrugs his shoulders and leaves. Musical reprieve of "Who's Going to Investigate" serves as a transition to the next scene, along with slides/film clips of the McCarthy Hearings.*)

SCENE SEVEN: THE LUCY SHOW

*JEAN:* Now, I was born at the height of the baby boom, so I don't have any memories of the McCarthy era. Just the stories my mother told me. When I was growing up, I remember her always going to meetings, or having meetings at our house. It seemed as though she was on a million committees—the NAACP, the Fair Housing Committee. She said she had some kind of disease. It was . . . what did she call it? (*remembers*) "Committee-itis." She would walk into a meeting with full intentions of resigning from, whatever committee it was. And before the meeting had ended . . . she had somehow been made the new chair of that committee. Committee-itis. I think it's genetic. Anyway, my favorite story was about the day my oldest sister was born, which was

*Voicings, (left to right) Eva Rodman and Annette (Rodman) Lement, family photo, photographer unknown.*

in 1953. And as she would tell the story, I couldn't get the *I Love Lucy Show* out of my head. You know the one, when Lucy's pregnant with Little Ricky and she's wearing this little white puffy, maternity blouse, and Ricky's holding the little suitcase and they're ready to go the hospital. (*The actors enter wearing flowers on their outside wrists, and move as Hollywood show girls. They enter singing the "I Love Lucy" theme: "I love Lucy, and she loves me." They stop momentarily, as no one knows the rest of the words. After a brief moment they continue the song singing "da da da." They form a heart. The company runs off revealing Lucy on a bench very pregnant. She mimes eating a box of chocolates. She deals a deck of cards and gets chocolate all over them. She wipes the chocolate off on various places, making more and more of a mess. Throughout the "bit," we hear canned laughter provided by the actors off stage. Laughter and applaud signs are flashed at appropriate times.*)

LUCY: (*yells to Ricky*) Ricky!

RICKY: (*from off*) Just a moment, Dear.

LUCY: (*yells*) Ricky, you promised you'd play cards with me.

RICKY: (*off*) In a minute, honey. I told you, I have to finish this arrangement, before I go to the club.

LUCY: (*yells*) Ricky, if you don't come and play cards with me, I'll . . . I'll call my mother and ask her to move in here till the baby's born, (*starts to cry*) so I'll have someone to play with, and I won't have to sit here by myself.

RICKY: (*enters and goes to her*) Now, Lucy you don't have to do that.

LUCY: (*crying*) It's just that I feel so fat . . . and I can't go to the club . . . and you won't play cards with me.

RICKY: Oh, honey, I'll play cards with you.

LUCY: (*sniffling*) You will?

RICKY: Yes.

LUCY: I love you, Ricky. (*She hugs him, getting chocolate all over him—canned laughter.*)

RICKY: Look what you're doing! (*He speaks in Spanish.*) Lucy, you've got chocolate over everything.

LUCY: You sit right there, I'll clean it up. (*She stands and bends to pick up a cloth, but gets a labor pain. Her head shoots up and her eyes get big.*) Ohhhh.

RICKY: Lucy, what is it?

LUCY: Ricky . . .

RICKY: What? What's happening?

LUCY: Ricky, I think it's . . .

*RICKY:* What?

*LUCY:* Ricky, it's the baby.

*RICKY:* The baby? (*Lucy nods.*) He's coming? (*Lucy nods.*) Now? (*Lucy nods.*) AHHHH!! Oh my God! Oh my God! (*He starts running around the room in a panic.*) Keep calm, Honey. I got everything under control. (*He takes deep breaths and then runs out of the room speaking Spanish very quickly.*)

*LUCY:* (*Lucy calmly walks over to the phone.*) Gladys, honey, give me Murray Hill 6-5198. . . . That's right, Gladys, it's the baby. . . . Yes, I remember when you had little Henry . . . (*She puts on a jacket.*) Well, not everyone says he's trouble. . . . No, dear. . . . Honey, Can you put me through to the doctor? . . . Thank you, Gladys. I hope to see you there, too. (*pause*) Hello, Dr. Rose, . . . This is Mrs. Ricardo . . .

*RICKY:* (*bursts into the room with a little suitcase half closed with a negligee hanging out. He runs into the phone cord, accidentally disconnecting it. He then grabs Lucy and sits her down on the couch.*) Lucy, honey, what are you doing on your feet. You sit here while I call the doctor.

*LUCY:* But, Ricky . . .

*RICKY:* No buts, you sit right there. (*He fumbles in the phone cord, again speaking Spanish very fast, with phrases like "We're having a baby," coming through in English. Suddenly, there is a very loud knock on the door.*) How did he get here so fast? (*Lucy starts to cross to the door. Ricky tries to stop her.*) No, Lucy, don't move. I'll get it. (*He trips over the phone cord.*)

*LUCY:* (*crosses to the door, and opens it*) May I help you?

*FBI AGENT ONE:* Are you Mrs. Ricardo?

*LUCY:* I am?

*RICKY:* Who is it, Lucy?

*MRS. CARMICHAEL:* (*from off*) What's all the racket down there?

*LUCY:* (*shouts up*) Nothing, Mrs. Carmichael. Go back to bed.

*FBI AGENT TWO:* We'd like you to come downtown to the station with us.

*RICKY:* What are you talking about?

*MRS. CARMICHAEL:* (*off*) There's *something* going on down there.

*LUCY:* (*shouts up*) Shove it, Mrs. Carmichael. (*sound of a door slamming*)

*FBI AGENT ONE:* We have a few questions, about your Communist activities. (*Lucy makes her famous "eww" sound.*) So you if you don't mind coming with us.

*RICKY:* Communist activities! The only thing *Red* about Lucy is her hair. (*canned laughter*)

*FBI AGENT TWO:* We'll determine that, Mr. Ricardo.

LUCY: (*gets that "I've got an idea" look in her eye*) Well, I'd love to talk to you, gentlemen . . .

RICKY: Lucy, what are you saying?

LUCY: But, I'm just about to give birth. (*She points to her pregnant stomach.*) So if you gentlemen will excuse us.

FBI AGENTS ONE & TWO: (*very embarrassed, fumbling over each other*) Oh . . . um . . . of course . . . we'll catch you at a better time . . . um . . . good luck with the kid and all . . . (*They leave.*)

RICKY: (*moves to her*) Lucy, you were wonderful.

LUCY: Was I?

RICKY: (*hugs her*) You were great.

LUCY: I was, wasn't I? Did you see how those FBI agents turned red when I told them about the baby? (*Ricky pauses for a second, then laughs uncontrollably.*) What! What are you laughing at? Ricky tell me!!

RICKY: (*gets his laughter under control*) Lucy, you just called the FBI: RED!!

*They both laugh—LUCY with her famous laugh. Actors enter with the "I Love Lucy" theme—"da da da." This time the heart reveals LAURA standing downstage.*

## SCENE EIGHT: A VOICE OF RESISTANCE

LAURA: They wanted to get me as a Communist, and I took the Fifth Amendment. It's my right not to tell them who I am. That is a matter of my own personal opinion. That's what the Constitution says, of the United States. We are not going to lay down by the witch hunters. (*corrects herself*) In front of the witch hunters, "by the witch hunters," I said. (*She laughs.*) It's a long, long struggle.

## SCENE NINE: THE ROSENBERGS' ARREST

*Various headlines and newspaper clips about the arrest and the start of the case are displayed on slides. A drum punctuates each speech.*

ANNOUNCER: July 17, 1950: FBI agents reported to Hoover on the day of Julius Rosenberg's arrest:

FBI AGENT: Ethel, his wife, made a typical Communist remonstrance, demanding a warrant and the right to call an attorney. She was told to keep quiet and get in the other room with the children.

Voicings, *(left to right) Ethel Rosenberg and Julius Rosenberg, photo by Roger Higgins.*

*ANNOUNCER:* August 11, 1950: Myles Lane of the Justice Department to reporters, the day before Ethel Rosenberg's arrest:

*LANE:* Her crime jeopardizes the lives of every man, woman, and child in this country.

*ANNOUNCER:* August 12: *New York Times*, Ethel Rosenberg's arrest:

*REPORTER:* Atomic spy plot is laid to a woman.

*Lights up on* LAURA *sitting by the fire, reading a letter.*

*LAURA:* Well, they were in separate cells. They used to write notes to each other and poems. They were like two lovers in jail, under the most awful circumstances possible.

*Lights up on* ETHEL *and* JULIUS *in their separate cells.*

*JULIUS:* August 12, 1950. Dearest Ethel, I heard the news over the radio last night and after strenuous efforts to see you or contact you I've been given permission to write this letter. Let me know as soon as possible how you are feeling. How are the children? Has any provision been made for them? I am fine and all's well. I expect the lawyer to see me this morning and I'll instruct him to send you commissary money, newspapers and all the little things he can do to make it easier. Tell me your plans for the children and I'll try to have the lawyer arrange a meeting for us to decide on the children. Keep a stiff upper lip. All my love. Your Julius.

ETHEL: August 12, 1950. My dearest darling Julie, By now you must know what has happened to me. Darling, I wish I could say that I am cool, calm and collected but the fact is that although, contrary to newspaper reports, I have not been hysterical at any time, I have shed many anxious tears on behalf of the children and have been feeling badly that I won't be seeing you on Sunday. My heart cries aloud for you and the children. Now indeed it is harder to be inside than out because each of us knows the other is not free to care for our dears. How unfortunate it was that I never got around to discussing arrangements for them with the proper people. I had been planning to do that very thing this week so that the kids should be subjected to as little strain as possible, in the event I was detained—and I must confess my mind does leap ahead to the frightening possibilities for them. However, I guess I will feel lots better after I see Mr. Bloch and ask him to get in touch with those people who can help us in the matter of the care of the children. By all means, sweetheart if you have any ideas about this and/or any of our other problems, please communicate with our lawyer and also write me about same.

Sweetheart, I talk with you every night before I fall asleep and cry because you can't hear me. And then I tell myself that you too must be choking with the same frustration and wondering if I can hear you. Darling, we mustn't lose each other or the children, mustn't lose our identities. I try to think of the good, fine life we've led all these years and I am agonized with my longing to go on leading it. All my love and my most devoted thoughts to you, my dearest loved one. Please write me as soon as you can. I love you, Ethel.

(A sound cue of cell doors closing gives the sense that time has passed.) August 29, 1950. My dearest darling Julie, I am hoping that by now you have received my second letter. By now I know that my first one finally reached you. Oh darling, even though we were able to spend some time together the day we went to court, it seemed to me when I had returned here that there were so many other ways I might have expressed my feelings to you, so many other things I might have said. So let me say them now, my dear one. And yet, I couldn't ever say enough what pride and love and deep regard for you I feel. What you wrote me about ourselves as a family, and what that family means to you made my eyes fill. There came to me such an abiding sense of faith and joy, such a sure knowledge of the rich meaning our lives have held that I was suddenly seized with an overwhelming desire to . . . (*They turn to each other and, the lines begin to overlap.*)

*JULIUS:* . . . see you and say it to you and kiss you with all my heart. Sweetheart, we must go on pouring out all that we feel towards each other, in our letters as I know how this strengthens the deep bond between us.

*ETHEL:* That bond you described as well in your last writing.

*JULIUS:* How frustrating it is, though when we have been accustomed to day-to-day association to have only this means of communication.

*ETHEL:* I treasure the time we spent together last Wednesday—which already seems so long ago—and can't wait for our next meeting.

*JULIUS:* Love you sweetheart.

*ETHEL:* Your, Ethel. (*Ethel's theme plays. They turn away as they realize they are indeed alone, as lights fade.*)

ACT TWO
SCENE ONE: UNANSWERED QUESTIONS

*A theme song plays, and a slide that reads "Unanswered Questions, 1998" is projected. Characters are in today's dress.*

*HOST:* Welcome to "Unanswered Questions." The show that answers the most difficult questions of the century—in a fifteen-minute format. (*overly dramatic*) According to Hugh W. Hunter of the Yale Herald "The Rosenbergs were sent to the electric chair on June 19, 1953, after what then FBI Director J. Edgar Hoover called: The Trial of the Century." The Rosenbergs, who were suspected to be Communist sympathizers during the Red Scare of the 1940s and 50s, were tried for allegedly transmitting the secrets of the Manhattan Project—the scientific effort that produced the atom bomb—to the Soviet Union. Today's question is: Were the Rosenbergs guilty? Now to help us answer this question we've selected people from our audience, people like you. Let's begin with you Ms . . .

*JONES:* Jones.

*HOST:* Ms. Jones, were the Rosenbergs guilty?

*JONES:* Umm . . . Were they the ones that had that day care center?

*HOST:* Nnno . . . We'll get back to Ms. Jones.

*KATZINSKY:* Excuse me, I don't mean to interrupt, but you said the Rosenbergs were tried for transmitting the secrets of the Manhattan Project, or in effect "the Bomb."

*HOST:* That's correct, Ms . . .

*KATZINSKY:* Katzinsky. See, that's the thing. They were actually tried for conspiracy to commit espionage. *Conspiracy*, that's like saying they had a conversation about it.

*MILLER:* Wasn't it her brother or someone who implicated them?

*KATZINSKY:* There were two witnesses, David and Ruth Greenglass—Ethel's brother and sister-in-law—who were both facing the death penalty if they didn't testify against the Rosenbergs. At first, Greenglass even said his sister was innocent, and then he changed his story.

*HOST:* Yes. But they were found guilty of selling the bomb.

*KATZINSKY:* No. On the basis of these two, unreliable witnesses and some very shaky evidence, like a Jell-O box, the jury found them guilty of conspiracy. Then Judge Kaufman comes along and sentences them for selling the secret of the atomic bomb, which even all the scientists say is ridiculous, causing the Korean War, and causing the future deaths of millions of people.

*BELIOT:* You know, you people on the left keep saying that the Rosenbergs were martyrs. But the truth is, it came out last year that they were guilty.

*MILLER:* I saw that in the papers.

*HOST:* So you disagree with our guest, Ms . . .

*BELIOT:* Mrs. Beliot. Now we finally have proof that they were guilty.

*KATZINSKY:* Guilty of what, exactly?

*BELIOT:* Guilty. A Soviet agent, Alexander Feklisov, admitted that he met Julius Rosenberg on a regular basis from 1943–1946. And that Rosenberg passed on secrets to the Soviets.

*KATZINSKY:* All right, let's say you buy everything Feklisov says. I personally happen to be suspicious of his motives, but for the sake of argument, let's say it's all true. At the very worst, he says that Julius Rosenberg gave him very low-level stuff, information that wasn't of any real use. *And* he says that he never met with Ethel Rosenberg and that she had nothing to do with it. So right there, a man was executed for something that normally he would receive a jail sentence. And on top of that, an innocent woman was killed.

*MILLER:* Yeah. . . . But what about those papers the Ve . . . the something papers that were just released.

*KATZINSKY:* The Venona Papers.

*MILLER:* Yes. That was it.

*HOST:* Miss Jones, you wanted to say something.

*JONES:* (*proudly*) Well, my sister went to Verona once . . . (*She looks around and sees everyone staring at her.*) when she was in High School.

*HOST:* (*pause*) I see. Yes, what about the Venona Papers? They were *communiqués* sent by Soviet agents in the United States to the Soviet Union, during World War II.

*BELIOT:* They were intercepted by U.S. Intelligence and decoded. And they say point blank that the Rosenbergs were the masterminds of a spy ring and that they recruited other spies.

*HOST:* Miss Katzinsky, no doubt you have something to add.

*KATZINSKY:* First of all, if you actually read the papers, which I have, you'll notice some very peculiar things.

*HOST:* Such as?

*KATZINSKY:* Well, of course the *communiqués* are written in code. Then the agents' names are coded. So in a sense, it's a double code—because the KGB took great pains to make sure their agents weren't discovered. Now the U.S. agents claim that the code name for Julius Rosenberg was "Liberal." And when you read through the stack of papers you'll see the name "Liberal" used dozens of times. Now in this one particular communiqué it says that "Liberal" recommended the wife of his wife's brother, Ruth Greenglass. Thus pointing directly to Julius Rosenberg.

*BELIOT:* Exactly!

*KATZINSKY:* If you were a KBG agent, would you send a *communiqué* to Moscow that explicitly gives the name of two agents? I don't think so. You'd be shot.

*BELIOT:* You people will grab at anything, even when the evidence stares you in the face.

*HOST:* What about it, Ms. Katzinsky? Are you in denial?

*KATZINSKY:* Look, once again, even if you take the Venona Papers at face value, they clear Ethel Rosenberg. They say, due to her health, "Liberal's wife does not work," meaning she isn't an agent. And once again, the information allegedly passed on by Julius Rosenberg was insignificant. The papers mention an antenna. And another thing, you have to remember that the Soviets were our allies during World War II, against Hitler.

*HOST:* Well, we are running out of time. So I'll pose the big question: (*drum roll*) Were the Rosenbergs guilty? Ms. Miller?

*MILLER:* Me . . . well . . . I don't know . . . I mean, there doesn't seem to be any evidence against Ethel. But there's . . . um . . . all this incriminating stuff against Julius. But it's not really clear what exactly he . . .

HOST: We're running out of time, Ms. Miller. Just answer the question: yes or no.

MILLER: (*starts to panic*) I . . . Oh, gosh . . . I just don't know. (*She starts to cry.*)

*the sound of a buzzer*

HOST: (*trying to cover*) Well, it looks as if . . . we have a tie. We'll just have to invite the Rosenbergs on next week's show, and ask them. (*All the guests turn to him in horror.*) Oh, I guess it's too late for that. (*suddenly bright, the theme song plays under*) Tune in next week to "Unanswered Questions," the show that answers the most difficult questions of the century—in a fifteen-minute format. (*theme song up to cover transition to next scene*)

SCENE TWO: OFFICE FOR CLEMENCY

*The year is 1951. The three women are busy at work—mimed. One is taking notes from the* New York Times. *One is at the typewriter. The third is stuffing envelopes.*

NORA: (*The scene is the office for clemency. Nora sits with the* New York Times.) We used to get the *New York Times* every day and I read the reports of the Rosenberg trial as it was going on. And what sprung out at me was Elizabeth Bentley, who was a paid informant for the government. It was her testimony that established a so-called fact that being a Communist was equal to being a traitor. In other words, your allegiance was not here, it was to the Soviet Union. And so that startled me and disturbed me. Because I knew it wasn't true. And I felt that the case itself was not proved. That we had to come to the defense of the Rosenbergs, because there was a terrible, a terrible *mis*-justice that was already in the works. And that summer, the *National Guardian* had a series of articles exposing what was in back of the Rosenberg case. So a number of people around the Dorchester, Roxbury, Mattapan area where I was living, in a modest apartment in a three-decker, we got together to talk about this. And early that fall, a professor named Stephan Love, spoke at the Harvard Law School. So I was asked if I would take notes, I knew shorthand, which was just like knowing another language, and I have used it all my life since. (*She hands notes to Anna who takes them and types them up.*)

ANNA: (*at the typewriter*) And then, we, we just started having an office. We got an office on Mass. Ave. We had practically no money, any of us. I think my husband Paul and I were among the poorest ones cause he had been, it was a tough time and he had been working in unions and we had come back to Boston, and there were just no jobs around. So they offered to have me work for the cause for thirty-five dollars a week. It was supposed to be a part-time job, but when you are committed to something there is no time limit on what you do. My son was about six years old then. We were involved on the case for a few years and he was eight when they were executed. It was a difficult time. There was an old typewriter somebody had given the office. We didn't have any money to have letterheads printed. So every time I wrote a letter to a rabbi or minister, a union or lawyers, I typed the letterhead and I figured out the exact spacing so I wouldn't have to re-center for each line. (*Anna hands the typed page to Carol who is stuffing envelopes.*)

CAROL: (*stuffs the paper into envelopes*) Well, a committee in New York printed the complete transcript of the trial, amounting to ten little thin books. And Professor Love had folded down pages over one hundred times, of, of irregular, I'll call it, irregular actions by Judge Kaufman. I mean there were so many strange things. He, the judge, interjected himself to help out any prosecution witness, putting words in their mouth and helping them along in what they were trying to say. And people can second guess poor Emmanuel Bloch, who worked like a tiger to defend those people. So, it was just, the whole thing was so tragic, and we were completely dedicated to trying to get some kind of either a new trial or something, and appealing to the Supreme Court.

NORA: We made appeals to all kinds of people around Boston.

ANNA: At one point, I mean there's funny things that you do, at one point we looked up addresses in the phone book of everybody named Rosenberg.

ALL THREE: We tried all kinds of things.


SCENE THREE: THE GIRLS' ROOM


*A school buzzer sounds as actors run on giggling in pairs from opposite ends of the stage. They run to an imaginary mirror downcenter and primp for a moment before taking their positions as the walls and sinks of the girls' room. YOUNG JUDITH and JULIE are the last to enter. They freeze in a pose under the following.*


JUDITH: When I was in junior high, my social studies class held forums on current events. I remember one particular day we were told that we would be discussing the Rosenberg case that afternoon. Right before class I happened to bump into Julie Tanner in the bathroom. She was in front of the mirror, as usual, combing her hair and putting on lipstick. Julie Tanner was very popular. She had many friends and hung out with the "in crowd." She was beautiful, trendy and outgoing. She was everything that I wasn't. But we did have one thing in common and today was the day to show it. So I turned to Julie and I said:

YOUNG JUDITH: Julie . . .

JULIE: (*half paying attention to Judith, half to herself*) Yes . . .

YOUNG JUDITH: You know how they're going to be talking about the Rosenbergs in social studies today?

JULIE: Yes.

YOUNG JUDITH: Well, I know that your family, like mine, stands behind their innocence and is really involved with trying to save them from execution. My mother told me that your family has raised a lot of money in support for their clemency.

JULIE: Oh, yes, tons of money.

YOUNG JUDITH: Well, today in class I would like to stand up and say how I believe the Rosenbergs are innocent.

JULIE: Yes . . .

YOUNG JUDITH: But people never listen to me. And I was thinking, well, since you are so popular, that if you stood up then the rest of the class would listen to you.

JULIE: Oh, yes.

YOUNG JUDITH: So if I stand up, you will stand up with me, then?

JULIE: Of course I will.

YOUNG JUDITH: Oh great. I need you to promise me though, because I'm not going to do it without you.

JULIE: Of course, I'll go with you.

YOUNG JUDITH: (*holding out her pinky*) Promise?

JULIE: (*taking hold of Judith's pinky*) Pinky. (*exit*)

JUDITH: (*to audience*) So I was really excited at that point that Julie was going to get up there in front of the class with me. I even tried to make myself look a little bit more glamorous. (*She fixes herself in the mirror, imitating Julie. At the sound of the bell, walls and sinks transform into students in class.*) When class began and the teacher announced:

TEACHER: Good afternoon class. Today we are going to be talking about the case of Julius and Ethel Rosenberg. Does anyone have anything to say about the Rosenberg spy ring?

JULIE: (*Young Judith looks to Julie who whispers back.*) You go first.

YOUNG JUDITH: (*whispers*) You promise to back me up?

JULIE: (*whispers*) I said, yes.

TEACHER: Did anyone do the reading last night?

JUDITH: I raised my hand with poised confidence and took my place at the head of the class. I stood there and said:

YOUNG JUDITH: I believe that the Rosenbergs have been wrongly accused . . . (*pause, quiet laughter*) I believe that the Rosenbergs are innocent. (*scattered laughter*) And I know I'm not the only one who feels this way. (*More laughter as the class becomes an ugly laughing mob, and the teacher joins in.*)

JUDITH: I looked toward Julie to signal her to come up to the front with me. She didn't budge. I could feel my face get redder as more and more kids continued laughing at me. I thought, c'mon Julie, stand up here with me. The kids will listen to you. But, to my horror, not only did she not stand up here with me, (*Julie joins the mob.*) but she began laughing alongside everybody else. I never felt so betrayed and so alone. I stepped off the platform and the laughter slowly ceased. (*school bell rings*) Later that day, I bumped into Julie again in the bathroom.

YOUNG JUDITH: Julie, why didn't you get up there with me? You promised me that you would.

JULIE: (*fake sympathy*) I know, I would have stood up there with you, but I saw how everyone was laughing at you. And I just didn't want them to laugh at me, too. You understand, don't you?

YOUNG JUDITH: No, I don't. Your whole family is working so hard on behalf of Ethel and Julius—sacrificing their time and money—and you don't even have the courage to stand up for it.

JULIE: No, it's not that. I just didn't want to upset anyone. I just want everyone to like me, that's all.

JUDITH: (*angrily speaking Young Judith's thoughts*) I can't believe you promised me and then you turned around and laughed at me.

JULIE: (*comforting*) Oh, it's not really a big deal. Really. (*Julie takes her place as part of the wall.*)

JUDITH: And she left. I never did speak to her again after that day. It made me wonder, though, how many more Julie Tanners were out there, afraid to speak out, afraid to be their own voice amidst all the madness? Afraid. (*A buzzer sounds and the actors freeze, covering their faces with crossed hands, and then move quickly off.*)

SCENE FOUR: SENTENCING

*ANNOUNCER:* At a February 1951 Congressional committee on atomic energy, six months after Ethel Rosenberg's arrest, U.S. attorney Myles Lane said:

*LANE:* The case is not strong against Mrs. Rosenberg. But for the purpose of acting as a deterrent, I think it is very important that she be convicted, too—and given a stiff sentence.

*(ETHEL and JULIUS stand downcenter listening to their sentence. Their focus is center, above the heads of the audience. The actor playing KAUF-MAN sits facing upstage on a platform above and behind them. He speaks into a microphone. A slide of KAUFMAN is seen above him.)*

*ANNOUNCER:* On April 5, 1951, Julius and Ethel Rosenberg were found guilty of conspiracy to commit espionage. Judge Kaufman handed down the following sentence:

*KAUFMAN:* The issue of punishment in this case is presented in a unique framework of history. It is so difficult to make people realize that this country is engaged in a life-and-death struggle with a completely different system. This struggle is not only manifested externally between these two forces, but this case indicates quite clearly that it also involves the employment by the enemy of secret as well as overt outspoken forces among our own people. All of our democratic institutions are, therefore, directly involved in this great conflict. I believe that never at any time in our history were we ever confronted to the same degree that we are today with such a challenge to our very existence. The punishment to be meted out in this case must therefore serve the maximum interest for the preservation of our society against these traitors in our midst.

Julius and Ethel Rosenberg, I consider your crime worse than murder. Plain, deliberate, contemplated murder is dwarfed in magnitude by comparison with the crime you have committed. The evidence indicated quite clearly that Julius Rosenberg was the prime mover in this conspiracy. However, let no mistake be made about the role which his wife Ethel Rosenberg played in this conspiracy. Instead of deterring him from pursuing his ignoble cause, she encouraged and assisted the cause. She was a mature woman—almost three years older than her husband and almost seven years older than her younger brother. She was a full-fledged partner in this crime. Indeed the defendants Julius and Ethel Rosenberg placed their devotion to their causes above their own personal safety and were conscious that they were sacrificing their own children, should their misdeeds be detected—all of which did not deter them from pursuing their course. Love for their cause dominated their lives—it was even greater than their love for their children.

Your spying has already caused the Communist aggression in Korea, with the resultant casualties exceeding fifty thousand and who knows but that millions more of innocent people must pay the price of your treason. By your betrayal you undoubtedly have altered the course of history to the disadvantage of our country. By immeasurably increasing the chances of atomic war, you may have condemned to death tens of millions of innocent people all over the world. It is not in my power, Julius and Ethel Rosenberg, to forgive you. Only the Lord can find mercy for what you have done. The sentence of the Court upon Julius and Ethel Rosenberg is, for the crime for which you have been convicted, you are hereby sentenced to the punishment of death, and it is ordered upon some day within the week beginning with Monday, May 21, you shall be executed according to law.

SCENE FIVE: THE ROSENBERGS AT SING SING

ANNOUNCER: Ethel Rosenberg was transferred to the Death House at Sing Sing, and was housed in solitary confinement, as the only female prisoner in the Condemned Cells. Immediately, their lawyer, Emanuel Bloch filed in court for a writ of habeas corpus. In her supporting affidavit, she stated:

ETHEL: (She stands center stage.) My removal to and detention in the Sing Sing Death House was made with the object and purpose of demoralizing my spirit and overcoming my will to resist efforts of the government to compel me to admit guilt of the crime for which I have been convicted although I am innocent of any such charge. I am sealed in the gray walls of this prison as if in a tomb. I am alone in an entire building except for the matron who guards me. I see no other human being from morning to night and from night to morning. I have no occupation other than to sit immured in the aching soundlessness of my narrow cell. I have no recreation other than to walk on a bare patch of ground, surrounded by walls so high that my only view is a bare patch of sky. Sometimes I can see an airplane passing by; sometimes, a few birds; sometimes, I hear the noise of a train in the distance. Otherwise, there is always dead silence. The power to transform a vital human being into a caged animal is a power to coerce that rivals the deliberate infliction of physical torture and pain.

*Lights up on* ETHEL *and* JULIUS *in their cells.*

ETHEL: April 17, 1951. My very own dearest husband, I don't know when I've had such a time bringing myself to write you. My brain seems to have slowed to all but a complete halt under the weight of the myriad impressions that have been stamping themselves upon it minute upon minute, hour upon hour, since my removal here. I feel, on the one hand, a sharp need to share all that burdens my mind and heart and so bring to naught, make invalid the bitter physical reality of our separation, yet am stabbed by the implacable and desolate knowledge that the swift spinning of time presents a never-to-be-solved enigma.

JULIUS: Precious Woman, Ethel, my darling, you are truly a great, dignified and sweet person. Tears fill my eyes as I try to put my sentiments on paper. I can only say that life has been worthwhile because you have been beside me. I firmly believe that we are better people because we stood up with courage, character and confidence through a very grueling trial and a most brutal sentence, all because we are innocent. All the filth, lies and slanders of this grotesque political frame-up, in a background of world hysteria, will not in any way deter us, but rather spur us on until we are completely vindicated. We didn't ask for this; we only wanted to be left alone, but the gauntlet was laid down to us and with every ounce of life in our bodies we will fight till we are free.

ETHEL: (*The two letters begin to overlap.*) I shall seek to console myself by recounting for you all that it is humanly possible for me to do, at one writing or another, though the incident described, the thought circumvented, the emotion captured be not of that exact moment's making.

JULIUS: Honey, I think of you constantly. I hunger for you. I want to be with you. It is so painful that such a great hurt can only mean that I love you with every fiber of my being. I can only repeat over and over again that the thought of you more than compensates for this pain because of all the happiness you have brought me as my wife. Sweetheart, I can't let go of you; you are so dear to me. If you are able to get just part of the sustenance you engender in me I am sure you will have the strength to withstand the hardships that face us.

*ETHEL:* Darling, do I sound a bit cracked? Actually, I am serious about it and find that I must at least express my deep-seated frustration so that you will comprehend, all I must endure in order to "wrest from my locked spirit my soul's language." As you see, sweetheart, I have already embarked on the next lap of our history-making journey. Already there appear the signs of my growing maturity. The bars of my large, comfortable cell hold several books, the lovely, colorful cards—including your exquisite birthday greeting to me—that I accumulated at the House of Detention line the top ledge of my writing table to pleasure the eye and brighten the spirit, the children's snapshots are taped onto a "picture frame" made of cardboard, and smile sweetly upon me whenever I so desire.

*JULIUS:* Now I'd like to talk about our greatest possession, our two dears. I got a wonderful letter from Michael and it moved me very deeply. I promptly wrote, reassuring him of our love and answering his two questions on a level he could comprehend. I told him we were found guilty and I also explained about the appeal to the higher courts and let him know everything will finally come out all right. That we want very much to see him and we are making every effort to get permission from the court for us to have a visit with the children. On the whole I think Michael will be able to understand. I did not tell him of our sentence. I said we will tell him all about our case when we see him. It is cruel to be separated from our children but it is good to know they are well and growing up.

*ETHEL:* Within me there begins to develop the profoundest kind of belief that somehow, somewhere, I shall find that "courage, confidence and perspective" I shall need to see me through days and nights of bottomless horror, of tortured screams I may not utter, of frenzied longings I must deny! Julie dearest, how I wait upon the journey's end and our triumphant return to that precious life from which the foul monsters of our time have sought to drag us!

*JULIUS:* It all seems so unreal, but yet the cold reality of the steel bars are all around me. I eat, sleep, read and walk four paces back and forth in my cell. I do a lot of thinking about you and the children and I intend to write at least once a week to each of you. My family is one hundred percent behind us and it encourages me. I know as time goes on more and more people will come to our defense and help set us free of this nightmare. I caress you tenderly and send all my love.

*BOTH:* Darling, I love you.

*ANNOUNCER:* On May 16, 1951, Julius was also transferred to the Sing Sing Death House.

ETHEL *sings "What Shines from my Cell," by Edith Segal.*

*ANNA:* During that period, we read the letters as they were being . . . some of them were published while they were still in jail and were writing to each other. And I, having been separated from my husband when he was in jail, and knowing the stiffness, the stiffness in expressing his feelings. I read into those letters by Julius, you know, the hesitancy about expressing his feelings or his love or things like that, and how they opened up. Now maybe only because it had happened to me on a much lesser scale, much less dangerous scale.

ETHEL *sings "Ave Maria." Julius' letter overlaps the end of the song.*

*JULIUS:* My Lovely Nightingale, Oh joy of joy, I caught a couple of bars of your rendition of Gounod's "Ave Maria" and the "Alleluia." Imagine if only your door were open, what a lovely concert we would have. I reminisced a bit of the many times you would sing my favorite arias and folk tunes. Honey, as I thought of it I just adored you. Too bad you weren't closer. I'm sure I would have conveyed my deepest feelings for you in a way that is very proper indeed for two lovebirds.

*LAURA:* It was like they were out in a garden having love with one another.

*JULIUS:* I send you my tender kisses as messages of my heart.

*LAURA:* They were saying such exuberant things in their letters.

*JULIUS:* I've got a little secret to tell you my wife, that I am very deeply in love with you—as if you didn't know it.

*LAURA:* Like they had just been married or had not been married yet.

*JULIUS:* Well what do you say?

*LAURA:* They were talking as though tomorrow they were going to be free and they were going to do all these wonderful things that they had been doing all these years.

ETHEL *and* JULIUS *sing and waltz to "I'm Dreaming of Waltzing," by Edith Segal.*

*LAURA:* It was so terrible to read these letters. I had a stack of poems that Ethel had been sending to her husband in jail. Every time I read them,

I would start . . . I couldn't read them anymore. I threw them out. (*She tears up the letters and cries.*)

ETHEL *sings "Eitz Chaim Hi" a Hebrew song of peace to comfort* LAURA. ANNA *and* LAURA *join in singing during the transition to the next scene. A collage of photos and headlines are projected, which chronicle events between Julius Rosenberg's move to Sing Sing and the eve of the execution.*

SCENE SIX: THE DEMONSTRATION

*The scene starts in the office for clemency where* ANNA, NORA, *and* CAROL *are making picket signs for clemency.*

*ANNA:* Well, the things that took place the last week, that week of the ups and downs. The case had been appealed to the Supreme Court. But the Court was out of session for the summer. The Rosenbergs were going to be safe for the next, till October. Then all of a sudden, through a series of covert visits and phone calls, the Supreme Court was called back from their recess. I mean it had never been done in our history. Having these people, they had already left and gone to Maine and all kinds of places. They had to come back. Then one judge gave them a stay of execution, and then he was forced to rescind that. So every single day it was a different position, ups and downs. It was crazy.

*NORA:* One day we're reeling from happiness. At least we have the summer to try to get more proof that they never had a table with an x-ray machine, whatever you call it. But it would have meant four months of gathering more proof and more opposition to the death sentence. The next day it was gone. Hope was gone. (*She grabs a picket sign defiantly.*)

*The scene moves out onto the street. Slides of the Massachusetts Statehouse and other Rosenberg demonstrations are projected. Sounds of a rally are heard by* OPPOSITION PROTESTERS, *who stand facing upstage on either side of the stage.*

*CAROL:* We held a vigil outside the statehouse, all day. I mean it must have been at least twelve hours with signs and all that. And here's what happened. This is a very important thing, cause it shows the opposition had help, from many sources, including some reporters. Because that day, they had signs that said: "Ethyl Burned." Cause there's *ethyl* gasoline, so her name was spelled E-T-H-Y-L. Ethyl will burn. (*dodging a rock*) And they were starting to throw things at us.

ANNA: (*taking control*) When you are having a picket line, a demonstration, and it's for a specific cause, you can't have everyone on that line talking to the reporters, the policeman, whatever. Because each one may have, a . . . an individual personal opinion or observation which is not the position of the whole line. So I was the spokesperson for that line. The first thing I did was speak to the policeman in charge. (*She stops a policeman and speaks to him. Noise from the crowd covers their conversation.*) Thank you. (*yells after him*) And by the way, we expect our civil rights to be upheld, our right to free speech, our constitutional rights. (*to audience*) So I got his name, and when opposition people harassed, and the police that were supposed to protect us turned their heads, I'd say, (*to nearby officers*) I spoke to Captain Joe Blow. (*to audience*) I don't remember his name. (*to officers*) And he said he would protect us. We have our rights! (*to audience*) Blah, blah, blah. So I would quote that captain. That was one of the things. Another thing is that as a few of the representatives came out of the state house, (*actors perform the following*) and one of them was frankly attacking somebody. I had my sign. I just punched him like this. (*She jabs her sign into the representative and yells at him.*) Hey, you can't attack someone on my picket line, Buster. (*She hits him with the sign again, then speaks to the audience.*) I was not what you'd call a mute person.

## SCENE SEVEN: DROP DEAD

*The scene is a market on the Lower East Side.* LAURA *is picketing and handing out fliers about the Rosenbergs' innocence to passersby. She stops and speaks to the audience.*

LAURA: Well, I lived in a Jewish community and they thought that the Communists, instead of helping them, were hurting them. They thought if the government was pouncing on you, you must be doing something wrong. I remember one case when I was giving out fliers on the Rosenbergs, and this little old man he was about four feet eleven, and had a beard about four feet eleven. He was walking and said:

MAN: (*spelled phonetically*) Vet za haget.

*LAURA: (to audience)* It means "drop dead." So he came back with his chicken, the chicken head was outside his parcel. He didn't have the chicken plucked, because it cost ten cents. So he was going to take it home and pluck it.

*MAN:* Vet za haget.

*WOMAN ONE: (a passerby)* You're defending those good for nothings? They bring nothing but shame on our community. Everyone knows they're guilty.

*LAURA:* Well if they're are guilty, I don't know that. I haven't seen proof that they're guilty of anything.

*WOMAN TWO:* They had a trial. The jury examined the evidence and . . . they're guilty. So you can take your fliers and your Communist ideas and get out of our neighborhood.

*LAURA:* You call that a trial? It was absolute nonsense. It was like a Nazi trial. It was all these people who brought forth obscene, unimaginable things against them. There were plants everywhere. That wasn't justice.

*WOMAN ONE:* Yeah, well, the Judge said they tried to give the atom bomb to the Russians. Jews have enough problems in this country. Now we need to be tied to the KGB?

*LAURA:* The Rosenbergs' only guilt was that they worked too hard to help the people. People like you. Maybe they worked too hard to do things, that they didn't get enough people behind them. I do not know. But I can tell you that I don't blame them for anything.

*WOMAN THREE:* Well I do. So stop cluttering up the street.

*LAURA: (on a soapbox)* Look, we are all trying to keep our heads above the water. Don't you see they're trying to divide us? What side are you on? Goons and Gings and Company Finks, is that what side you're on? You have to know that capitalism is not going to just give away. Our earnings are not going to increase by themselves. Can't you see you are being used as pawns? You know, anti-Semitism, anti-Negro, all these things. Pit one roof against the other. Defending the Rosenbergs means taking a stand against the real enemy. *(to audience)* They all just stared at me, and then the old man, the one with the chicken. He comes up and spits at me, and he says:

*MAN:* Vet za haget. Vet za haget. Ve za haget en stuck a no.

*LAURA:* Meaning: "I told you to drop dead and you are still standing there." *(crowd leaves)* So that was some of the atmosphere. Some people felt that the Rosenbergs were bringing bad things on Jewish communities.

They were separating the Jews from the rest of the community. And this was a Jewish ghetto.

## Scene Eight: Facing Death

*ANNOUNCER:* On June 15, 1953, the Supreme Court turned down a stay of execution for the Rosenbergs.

*MICHAEL:* Dear President Eisenhower, I saw on television on Monday, Mr. Otis is not in prison anymore because the President of the country let him go. It said that his wife wrote a letter to the President over there and she told why Mr. Otis should be let go. I think it is a good thing to let him go home because I think prison is a very bad place for anybody to be. My mommy and daddy are in prison in New York. My brother is six years old. His name is Robby. He misses them very much and I miss them too. I got the idea to write to you from Mr. Otis on television. Please let my mommy and daddy go and not let anything happen to them. If they come home Robby and I will be very happy and will thank you very much. Very Truly Yours, Michael Rosenberg

*ANNOUNCER:* Denying clemency, President Dwight Eisenhower explained to his son, John:

*EISENHOWER:* To address myself to the Rosenberg case for a minute. I must say that it goes against the grain to avoid interfering in the case where a woman is to receive capital punishment. Over against this, however, must be placed one or two facts which have greater significance. The first of these is that in this instance, it is the woman who is the strong and recalcitrant character. The man is the weak one. She has obviously been the leader in everything that they did in the spy ring. The second thing is that if there would be any commuting of the woman's sentence without the man's, then from here on the Soviets would simply recruit their spies from among women.

*Lights up on* JUDITH *who sits next to* YOUNG JUDITH *in bed.*

*JUDITH:* Every night I use to lie in bed and think . . .

*YOUNG JUDITH:* (*in bed*) If I were Ethel Rosenberg, what would I do? Could I be Joan of Arc? Could I really do that?

*JUDITH:* At that particular time, being a mother, was very definitive, it was like, being a mother versus being a revolutionary. I grew up very much with St. Joan. I met all those people who were revolutionaries. I was raised to be a revolutionary, as a child. My father believed that we should . . . Well, I think I was raised . . . possibly to die. Which is why the story of St. Joan was so close to me.

*YOUNG JUDITH:* Ethel is so much like St. Joan, if St. Joan had children. (*wide eyes*) What if St. Joan had children in addition to her other problems?

*Lights up on the* ROSENBERGS *in their cells. They move toward each other downstage and hold hands as they speak.*

*ETHEL & JULIUS:* Dearest Sweethearts, Our most precious children,

*ETHEL:* Only this morning it looked like we might be together again after all. Now that this cannot be, I want so much for you to know all that I have come to know. Unfortunately, I may write only a few simple words; the rest your own lives must teach you, even as mine taught me.

*JULIUS:* At first, of course, you will grieve bitterly for us, but you will not grieve alone. That is our consolation and it must eventually be yours. Eventually, too, you must come to believe that life is worth the living. Be comforted that even now, with the end of ours slowly approaching, that we know this with a conviction that defeats the executioner!

*ETHEL:* Your lives must teach you, too, that good cannot really flourish in the midst of evil; that freedom and all the things that go to make up a truly satisfying and worthwhile life, must sometimes be purchased very dearly.

*JULIUS:* Be comforted then that we were serene and understood with the deepest kind of understanding, that civilization had not as yet progressed to the point where life did not have to be lost for the sake of life; and that we were comforted in the sure knowledge that others would carry on after us.

*ETHEL:* We wish we might have had the tremendous joy and gratification of living our lives out with you. Your Daddy, who is with me in the last momentous hours, sends his heart and all the love that is in it for his dearest boys. Always remember that we were innocent and could not wrong our conscience.

*ETHEL & JULIUS:* We press you close and kiss you with all our strength.

*JULIUS:* Lovingly, Daddy—Julius,

*ETHEL:* and Mommy—Ethel.

*Ethel's theme plays in the transition to the next scene.*

Scene Nine: The Execution

*Lights up on ANN, NORA, and CAROL in their office.*

ANNA: We were so . . . it was as though we were losing close relatives. Close relatives. I never saw them in life, but my husband Paul and I and the other women—here's what happened.

NORA: On Friday, they were going to be put to death. And out of respect for the Jewish Sabbath, they were going to be put to death before sundown Friday night because the Sabbath, every holiday of the Jewish religion, begins the evening proceeding the full day. So they were gonna be murdered, executed, at eight o'clock or eight something, right before sundown.

CAROL: It's like you've been put through a ringer, up, down, and sideways. A few of us gathered at this couple's house. We didn't have television, it was radio at that time and you heard the news.

*Lights up on JUDITH on the street.*

JUDITH: I never told my parents, in fact, but I was so worried that she would be . . . especially Ethel. I think most of us identified . . . she had those big doe eyes, and she looked totally like she had been trapped, you know. I knew about her mother, we had read all these stories about how her mother made her miserable, and she was so alone. So anyway, on the evening they were to be . . . killed, I decided that that only thing that might save them was God. But I didn't know where to find him.

*Lights up on LAURA in the factory. We hear the sound of the machines, and actors are working the looms.*

LAURA: I lived in New York, and I happened to be working at the same place that Ethel Rosenberg had worked at years before. And I was a union organizer in my shop, Bell Textiles. So I closed down the shop and we joined the march. We went from Union Square to, we walked to the Rosenberg's house. That was at the time, at sundown, when they were executing them.

*Lights up on JUDITH. A crowd forms in the street. YOUNG JUDITH is lost among them.*

JUDITH: I got on the subway and went to St. Patrick's Cathedral. I actually went there by myself. Of course I was Jewish, and I wasn't much of a believer because, well—given the world in which we live—I didn't see that praying to anything really helped. It seemed to me that it was more of a comfort for you than anything that would actually intercede on your behalf. However, I was willing, being a child, to suspend disbelief. (*In a dance, the crowd transforms into worshippers in the Cathedral, singing a Gregorian chant, which continues under the scene. Young Judith enters the church.*)

JUDITH & YOUNG JUDITH: As I entered the church, everything looked so huge.

YOUNG JUDITH: And it felt cold.

JUDITH: I couldn't take my eyes off of the stain glass windows.

YOUNG JUDITH: People were kneeling, saying some chant I couldn't understand.

JUDITH: And some people walked in a line to this man in white.

YOUNG JUDITH: So I got in line. It looked like the man in white was putting something in their mouths. And he was saying something . . .

PRIEST: Body of Christ.

WORSHIPPERS: Amen.

PRIEST: (*to Young Judith*) Body of Christ.

YOUNG JUDITH: Oh. I'm not really here for that. I was hoping maybe I could get in touch with God here. (*She speaks to each person as they step forward to receive Communion.*) This really shouldn't be happening.

WORSHIPPER ONE: Shhh.

YOUNG JUDITH: Ethel and Julius simply can't die. They just can't.

WORSHIPPER TWO: Shhh.

YOUNG JUDITH: This is all wrong, can't you see?

WORSHIPPER THREE: Shhh.

YOUNG JUDITH: Please, God, hear my prayer.

JUDITH: (*to audience*) I wasn't sure if God heard me, so I thought I better go to another place, just to make sure. (*As Young Judith steps out of the church, the actors transform back into the street scene as Laura emerges.*)

LAURA: We had a thousand people on that march. All the union people and the people supporting us left from Union Square to the Rosenberg house. I had never been able to meet Ethel. She was in Sing Sing. I couldn't go to see her. So, I went to see her before she died, well, the home she lived in.

*The street scene transforms into a Hindu Temple.* WORSHIPPERS *sing a Hindu prayer, which continues under the scene.* YOUNG JUDITH *stands in the center of the* WORSHIPPERS *who sit in a yoga position around her. Lights up on* JUDITH.

JUDITH: I had never seen anything like this place before, so I thought . . .

JUDITH & YOUNG JUDITH: Maybe, just maybe I could find Him here.

YOUNG JUDITH: People were sitting strangely. I guess they were praying, and there was music that sounded so peaceful that God must be here. (*She looks up.*) Please, God, please hear my prayer. This execution must be stopped. I need your help.

JUDITH: (*to audience*) So I waited . . . but I wasn't sure if he heard me. (*The crowd stands and moves to another part of the stage singing a Muslim prayer, and transforming into a Mosque with people bowing in prayer. The prayer continues under the scene.*)

JUDITH: I walked into this great mosque, and saw people on their knees, bowing in prayer.

YOUNG JUDITH: And I thought they looked very serious and very devoted.

JUDITH & YOUNG JUDITH: If God was anywhere, he was certainly here.

YOUNG JUDITH: So, I got on my knees and begged. God, don't you understand? They have two children, littler than me. (*She starts to cry.*) How can you take them away? They didn't do anything bad, God. I'll do anything. Please let them live. (*She sobs. Lights fade out on Young Judith and up on the Radio Announcer standing at a microphone.*)

ANNOUNCER: On June 19, 1953, the official observer of the execution gave the following report to the press:

OBSERVER: Julius and Ethel Rosenberg have gone to the electric chair. The first to go into the death chamber was Julius Rosenberg. The first volts of electricity entered his body at 8:04 p.m. She died a lot harder.

ANNOUNCER: Hearst reporter Bob Considine also witnessed the execution:

CONSIDINE: Ethel wore a Mona Lisa smile. Her little minnow of a mouth was curled at the edges in the faintest possible way. She was dressed in a dark green print of cheap material, a prison dress that revealed her plump legs below the knee. Her dark brown hair was set in an almost boyish manner. As the hood was lowered over her eyes and the black strap placed across her mouth, she was looking straight ahead almost triumphantly. As the torrent of electricity swept through her body . . . from every pore there seemed to emanate a strange, unearthly sound made up almost exclusively of the letter Z. Now she seemed about to stand. Her hands contracted into fists. Thus she sat, lifted off her seat as far as the straps would permit, and I had the startled feeling that she would break those bonds and come charging across the floor, wielding those tight little fists.

OBSERVER: Believing she was dead, the attendants had taken off the ghastly strapping and electrodes and black belts and so forth. These had to be readjusted again and she was given more electricity, which began again the ghastly plume of smoke that rose from her head and went up against the skylight overhead. After two more of those jolts, Ethel Rosenberg had met her maker, and she'll have a lot of explaining to do.

CONSIDINE. She could relax now. Her face possessed the same quizzical half smile that had been painted upon it minutes before. As she was pushed out of sight on a wheeled table her right leg was flexed in an easy and almost nonchalant posture. It was a trying experience when, a few minutes later, briefing thirty-eight reporters from half a dozen countries, the first question asked was a shrill one from a lady reporter. "What did Mrs. Rosenberg wear tonight?" she called up to me. It just seemed so damned callous. (*lights out on the Announcer and Observer and up on Anna*)

ANNA: We drove that night. We got to New York. We must have left in the middle of the night, because we got to New York in the morning. And it was roasting, and I had very few clothes to my name. So, I had a dress that I was going to put on for the . . . I presume . . . it was black. We arrived at the street where the office or whatever the building is, around noontime. There were thousands, there were maybe a hundred thousand people crowding the streets all around there. But, we were taken in, cause we had been running the office in Boston. Somehow we had something that let us in. How did we get into the . . . into the Rosenberg . . . not the committee . . . where the two . . . the two, um, coffins, the open coffins were there. And we were there. (*pause*) And we saw the bodies. It was just weird. It was . . . I felt as though I had lost a sister, when I looked at her. It was an amazing thing for me to see those two faces, those two bodies lying there. The courage they . . . the courage she had of knowing that she will never see her children again. And that those children would never have their mother and father who love them very much, all through their growing years. That's all things they gave up. (*She fights back tears.*) And there was my political and spiritual sister. It's so sad. I never met her, till she was dead. Until my Ethel, my sister, was gone. (*The scene transforms to the funeral of the Rosenbergs. A Rabbi leads mourners in "Eli Eli," a traditional Hebrew hymn. Laura turns from the funeral to address the audience. The hymn continues under the following.*)

*LAURA:* I went to their funeral. It was a Jewish place. It was a Jewish undertaker. We all marched there from different parts of the city, and we had a cortege watching over her and her husband. And it was a very . . . very touching thing. It was near a Brown Stone where I lived. (*speaks as if giving a eulogy*) Ethel to me was a strong woman. And she to the end, stuck to her principles. And that is what I want to take away with me. She is a great force in my life, when things get dreary—I live alone . . . I'm not always friendly—I look to her. Ethel stood out, as a woman and as a Communist, as a free person and as a union leader. And that's all I have to say. (*She breaks down crying.*)

ETHEL *enters and sings "If We Die," by Ethel Rosenberg, as if comforting her.* LAURA *and* SARA *join in. The cast enters and sings, "The Case Is Not Closed," from "A Time for Remembering" by Lewis Allan. Individual cast members sing each verse and the whole cast sings the chorus and the repeated verse. The play ends with a voice collage of the women who were interviewed and a slide of Ethel and Julius Rosenberg.*

## *Voicings* Study Guide

### *Learning Goals*

1. to review the political climate of the early 1950s, particularly as it relates to the Red Scare
2. to examine a controversial moment in history from different viewpoints
3. to understand how ordinary women experience and impact historical events
4. to place the Rosenberg case within a larger historical context

### *What Happened in History*

In the early 1950s, the fear of Communism was at the forefront of American politics and the news. Senator Joseph McCarthy revealed that he had the names of over two hundred Communist agents employed by the U.S. State Department, launching the McCarthy Hearings and the Red Scare. At the same time, suspected Communist spies were arrested for allegedly selling secrets of the Manhattan Project to Russian agents. In June 1950, the FBI questioned Ethel Rosenberg's brother David Greenglass, a scientist who had worked on the top-secret project to design an atomic bomb. Greenglass, whose wife was also under investigation, implicated his brother-in-law Julius Rosenberg as a member of a Soviet spy ring. Julius was arrested soon after, shortly followed by his wife Ethel. The Greenglasses, fearing for their own imprisonment, agreed to testify against Ethel and Julius. The Rosenbergs were tried and sentenced to death in April 1951. That sentence outraged some Americans, particularly those involved with the Socialist and labor movements, many of whom fought to have the Rosenbergs' sentence commuted. Ethel and Julius were executed on 19 June 1953. Years after the trial, Greenglass admitted that, under pressure from the government, he and his wife falsified their testimony against Ethel.

## Historical Timeline

*28 September 1915:* Ethel (Greenglass) Rosenberg is born.

*March 1917:* The Russian Revolution begins.

*1917:* The Espionage Act is enacted as a means of arresting and imprisoning war protesters during World War I.

*12 May 1918:* Julius Rosenberg is born.

*1920:* Attorney General A. Mitchell Palmer uses the Espionage Act to arrest and deport thousands of immigrants suspected of communism during the first U.S. Red Scare.

*1929:* The Communist Party of the United States is founded.

*Summer 1939:* Ethel and Julius Rosenberg marry.

*7 December 1941:* The United States is attacked by Japanese forces in Pearl Harbor and enters into World War II.

*1942:* The Manhattan Project begins.

*1943:* Julius Rosenberg meets Soviet spymaster Aleksandr Feklisov.

*February 1943:* The Venona Project begins.

*November 1944:* Julius Rosenberg allegedly asks David and Ruth Greenglass to help him obtain information about the Manhattan Project.

*December 1944:* Julius Rosenberg allegedly provides Soviets with a proximity fuse.

*16 July 1945:* The United States tests the first atomic bomb at Alamogordo, New Mexico.

*6 August 1945:* The United States drops an atomic bomb on Hiroshima.

*2 September 1945:* Japan surrenders to Allied forces, ending World War II.

*1946:* Julius Rosenberg and Aleksandr Feklisov allegedly meet for the last time.

*Late 1946:* The Venona Code is broken.

*28 August 1949:* The Soviets detonate their first atomic bomb.

*15 June 1950:* David Greenglass names Julius Rosenberg as the man who recruited him to spy for the Soviet Union.

*16 June 1950:* The FBI interviews Julius Rosenberg for the first time.

*30 June 1950:* The United States enters into the Korean War.

*17 July 1950:* Julius Rosenberg is arrested.

*11 August 1950:* Ethel Rosenberg is arrested.

*31 January 1951:* A grand jury indicts the Rosenbergs, Morton Sobell, and David Greenglass.

*6–28 March 1951:* The Rosenbergs, Sobell, and Greenglass are put on trial.

*29 March 1951:* The jury finds the Rosenbergs guilty of conspiracy to commit espionage.

*5 April 1951:* Judge Kaufman sentences Sobell to thirty years and sentences the Rosenbergs to death.

*10 January 1952:* The Rosenbergs appeal their case to the U.S. Court of Appeals. Judge Jerome Frank denies the appeal.

*13 June 1953:* The Supreme Court denies a stay of execution.

*17 June 1953:* Supreme Court Justice William O. Douglas grants a stay of execution.

*19 June 1953:* In a special session, the Supreme Court vacates Justice Douglas' stay of execution. Ethel and Julius Rosenberg are executed that same day.

*21 June 1953:* A funeral is held for the Rosenbergs in New York City.

*1960:* The Soviets shoot down an American U-2 spy plane over Soviet territory; this action is made possible by the proximity fuse allegedly supplied by Julius Rosenberg.

*1969:* Morton Sobell is released from prison.

*11 July 1995:* The CIA and NSA release decoded Venona cables, which indicate that Julius Rosenberg was involved in espionage activities.

*1997:* Feklisov claims in interviews that he met with Julius Rosenberg between 1943 and 1946.

*2001:* David Greenglass admits that his testimony concerning Ethel Rosenberg's role in conspiracy was perjured.

## *Vocabulary*

*Manhattan Project:* Initiated in 1942 under the U.S. Army Corps of Engineers, the project's goal was to design an atomic weapon before Japan and Germany completed one.

*Venona Papers:* documents resulting from a secret program launched by the U.S. Army's Signal Intelligence Service that decoded communications between alleged spies in the United States and their contacts in the Soviet Union (The Venona Papers were used in evidence against Julius Rosenberg.)

*Espionage Act:* Passed by Congress in 1917 during World War I, it prescribed a ten-thousand-dollar fine and twenty-year prison sentence for interfering with the recruitment of troops or the disclosure of information dealing with national defense. This controversial law was used to prosecute war protesters, and later applied to convict the Rosenbergs.

*Wobbly:* a member of the Industrial Workers of the World, a radical industrial labor union

*Communism:* the form of government used by the Soviet Union, China and other countries, characterized by a classless society and the equal distribution of goods; also the term used for a political movement dedicated to establishing such a system

*Blacklist:* a list of people who are ostracized and refused employment (During the Red Scare in the 1950s, many alleged members of the Communist Party were blacklisted.)

*Witch Hunt:* accusations made against individuals based on insufficient evidence (The term is often used to describe the Red Scare of the 1950s.)

*McCarthy Hearings:* In 1950, Senator Joseph R. McCarthy accused hundreds of U.S. State Department employees of being card-carrying Communists, launching our nation's second Red Scare.

*Red Scare:* a term used to describe the fear of Communism felt by Americans in the 1920s and 1950s

*Espionage:* the act of spying, or the use of spies by a government

*KGB:* the Russian intelligence agency—the Soviet Union's version of the CIA

*Treason:* betrayal of one's country (In the U.S. Constitution, treason is defined as levying war against the nation or giving aid and comfort to its enemies.)

*FBI:* The Federal Bureau of Investigation was founded in 1908 as part of the U.S. Justice Department to investigate federal crimes. Under the direction of J. Edgar Hoover, the FBI substantially expanded the scope of duties, targeting persons considered "subversive," such as the Rosenbergs.

*CIA:* Founded in 1947, the U.S. Central Intelligence Agency collects information relevant to national security.

## Key Players in the Rosenberg Trial

### The Defendants:

JULIUS ROSENBERG was arrested, tried, and executed as a spy.

ETHEL ROSENBERG was accused along with her husband and also sentenced to death.

MORTON SOBELL was a friend of the Rosenbergs and was indicted with them. He evoked his Fifth Amendment right not to testify at trial. He received a thirty year sentence and was released in 1969. Sobell maintains his innocence to this day.

### Defense Attorney:

EMANUEL BLOCH was the defense attorney for the Rosenbergs and also a personal friend. He defended American Communists in earlier cases, including the leader of the Communist Party of Pittsburgh.

*Prosecution Attorneys:*

IRVING SAYPOL was the U.S. Attorney for the District of New York. He was the Chief Prosecutor in the Rosenberg case and that of other suspected Communists. Shortly after the Rosenberg trial, he was appointed to the New York Supreme Court.

ROY COHN assisted Irving Saypol as part of the prosecution team. The trial was an important stepping-stone in his career, and Cohn went on to aid Senator McCarthy during the Red Scare. In his autobiography, Cohn admitted to framing the Rosenbergs.

*Soviet Spies:*

KLAUS FUCHS was a British scientist who worked on the Manhattan Project and confessed to being a spy in 1950.

ALEKSANDR FEKLISOV was a KGB agent who claimed to have recruited and handled Julius Rosenberg as part of a network of spies. Although he claimed to have met with Rosenberg over fifty times between 1943 and 1946, he denied that Ethel Rosenberg was involved in her husband's activities.

*Prosecution Witnesses:*

HARRY GOLD was an American spy and courier for the Soviets in their efforts to obtain information on the atomic bomb. He named the Greenglasses and the Rosenbergs as spies.

DAVID GREENGLASS was Ethel Rosenberg's brother. He worked on the Manhattan Project and allegedly provided Julius Rosenberg with information about the atomic bomb. After interrogation by the FBI, Greenglass agreed to testify against Ethel and Julius in exchange for his wife's freedom and a lighter prison sentence for himself. He later recanted his testimony against his sister and brother-in-law.

RUTH GREENGLASS was David Greenglass' wife. She testified against Ethel and Julius Rosenberg in exchange for immunity.

*Judges:*

IRVING KAUFMAN presided over the Rosenberg case at the age of forty.

JUSTICE WILLIAM O. DOUGLAS was the controversial Supreme Court Justice who granted the Rosenbergs' stay of execution.

*Rosenbergs' Sons:*

MICHAEL MEEROPOL, the elder son of Ethel and Julius Rosenberg, was ten years old at the time of their execution.

ROBERT MEEROPOL, the younger son of Ethel and Julius Rosenberg, was six years old at the time of his parents' execution.

## Preperformance Lesson Plans

### Background: The Rosenberg Case

*Goal:* to gain a deeper understanding of the Rosenberg story and the events surrounding their conviction

*Objectives*

1. to survey historical information about the Rosenberg case
2. to consider various arguments for and against their conviction
3. to take a stand on a controversial issue and develop arguments to support each side

*Method*

1. Ask the class what they already know about the Red Scare of the 1950s. What images come to mind? What events have they heard about? Write their thoughts on the board.
2. Review the historical information included at the beginning of this study guide.
3. Ask students to imagine themselves as American citizens during World War II. Remind them that:
   a. The Soviets and Americans were allies fighting against Germany.
   b. Many Jewish Americans were aware of the Holocaust and felt that the United States was not doing enough to end it.
   c. Can they think of a reason why an American might want to share military intelligence with the Soviet Union?
4. Now ask students to consider why Americans were fearful of the Soviet Union after World War II.
5. Ask students to choose from among the following historical characters. They are to research and write a one to two page, first person account of their role in the trial:
   a. Ethel Rosenberg
   b. Julius Rosenberg
   c. Irving Saypol
   d. Roy Cohn
   e. David Greenglass
6. Separate the class into groups according to the person they researched (all the Ethel Rosenbergs in one group, all the David

Greenglasses in another group, and so on). Ask each group to brainstorm what the person they researched would say about the outcome of the Rosenberg case. What points would they want to communicate to a modern-day audience?

7. Next, ask the students to imagine that they are modern-day historians. They will have the opportunity to interview the historical characters mentioned earlier. Ask them to come up with two or three questions that they would ask each of the other historical figures.

8. Ask for a volunteer from each group to be interviewed in character as the person they researched. He or she will also have an opportunity to mention any of the points that arose during the group's discussion.

*Follow-up:* Ask students whether they had any opinions or assumptions about the Rosenberg case before this activity. If so, have any of these assumptions changed?

### Oral Histories

*Goal:* to understand the significance and process of recording and retelling oral histories

*Objectives*

1. to explore the effect of historical events on everyday people
2. to interview a person who participated in or recalls a historical event
3. to create an artistic interpretation of an oral history

*Method*

1. Choose a historical event of local and/or national significance that occurred before the students were born (e.g., the Civil Rights Movement of the 1960s). In class, give a brief overview of the event. Distribute and discuss historical information on the topic and its context.

2. Ask students to locate and interview someone in their community who participated in or recalls the selected event. (If you anticipate that students may have difficulty identifying interview subjects, you can make the initial contacts yourself.) Prior to the interviews, brainstorm possible questions with the class.

3. Ask students to write a monologue in character as the person they interviewed, to be performed for the class.

*Follow-up:* Split the students up into groups of three or four. Ask each group to choose one of the monologues, and to create a scene from it to perform for the class.

## Post-Lesson Plans

### A Community Crisis

*Goal:* to re-create the sense of hysteria present in the 1950s Red Scare and explore how a community can turn against a person or group of people

### Objectives

1. to relate to the thoughts and feelings expressed in the play *Voicings*
2. to examine group hysteria in a different context than the one presented in *Voicings*

### Method

*Warm-up*

1. In a large open space, ask students to walk in random patterns at their own pace. As they encounter their classmates, they should greet them (nonverbally) as if seeing them in the hallway at school.
2. As the students walk, ask them to picture the following scenario: someone has been breaking into students' lockers and stealing their belongings. The school is in an uproar over this, and whoever is caught could be expelled. Now tell each student to imagine that they have been unfairly accused of the thefts. They don't know who made the accusation. It could be anyone—even their best friend. As they continue to walk, they should suspect that each person they encounter could be their accuser.
3. End the warm-up with a brief discussion. Ask students to reflect on their thoughts and feelings as they walked around the room. How did their views of their classmates change after being told that someone accused them of stealing?

*Main Activity*

1. Tell students that they are going to create their own town. This community will have the usual key players: mayor, chief of police, teachers, local merchants, and so on. Ask students which role they would like to play in the community. The only role that is not

available to them is that of mayor, which will be played by the teacher.

2. Tell the class that they are responsible for determining what kind of a town they live in. What is important to the people who live there? Ask them to brainstorm, in groups, their top five values. Then, as a class, have them narrow down their lists to a top three (this can be done by a vote). Ask each student to consider how these values apply to their selected role in the community.

3. Next, tell the students that there will be a celebration of the founding of their new town. In anticipation of the festivities, citizens are asked to work with a partner to create something that symbolizes the community and its values. Examples include a song, a flag, a welcome sign for the town, or a pledge. Tell students that they will be presenting these at the founding celebration. This assignment may take a day or two to complete, and can be given as a homework assignment.

4. Tell the group that there is a crisis brewing in the town. A new political group has started to form. This group is considered dangerous because its beliefs are in opposition to many of the important values of the community. As a class, discuss what those opposing values are and create a description of this group. (*Extension:* The class can role-play members of the opposition party at a political meeting or rally to flesh out their belief system.)

5. In role as mayor, the teacher calls and facilitates a town meeting to discuss the crisis. Students must develop a plan of action. Brainstorm different possibilities and record them. Then, as a town, hold a vote on which course to take.

*Follow-up:* Discuss the activity with the students. What suggestions did they think of, and why? How did it feel to know that their way of life was being questioned, and even threatened?

### Modern-day Witch Hunts

*Goal:* to explore the modern-day relevance of the Rosenberg story

*Objectives*

1. to discover parallels between the Rosenberg case and current events
2. to research and thoughtfully debate recent historical events

*Method*

1. Brainstorm with the class: What are recent examples of when Americans feared for their safety? During those times, were certain groups of people singled out for suspicious behavior? Why might this have happened? Record their responses on the board.

2. Ask the students to research one of the examples mentioned in class, and write and present to the class a brief paper that compares and contrasts that story to the Rosenberg case.

3. After each student has presented, ask the class the following questions: Who thinks that public policy toward suspected criminals, particularly those seen as a threat to national security, has changed since the Rosenberg case? Who thinks it has not? If the Rosenbergs were accused today, would their trial have the same outcome? Facilitate a class debate.

# Resources

Bentley, Eric, ed. 2002. *Thirty Years of Treason: Excerpts from Hearings Before the House Committee on Un-American Activities, 1938–1968.* New York: Thunder's Mouth.

Fast, Howard. 1990. *Being Red.* Boston: Houghton Mifflin.

Fried, Albert, ed. 1997. *McCarthyism: The Great American Red Scare: A Documentary History.* New York: Oxford University Press.

Gardner, Virginia. 1954. *The Rosenberg Story.* New York: Masses & Mainstream, Inc.

Goldstein, Alvin. 1975. *The Unquiet Death of Julius and Ethel Rosenberg.* New York: Lawrence Hill.

McCarthy, Joe. 1952. *McCarthyism, the Fight for America: Documented Answers to Questions Asked by Friend and Foe.* New York: Devin-Adair Co.

Meeropol, Robert. 2003. *An Execution in the Family.* New York: St. Martin's Press.

Meeropol, Robert, and Michael Meeropol. 1986. *We Are Your Sons.* Urbana, IL: University of Illinois Press.

Okun, Rob A., ed. 1988. *The Rosenbergs: Collected Visions of Artists and Writers.* New York: Universe Books.

Philipson, Ilene. 1993. *Ethel Rosenberg: Beyond the Myths.* New Brunswick, NJ: Rutgers University Press.

Pilat, Oliver. 1952. *The Atom Spies.* New York: Putnam.

Radosh, Ronald, and Joyce Milton. 1983. *The Rosenberg File*. New York: Holt, Rinehart, & Winston.

Roberts, Sam. 2001. *The Brother: The Untold Story of Atomic Spy David Greenglass and How He Sent His Sister, Ethel Rosenberg, to the Electric Chair*. New York: Random House.

Segal, Edith. 1953. *Give Us Your Hand! Poems and Songs for Ethel and Julius Rosenberg in the Death House at Sing Sing*. New York: Peoples Artists, Inc.

*United States v. Rosenberg*, 195 F2d 583 (2d Cir, 1952).

*United States v. Rosenberg*, 200 F2d 666 (2d Cir, 1952).

*Rosenberg v. United States*, 346 US 273 (US Supreme Court, 1953).

*Meeropol v. Nizer*, 560 F2d 1061 (2d Cir, 1977).

*www.pbs.org/wnet/americanmasters/database/mccarthyism.html*

*www.eisenhower.archives.gov/dl/McCarthy/Mccarthydocuments.html*

The Venona History Page: *nsa.gov:8080/docs/Venona.htm*

FBI Files on the Rosenbergs: *www.fbi.gov/foipa/foipa.htm*

# 5

## Creating Your Own Plays Based on Primary Source Documents

There are countless resources available for teachers and playwrights to create plays exploring American justice. The playwriting process varies for each writer and may be influenced by the material and the dramatic genre. In this chapter, we look at how the plays in this book were created. *Salem's Daughters* was written by a single author for a children's theatre. *Justice at War* and *The Trial of Anthony Burns* are both TIE pieces, devised by a team. *Voicings* was written as part of a college course that involved students and women in the community. The structures that follow are offered as examples only and should be adapted to your needs and circumstances.

## Writing a Historical Play for Family Audiences: *Salem's Daughters*

The process of writing *Salem's Daughters* was more straightforward than that of the other plays in this collection. As the sole playwright, I determined what was important and proceeded at my own pace. Also, I wasn't concerned with learning goals or the reactions of the audience. I wanted to write a compelling piece of theatre for the actors to perform.

### Researching the Topic

At the beginning, it's helpful to immerse yourself in as much information as possible. An Internet search of the topic can provide you with general information, resources, and the names and locations of libraries, museums, state and town archives, historical societies, cemeteries, houses of worship, institutes, and historical sites. Before you go to these places, call to confirm the hours of operation, and ask who would be the best person to help you. If you can speak to that person before your visit, they may be able to save you time by collecting materials in advance. Try to schedule an appointment with an archivist or docent who can help you find resources and direct you to related institutions. Historical documents are often kept in the archives or special collections, so make sure to ask about this. Some libraries require particular forms of identification, an entrance fee, or an application process. Again, it is smart to call ahead.

In researching the Salem witch trials, I visited the following Massachusetts locations:

1. Salem: Essex Institute and Peabody Museum, Salem Witch Museum, House of Seven Gables, Witch House, Burying Point, and First Church

2. Danvers (formerly Salem Village): Rebecca Nurse Homestead, Wadsworth Cemetery, and the Public Library

3. Beverly: John Hale House and the Public Library

4. Boston: Massachusetts Historical Society and the Public Library

5. Cambridge: Widener Library at Harvard University

What are you looking for? You might not be able to answer this question at first, but the more information you have, the more you will discover what you need. Once you've acquired a general overview of the primary topic, make a list of subtopics and people to research, and update the list as you go along. While you will amass far more information than you can possibly use, seemingly minor details may end up being useful. Genealogical searches of the key players, including birth, marriage, and death records, may provide important information. Search for period newspapers and periodicals, focusing on key dates. Court records, such as warrants, summonses, trial transcripts, indictments, lawyers briefs, and court decisions are extremely useful, as are journals, letters, and diaries written by potential characters or important figures of the day. Jackdaw Publications Division of Golden Owl Publishing sells historical portfolios with replications of primary source documents, broadsheet essays, and study guides on dozens of topics.

Take good notes, not only on the information, but also on where you found it. You may want to return to that source. Some institutions are very generous with their documents and will let you photocopy as much as you want. Other locations ask you to fill out a form so they can mail you copies prepared by their staff. Prices can range from five cents to a dollar a page or more. Certain libraries prohibit photocopying and will only allow you to enter with paper and a pencil, or a laptop. Once you have collected the bulk of your information—the research process will likely overlap the writing—take some time to read and reread the information. You can use highlighters, colored sticky notes, file folders, and so on, to organize the material.

In *Salem's Daughters*, I incorporated text from Reverend Parris' sermons, and from various firsthand accounts and transcripts of the trials. Cotton Mather's writings on witchcraft helped me to understand the Puritans' belief in supernatural phenomenon. I researched subtopics including the history of witchcraft, childhood life in colonial New England, customs and superstitions of the period, and early American paintings and block prints. Visits to locations in Salem and Danvers provided tangible evidence of daily life in 1692, and an emotional connection to the place. On a chilly fall day, I walked through the burial grounds at the Rebecca Nurse Homestead. A plaque explained that Nurse was initially buried in a shallow, unmarked grave after she was hanged, as was the custom. That night, her family exhumed her body and buried it somewhere in the family plot; they couldn't mark the grave for fear of discovery. As I read the story, a flock of crows burst from a nearby tree, their wings flapping loudly overhead and chills went down my spine. Later, meeting with the composer, he was able to re-create that sound and incorporate it into the score.

## Starting to Write

If you've done a thorough job, you could likely create a dozen or more interesting plays from your research. You may be tempted to include every interesting fact that you've unearthed. If you have an impulse, go with it. You can always edit something out as you revise the script. The important thing is not to become so overwhelmed by the material that you can't begin to write. If it helps, write an outline of the play, a timeline of events or ideas for possible scenes. Pick one scene to explore and start writing.

One way to focus your energies is to ask: Whose play is it? This may be obvious or it could be a difficult decision; you may need to start writing before a main character emerges. I selected Ann Putnam as the protagonist of *Salem's Daughters* because she went through such a compelling journey. As a girl of twelve, she was highly influenced by her parents, who had prior personal and economic grudges against many of the persons who were later accused of witchcraft. Ann was described as a sincere little girl, and that sincerity made her an effective accuser. Her parents died shortly after the trials. In 1706, she wrote a confession to the congregation of Salem Village acknowledging that she was wrong in her accusations and begging for forgiveness.

I was reminded of a conversation I had with a friend in college about race. She told me that her parents raised her with many negative attitudes about black people. Growing up, she never actually met an African American, but she accepted her parents' beliefs. In college, she met people of all races and learned that her assumptions were unfounded. Like my friend, Ann had to be separated from her family before she could see the truth. Once I found my main character, the supporting cast fell into place.

While primary source documents provide inspiration for your play, remember that your goal is to create a compelling drama. One of the best ways to bring the material to life is to find a personal connection to the characters. This is not to say that you need to modernize the script in order to connect with the characters. The historical period will dictate much of the characters' speech and decorum, but their inner life can be fused with pieces of yourself and people you know. In addition to historical figures, you might want to include fictional characters in supporting or major roles.

Try to avoid having your characters stand around spouting a lot of historical information. It's okay, even desirable, for the audience *not* to know everything about the situation right away. Don't feel compelled to start at the very beginning. You can start in the middle and weave in the given circumstances along the way. A great way to hook your audience is to create a mystery. As long as they want to know more, the audience will stay engaged. In each scene, try to imagine your characters in a particular setting, preferably engaged in a physical activity (e.g., drinking tea in a parlor or rum in a tavern, planting flowers in a garden, or cleaning a gun on the front porch). The location, weather and objects all become part of the scene. Where was each character prior to the scene? The more you can flesh out the lives of the characters, the more you can avoid a bunch of talking heads.

Sometimes it's helpful to have actors improvise a scene while you transcribe it. If you provide actors with the given circumstances (i.e., time, location, previous action, etc.), their objectives and obstacles, and an activity, they may instinctively create a compelling scene. Later you can review your transcript and make necessary revisions. Three of the scenes in *Salem's Daughters* were created this way, in part because the script was unfinished when we started rehearsal.

## Revisions

Once you've completed a first draft of the play, it is helpful to hear it. Gather actors, students and/or friends to read and then discuss the play. I like to write down everything that's said in the discussion, let it sit, and then try to sort through it later. Ultimately, you are the writer and you should follow your own instincts—use what's helpful and set aside the rest. After hearing the play, you will have a good idea of what's working and what needs to be changed.

Censoring yourself in the first draft is usually counterproductive, but in revising the script you need become more of an editor. Have you cluttered the play with too much historical information? You may have included interesting facts, but if they don't serve the play, get rid of them. Do you need to show why a character is motivated to act in a certain way? Maybe you need to do more research on specific details. Do some scenes come to a climax too quickly, and need more of a build? Do you need to cut an unnecessary scene or add a new one? Read through the play several times making changes. Once you've made all the revisions you can, arrange for a second reading. Again, follow your instincts and revise the script. When the play is in fairly good shape, it can go into production. You can continue to rewrite the script throughout the rehearsal process and after the show closes.

## Devising a Theatre-in-Education Piece:
### *The Trial of Anthony Burns* and *Justice at War*

The process of creating an interactive TIE piece is very different than writing a traditional play as it is guided both by artistic and educational goals. This section describes how Theatre Espresso devised two of its historical TIE pieces for young audiences: *Justice at War* and *The Trial of Anthony Burns*. The process used was closely modeled on one created by theatre educators Chris Vine and Lynne Clark, formerly of the Greenwich Young People's Theatre. Chris now heads New York University's Creative Arts Team (CAT) and Lynne teaches theatre at Queen Anne's College in Scotland. In the early 1990s, Wendy participated in a workshop led by Chris and Lynne at Emerson College. Since then, Theatre Espresso has used this process in creating new work, adapting it to meet the company's working style and their artistic and educational objectives. We encourage you to do the same.

### *Determining the Needs of the Students*

The more you know about your target audience, the better prepared you will be to create a drama that serves their needs. Start by determining your target age range. Will the piece be performed for one specific audience or will it be performed multiple times for a variety of school groups? Assess the educational and cultural needs of your chosen audience. You may have firsthand knowledge of the students if you've worked with them before, or you may need to make some assumptions given what you know about their age group, the school they attend, and the educational standards set forth for their grade. Perhaps a school system or a teacher has asked you to create a TIE piece to address a particular educational or behavioral need. Finally, consider the interests and concerns of your chosen age group. Do they value material goods like money and clothes? Are they concerned about grades and their future or more worried about their social life and fitting in?

## Selecting and Researching a Topic

Based on the needs of your target audience, brainstorm what your team wants to do a TIE piece about. What excites you? What topics are studied in school by your target age range? Once the topic is selected, you can begin to research the general subject. The Young Adults section of your local library can be a very helpful place to start, as these books can provide an excellent overview of the major issues surrounding the time period, event, or trial you are studying (Review "Researching the Topic" at the beginning of this chapter for more hints on conducting historical research.)

## Segmenting the Topic

Once you've selected a historical period and/or an event, there may be a variety of subtopics that would make a compelling drama. One way to determine which aspects of the topic you want to focus on is to list all the possibilities, narrow it down to your top three choices, and then select the central theme of the drama. List as many subtopics as possible. For example, when devising *The Trial of Anthony Burns*, we made the following list:

1. states' rights—pre-Civil War
2. goals of the abolitionists
3. Burns as a test case for Fugitive Slave Law
4. galvanizing the literary world, the start of the Republican movement
5. manipulation of an individual (Burns) for a cause
6. concepts of heroism
7. evolutionary nature of the law
8. tension between human and moral law
9. civil disobedience as a protest method

## Determining a Central Question

What issue do you want to present to the audience? Take your selected theme and transform it into a question. Try to develop a question that is complex— something that the students will need to grapple with. Using the previous list of subtopics as an example, sample questions might be: What is the impact on an individual whose trial is used as a test case? Why did literary figures such as Ralph Waldo Emerson and Henry Thoreau become political activists over the Burns trial? How did the Burns trial change Massachusetts law? Any of these questions could serve as a springboard for a drama.

In Theatre Espresso's dramas, the students are placed in decision-making roles, and the central question determines the decision they are asked to make. In *Justice at War*, the key question focused on the legality of interning a group of people during times of war. In creating *The Trial of Anthony Burns*, however, the process was not as straightforward. Early on, we decided to explore the divergent goals of the abolitionists. Later we discovered that the character of Judge Loring, a professed abolitionist, presented a compelling legal and moral dilemma. Questions surrounding Loring's actions arose. What else could he have done? If he had other options, what were they and why didn't he take them? Our key question became: What, if any, actions should a judge take when a human law violates his sense of moral law?

## Selection of Characters

You will likely find dozens of historical figures who could be included in the drama. One way to narrow down your selection is to determine which characters represent which viewpoints. This will also help you to ensure that you are presenting a balanced view of the issues. When re-creating a pivotal moment in history, you will discover strong, divergent, and often contradictory opinions espoused by several key players. In devising our initial concept of *Anthony Burns*, we considered characters with the following objectives:

1. Reverend Grimes, John Greenleaf Whittier, and society women who gave money to the Reverend—buy Anthony Burns' freedom

2. Reverend Thomas Wentworth Higginson and Samuel Stowell—initiate another possibly violent attempt to rescue Burns

3. Theodore Parker and Wendell Phillips— maintain peace at any cost, even if it means letting Burns go back to Virginia and buying him later

4. Richard Henry Dana and Wendell Phillips—continue with the trial despite the likelihood that Burns will be sent back into slavery, thus making a martyr of Anthony Burns

## Selection of Context

Given the central question, where and when in the course of events should you set the drama? Because our goal in *Justice at War* was to examine the legality of singling out a group of people for internment, we decided that the students would play Supreme Court justices ruling on the constitutionality of the camps. To explore this question, we would need to hear from lawyers, an official responsible for setting up the camps, and from someone who was interned. In devising *Anthony Burns*, we created the following chart:

| Characters | Context |
|---|---|
| abolitionists | meeting to decide how to protest Burns' arrest |
| Anthony Burns | in the courthouse with defense attorneys, deciding whether or not to take a defense |
| Judge Edward G. Loring | on the eve of his decision, contemplating his options |
| attorney for the claimant | before the trial, strategizing with Suttle |
| Charles F. Suttle, owner of Burns | deciding whether or not to sell Burns |
| abolitionists | debating whether to buy Burns or fight for his freedom |
| Massachusetts State Legislature | establishing the Personal Liberty Act |

## Devising a Framework

What activities can the pupils actually do? In Theatre Espresso dramas, students interrogate characters, take notes, debate, articulate their beliefs, defend their opinions, and challenge the characters and each other. In developing a structure for your drama, it is helpful to review drama-in-education techniques and methods that can be incorporated. Given your knowledge of the target audience, consider what activities are most appropriate for them. Here are some suggestions:

1. *teacher in role*: The teacher takes on a character and plays an active role in the drama to provide a problem or conflict.
2. *mantle of the expert*: Students are given roles that are presumed to have some expertise in an area central to the drama.
3. *tableau*: A frozen picture—this is often a starting point for a drama.
4. *role play*: Students play characters in the drama.

5. *story building*: Students help create the story line that will be acted out.

6. *forum theatre*: Students view a scene about a conflict, and are then asked what the characters could have done differently in order to resolve the conflict. Students either direct the actors to pursue different tactics, or show them by actually taking on their roles.

7. *hot seating*: A character is interrogated by students who are either in or out of role.

## Determining Your Strengths

What skills do you have in your team? Consider the particular talents of individual team members, such as playwriting, directing, acting, photography, computer graphics, dance, movement, juggling, singing, or playing an instrument. These skills may useful in the creation and performance of your piece.

## Writing the Play

Primary source documents will provide both inspiration for original dialogue, and direct quotes from articles, letters, journals, and transcripts. Review and sort your collected materials. There are many models to follow once you start writing. You can meet as a group to brainstorm/improvise ideas, and then have a single playwright go off and write scenes. You may want to assign members of your team to write specific scenes and then meet periodically to review them. The team may want to work collectively to write the play. If more than one person is involved in the writing process, you need to take extra care that the final script has a cohesive through-line.

While writing the play, issues of dramatic license versus historical accuracy will likely arise. As stated previously, there is no set rule or easy answer to this dilemma. As a play is an entirely different medium than a lecture, altering "the facts" is sometimes necessary in order to portray historical events dramatically. It is up to the playwright to decide whether a specific change will affect the integrity of the piece. To help ease concerns about whether your choices are appropriate, you can consult an historian or legal expert.

It is important to hear the script read aloud both during the writing process and once a first draft is complete. Readings in front of an audience can help you determine which parts of the script are strong and what needs to be clarified. You can expect that script will go through several revisions before it is ready to be performed.

## Program Implementation and Revisions

Once the TIE piece is written and rehearsed, it can be previewed before a student audience. At this point you will quickly learn what is working and what needs to be revised. To evaluate your program's effectiveness, document and review the questions and comments offered by students during the interactive portion of the drama. If the students offer thoughtful comments and queries about the central question, you'll know that you're meeting your goal. If they are confused or seem fixated on a minor point, you'll know that, too. You should continue to refine the structure once it's in production. Since many variables can factor into an audience's response (e.g., age and level of preperformance preparation), it is helpful to document several performances and determine whether common threads emerge, which indicate that revisions are necessary. Script changes, additional research, and directorial choices can alleviate most problems. Each time you rehearse and perform the drama, you will find new ways to clarify the action.

## Preparing Actors for the Interaction with the Audience

Actors of TIE need to be skilled educators who can communicate directly with the audience. Theatre Espresso practices the interactive portion of the drama during the rehearsal process. We hold mock questioning sessions during which we try to anticipate what students will ask. The moderator is a key role in any Theatre Espresso drama, and these rehearsals provide the actor with an opportunity to practice her moderating skills. In fielding questions and comments, the actor needs to listen *carefully*, and then repeat or rephrase (if necessary) what the student said to make sure that everyone heard it. In rephrasing a question or comment, the moderator lifts and clarifies the language and, if the student uses words or terms that are not of the period, brings it back into the historical context.

To avoid changing the student's intent, the actor can work with the student to make sure their point has been made accurately (e.g., STONE: So you're saying that the government was protecting Japanese Americans from racist attacks?). The student then has an opportunity to confirm or correct the moderator's interpretation. The preceding process also allows the other actors time to think of their response. We take every question seriously and answer it even if it has been asked before.

No matter how much you prepare, there will occasionally be questions that the actors can't answer. While the actors are in character, we have several ways of dealing with this. If possible, the actor will try to deflect the question (e.g., DEWITT: I don't know where you heard that, but that information is confidential.). If the question can't be reasonably avoided (e.g., STUDENT: Miss Endo, how many sisters and brother do you have?), the actor will make up an answer during the play. In either case, the actor will make sure to return to the question during the postperformance discussion (e.g., ENDO, out of charcter: During the play, you asked me a really great question. I don't know how many sisters and brothers Mitsuye Endo had, but now that you've brought it up, I'm going to try to find out.). We then attempt to learn the answer to that question before the next show.

During the postperformance discussion, students ask questions about the drama, what happened in history, and about the company. The actor moderating this discussion repeats each comment or question so that everyone in the room can hear. We also encourage students to draw connections between current events and what happened in history. This conversation provides classroom teachers with a springboard for further discussion and/or research.

## Creating an Oral History and Performance Piece: *Voicings*

The following guidelines outline the process of writing a documentary theatre script during a college course, but these methods can easily be adapted for a high school group, theatre company, or single author.

### Selecting the Historical Topic

Here are several considerations to keep in mind:
1. Does the topic excite you?
2. Do you want to focus on a general phenomenon (women in the workforce during World War II), a single event (the assassination of John F. Kennedy), or a combination of both (radical women of the 1930s, 1940s and 1950s, with the Rosenberg Case as a central event)?
3. Do you want to explore history or current events?
4. Will you be able to identify interview subjects who have a personal connection to your selected topic?
5. Is your topic dramatic enough for a play?

### Selecting the Theatrical Genre

Once you have determined your topic, select a theatrical genre through which to tell the story. Your choice may be guided by the time period, the tone of the event, the location, or other considerations. Here are the topics and genres for three of our projects:

1. the Rosenberg case: epic theatre of Bertolt Brecht and Erwin Piscator
2. war brides of World War II: 1940s musicals of stage and screen—particularly those that juxtaposed fantasy and reality
3. the four church women who were raped and murdered in El Salvador in 1980: political puppet theatre—particularly that of Bread and Puppet

## Locating Interview Subjects

If you are creating the script as part of a course, it is important to identify the interview subjects in advance. How many subjects do you hope to interview? In determining the number of interviewees, decide whether you want to send students out individually or in pairs. Also, do you want students to interview one subject or two? Remember that each interview and transcription takes a considerable amount of time and effort.

One of the best ways to find interview subjects is to contact organizations to which potential interview subjects might belong. In preparation for *Voicings*, Susan and I attended the annual Julius and Ethel Rosenberg Commemoration at the Community Church of Boston. There, we met a majority of the women who were later interviewed for the project. For *I'll Be Seeing You* (our oral history and performance piece about World War II brides), we contacted a war brides organization and discovered that members were holding a reunion in Rhode Island during the time our course was offered. After speaking to the convention chairs, we arranged a field trip to the convention, where students interviewed foreign war brides.

Word of mouth is also a great way of locating subjects. If you start talking about the upcoming project with friends, colleagues, and family, you will likely find someone who knows someone connected to your topic. If your event took place fifty or sixty years ago, contact retirement communities. You can also place a targeted newspaper ad or a Web posting.

## Class Resources

In preparation for the course, compile a packet of readings that includes a historical overview of the event and its context, primary source documents, and information on the selected theatrical genre. (Review "Researching the Topic" at the beginning of this chapter.) Try to locate videotaped performances that employ the chosen style. Is there an upcoming local theatre production that can serve as an example of the genre? If so, arrange a field trip to see it.

## Guest Speakers

Is there someone who can provide valuable information about your topic to the whole class? For *Voicings* we invited Robert Meeropol, son of Ethel and Julius Rosenberg, to Regis College. He spoke to the class about his memories and experiences growing up (he was three years old when his parents were arrested), and his current thoughts and feelings about his parents and the case. His visit was an inspiring and moving experience for our students. To honor their parents' final wish that their sons avoid being bitter, and to turn the tragedy of their parents' deaths into something positive for humanity, Michael and Robert Meeropol started the Rosenberg Fund for Children, which raises money for the children of political prisoners.

## Structuring the Class

Conducting the Oral History and Performance course is a huge undertaking, one that Susan and I only attempt every three or four years. An extended class period is held once a week. Prior to each session, we meet to coordinate our teaching. We co-teach each class, and we draw connections between our two disciplines at every possible occasion. For example, after Susan led a class discussion on letters written by war brides, I divided students into small groups and asked them to use the letters as the basis for a short performance piece that juxtaposed fantasy with reality. The students rehearsed and then presented their scenes.

## Additional Research Projects

Divide the class into groups. Ask each group to research an art form from the target historical time period (e.g., music, art, dance, photography, or theatre—different than the target genre). The groups present a creative presentation based on their findings. These collected resources may be useful in creating the script, or incorporated into the final production.

## Preparing to Conduct Oral Histories

Interviewing a stranger can be an intimidating prospect for a student. Try to prepare them for what will happen. James Hoopes' *Oral History: An Introduction for Students* (University of North Carolina, 1979) provides an excellent overview of the process as well as practical advice. You can also invite an oral historian to your class to conduct a workshop. Students can practice by interviewing each other in class. Give students as much information as possible about the person they are going to interview, and ask them to write their interview questions in advance. They may stray from the list during the interview, but the preparation will be helpful. Discuss what kinds of questions they should ask. Open-ended questions provide the most fruitful replies. Here is a list of possible topics to cover:

1. personal history: birth, family, marriage, children, education, and employment
2. connection to the topic—try to get specifics
3. favorite songs, artworks, or plays—encourage the subject to sing her favorite song
4. views on related historical events
5. anything else they think is important

Take care in assigning a student to an interview subject. Keep in mind each student's strengths and weaknesses, the temperament of the interview subject, the location of the interview, which students own cars, their schedules and availability. Make sure the subject knows that a student will be calling them. Find out when each subject is generally available and give that information to your students. Assign students a window of time within which they need to conduct their interview, and follow up to make sure they have made an appointment. Students should bring a recording device to the interview; encourage them to practice operating the device and to check the batteries prior to their visit.

### Release Forms

Create a release form for the subjects to sign, giving permission for their interview to be used in the creation of the play. Hand out and discuss the forms with the class and ask students to turn in the signed forms soon after their interview.

### Transcripts

Ask students to transcribe their entire interview and submit both a hardcopy and an electronic version. To familiarize the entire class with the range of interviews, ask students to give an oral presentation that highlights the most interesting segments of their sessions.

## Transforming Interviews into Theatre

Once they have identified interesting sections of their interview, ask students to select the most compelling story to dramatize. Other parts of the interview may be woven into the play, but it is helpful to find a focal point. If two people interviewed a single subject, you can either ask them to work together on the script, or to each pick a different segment to dramatize. In writing their script, encourage students to think visually. There may be more interesting choices than having an actor walk on stage and deliver a monologue. The selected theatrical genre will help guide students in developing their script. Hold readings of the scripts in class. Once everyone has completed a first draft, they can start to rehearse. We found it useful to divide the class into groups; each student casts her play from the group and then directs it. Discuss a logical order for the pieces. Finally, groups perform their pieces for the rest of the class and invited guests.

## Developing the Script

The process of combining individual pieces into a cohesive script can be accomplished by a committee or a single playwright. If you plan to rework scripts written by your students, it is a good idea to get their permission in advance. For *Voicings,* I started with students' scripts—editing and revising as necessary. I then wrote additional pieces based on the interview transcripts, and on my mother's story. I incorporated letters by Ethel and Julius Rosenberg written to each other while they were in prison, newspaper headlines and articles, quotes from government officials, poems inspired by the Rosenberg case, and songs mentioned by the interview subjects as being important in their lives. Finally, I created transitions from one piece to another.

## Starting the Rehearsal Process

The cast may be selected from the class who wrote the script, or from a larger community. For *Voicings,* auditions were open to all students, but preference was given to students from the Oral History and Performance course. After casting the show, hold a reading of the script. If possible, invite the women who were interviewed, along with any members of the class who did not audition. Prior to the reading, mail scripts to all the people who were interviewed, regardless if they can attend. Following the reading, ask for honest feedback. If anyone has a problem with something in the script, it's best to know as soon as possible. Ask the interviewees to speak to the cast. Our subjects bonded not only with their interviewers, but also with the actors who played them. Some of these relationships have continued over a decade after the production ended.

### Honoring Your Interview Subjects

It is important to let the interviewees know how much you appreciate their involvement. Here are some suggestions:

1. Ask each of the students to write a thank-you card to their interview subject.
2. Send the subjects complimentary tickets to the show.
3. Make sure to thank the interviewees in the production program.
4. If many of the subjects plan to come to the same performance, hold a special reception in their honor. We bought corsages for each of the women on the opening night of *Voicings*.
5. Tour the production to a location that is meaningful to the people who were interviewed. We performed *Voicings* at the Community Church of Boston, where Susan and I originally met the women.
6. Raise money for a cause that is important to your subjects. One Regis College student was so inspired by Robert Meeropol's visit to our class, that she organized a "Blues Night" reception that followed a performance of *Voicings*; proceeds from the event were donated to the Rosenberg Fund for Children.

## Conclusion

We hope this book has inspired you to create your own plays and drama activities that explore American justice. The possibilities for content and form are vast, as are opportunities for unique collaborations and new and exciting venues. Whether working on your own, with a team of artists, or a group of students, the process of researching and developing historical plays is rich and rewarding. It brings us closer to the dilemmas faced by well-known figures and ordinary people, and challenges our assumptions about the past. By delving into our nation's messy—sometimes violent—struggle for justice, we can illuminate moments of true courage and insight. We are reminded that democracy survives through the actions of individuals, and that each of us has an important role to play.

## Suggested Resources on Famous Trials and Landmark Cases

Belknap, Michael R. 1994. *American Political Trials.* Westport, CT: Green-
    wood.
Irons, Peter, and Stephanie Guitton, eds. 1993. *May It Please the Court.* New
    York: New Press.
Knappman, Edward. 1995. *Great American Trials.* Canton, MI: Visible Ink.

### Websites

*www.landmarkcases.org*
*www.law.umkc.edu/faculty/projects/ftrials/ftrials.htm*